CU00734492

Copyrighted Material

Copyrighted Material

EGYPTIAN LIGHT
AND HEBREW FIRE

Copyrighted Material

SUNY Series in Religious Studies
Harold Coward, editor

Copyrighted Material

EGYPTIAN LIGHT
AND HEBREW FIRE

THEOLOGICAL AND PHILOSOPHICAL ROOTS OF
CHRISTENDOM IN EVOLUTIONARY PERSPECTIVE

Karl W. Luckert

State University of
New York Press

Copyrighted Material

Published by
State University of New York Press, Albany

© 1991 State University of New York

All rights reserved

Printed in the United States of America

No part of this book may be used or reproduced
in any manner whatsoever without written permission
except in the case of brief quotations embodied in
critical articles and reviews.

For information, address State University of New York Press,
State University Plaza, Albany, N.Y., 12246

Production by Marilyn P. Semerad
Marketing by Dana E. Yanulavich

Library of Congress Cataloging-in-Publication Data

Luckert, Karl W., 1934–
    Egyptian light and Hebrew fire : theological and philosophical
roots of Christendom in evolutionary perspective / Karl W. Luckert.
        p.   cm. — (SUNY series in religious studies)
    Includes bibliographical references and index.
    ISBN 0-7914-0967-8. — ISBN 0-7914-0968-6 (pbk.)
    1. Egypt—Religion—Influence. 2. Judaism. 3. Philosophy,
Ancient. 4. Christianity—Origin. 5. Egyptian literature—Relation
to the Old Testament. 6. Gnosticism. 7. Gnostic literature-
-Relation to the New Testament. I. Title. II. Series.
BL2443.L83 1991
270.1—dc20   91-11980
                                                            CIP

10   9   8   7   6   5   4   3   2   1

Copyrighted Material

Contents

Copyrighted Material

Copyrighted Material

Preface

As all creations in this changing world have begun, so also this book has made its first stirrings as something else. The entire breadth and length of the story of religions, of human religiosity caught up in the larger process of evolution, has occupied my mind for decades. This preoccupation has generated a hefty stack of preliminary pages, and the completion of that project, Religion in Evolution, at one point has called for a condensed chapter on the religions of the Near East.

This intended summary chapter, over the course of a year, has grown into an oversized tail. In the end it seemed preferable to snip it off and to publish it as a separate book, *Egyptian Light and Hebrew Fire*.

But then the inevitable happened. When the manuscript was given to friendly readers they promptly discovered that my few hundred pages of introduction were missing. To remedy this situation, some of the basic methodological and contextual presuppositions have been summarized in Chapter 1, as prolegomena. This summary chapter, though extensive, will not satisfy the curiosity of all readers in the history of religions field, but it suffices to outline the phenomenological and evolutionary background assumed for this book. Concepts, processes, categories, and special terms from this "methodological reorientation," will be referred to and used throughout.

A book of such broad scope could never have been written without the stimulation provided by good colleagues. A healthy and free academic environment, inhabited by daring dreamers of goodwill, is a blessing for anyone who ventures onto paths that have been obscured by the winds of time. Some colleagues from our department at Southwest Missouri State University have read the manuscript at various stages of completion or have contributed to my thinking in discussions. They are Victor Matthews, Stanley Burgess, Robert Hodgson, Charles Hedrick, James Moyer, Gerrit tenZythoff, Ramsey Michaels, Kathy Pulley, James Llewellyn—and from a neighboring department Garth Alford. Readers outside our university who have given advice were Gregory Alles, Arne Hassing, Don Benjamin, Carlos dela Pena, Burton Mack, Frank Reynolds, Robert Potter,

Copyrighted Material

James Stein, Douglas McGaughey, Dudley Brown, and Heidi Luckert. My special reference to these names is motivated by sincere gratitude for their time, their friendship, and their good suggestions. Not even the slightest hint is hereby intended to imply that these people ought to share responsibility for the shortcomings of this book. I consider myself quite capable of having manufactured all my errors by myself—even in spite of the good advice sometimes offered by others who might have known better.

In Memory

I dedicate this volume to the memory of my father, Wilhelm G. Luckert, whose restless mind appears, in hindsight, to have harbored the questions and doubts that I was predestined to imbibe during childhood, and for which this book was destined to attempt some answers. At the height of his powers and self-confidence, this blessed elder could easily have judged this book—without having to read it first—as "Egyptian Light, Hebrew Fire, Greek Embers, and German-American Smoke." Now that he has attained his fulfilled state of knowing, surely, he has no regrets that my academic offerings, which anyhow were perceived still "through a mirror darkly," have never caught up with him during his journey through dim sunlight.

And while this book is still awaiting to be printed, my dear mother, Emilie Luckert/Hilt, has departed from our realm of light and shadows as well. Probably more than I will ever understand, her temporal presence has caused me to perceive ancient Egyptian religion as Christendom's "mother religion," as surely as the presence of my father has helped me to recognize the Hebrew tradition as a more fiery paternal mode of piety. Thus, as their lives and loves survive in memory among their offspring, their *ka* souls will continue to shine from the shadow play among the *ba* structures in this book.

Copyrighted Material

Egyptian Light
and Hebrew Fire

Copyrighted Material

Copyrighted Material

1

Prolegomena
for Methodological Reorientation in the
History and Evolution of Religions

Some readers of this book may be better served by beginning in chapters other than this "Prolegomena." This introductory portion is nevertheless quite necessary. It has been written to serve as background for my peers in the history of religions field. For more than two decades I have been working mostly along the periphery of this discipline, along the boundary of primitive religions, ethnology, and general anthropology. Swept along by the dynamic of interacting with my subject matter—with religious people, while doing ethnological field work—my phenomenological, historical, and evolutionary categories evolved all the while. Inasmuch as it may not be useful to adopt the entire conceptual machinery of anthropology, I have explored an avenue of mediation between the history of religions and those concerns of anthropologists that might aid our understanding of religious phenomena. I have become convinced that without considering the new harvest of anthropological evolutionary insights, our discipline of history of religions—with its traditional accent on history—will soon lose its relevance within the landscape of modern academe.

Students of Neoplatonism and Augustinian theology may enter into the subject matter of this book more easily by reading first the summary chapter on "Helipolitan Theology" (Chapter 2) in dialogue with the chapters on Plotinus (Chapters 14 and 15). At the same time, this particular combination also may be the easiest entry for anyone else who is philosophically inclined and wishes to grasp the larger picture. In any case, that latter sequence and entry has led me onto my initial path of discovery.

In all likelihood more readers will be prepared, initially, to begin wrangling with the theological profile of ancient Egypt from the point of view of the Hebrew tradition than from the field of Neoplatonic philosophy. This is somewhat unfortunate because, as I now perceive the situation, the theological dependency of Christendom on ancient Egypt is much stronger than its theological link with the Hebrew tradition. All the while, I now also recognize more clearly than before that the religio-political Christian gospel of the "kingdom of heaven" owes some of its sparks to the ancient Hebrew fiery reaction to Egyptian imperialism.

Reorientation in the Phenomenology of Religions

The phenomenon generally referred to as *religion* has been defined by Western scholars over the years in many dozens of ways. Most of these definitions are still useful to all who take time to immerse themselves in the ontological contexts in which their originators conceived and formulated them. Different aims and methodologies among professionals require different emphases or foci. Different foci support different ontologies, and different ontologies invariably result in different working definitions.

For instance, a historian, philosopher, psychologist, sociologist, anthropologist, or theologian, each begins his or her train of specialized professional thought with a preferred ontological emphasis. Their respective methodologies are applied to help highlight the subject matter they are examining. Moreover, the decision to focus one's attention on specific types of data implies, by itself, the commitment of an academic discipline to a primary configuration of reality. For example, historians value events that have scored in their linear reckoning of time as their basic data and realities; philosophers evaluate axioms and propositions as fundamental; psychologists traditionally have focused on the "psyche" and have shifted, more recently, to more easily observable "behavior"; sociologists study societal units and their functioning; in a wider angle of view, anthropologists concern themselves with larger societal configurations or cultures; and finally, theologians begin their work with a focus on the nature of God or gods.

Copyrighted Material

The subject matter "religion," in the domains of all these specialized academic disciplines, has been examined by individual scholars with varying degrees of seriousness. But, inasmuch as religion seems peripheral to the ontological focus of such specialized academic disciplines, it easily disappears or is reduced to a mere aspect of other, more central realities. So for instance, viewed from the perspective of philosophy, various types of religious thought tend to be evaluated simply as irrationality. And frequently, in the psychological perspective, religion tends to be reduced to emotionality or to some type of abnormal behavior. For instance, in Freudian psychology a theistic religion may be seen as originating with the amplification or "projection" of the concrete model of a human father. Sociologists of the Dürkheimian persuasion regard gods and totems as "social representations;" that is, as projections or spiritualized expressions of concrete social togetherness. Marxists characterize religion by its role in the class struggle, as a means utilized by capitalists as an opium or tranquilizer in their exploitation of workers.

On the other hand, theologians who are committed to the ontology of a specific theistic tradition will focus first on the reality of their recognized God or gods. They will proceed to measure the gods of other people by that standard. In this manner theologians, like other scholars who either explicitly or implicitly operate on the basis of a presupposed ontology, may explain the wider world of religion, likewise, as epi-phenomenon of their envisioned central reality configuration. Some theological systems have gone so far as to depreciate the category "religion" itself—for instance, the theology of Karl Barth or the so-called philosophies held forth by numerous Hindu gurus. The latter reserve the label *religion* to designate the weaknesses they find in other people's outlook and behavior. Meanwhile, Barthian theologians and Hindu gurus classify their own ever-so-religious postures as respectable "non-religious" ontologies or philosophies.

Religion, defined to serve the needs of this discussion, and stated as briefly as possible, *is the response of humankind to so-experienced or so-perceived greater-than-human configurations of reality*. This definition is "relational" in that it focuses on the *Homo sapiens-religiosus* as he or she experiences and relates to the physical as well as socio-cultural environment. A religious person who becomes a historian's subject matter may or may not perceive the surrounding world in the same way as his or her academic observer. Nevertheless,

Copyrighted Material

religion always belongs to a person's own perception of the larger world, to his or her ontology. That larger ontology helps categorize one human experience as aggressive, another experience as religious, and still another as egalitarian or social. A passive observer therefore can do no better than to note how another person's religious behavior varies from his or her ordinary egalitarian or societal behavior, or how it differs from aggressive behavior in that person's quest for survival.

On the other hand, every person does encounter greater-than-human configurations of reality, religiously. By the very fact that a superior reality configuration is greater, it can never be fully comprehended or explained, neither by a subjective experiencer nor by an objective observer. Nevertheless, with the same humility that a person acknowledges, religiously, one's relational inferiority toward greater-than-human reality, a historian of religions may note instances of such humble behavior and expressions as religious data.

Some historians of religions may object to this quantified delineation of the subject matter "religion." They may offer the fact that elves and dwarfs are less-than-human beings, and that meanwhile human responses toward them in ancient times have been classified as religious phenomena. A historian of religions must answer that, indeed, sincere responses to elves and dwarfs are still today religious behavior, as in the case of northern European peasants who, occasionally, still pray for blessings and protection from these unseens. Although, admittedly, the recipients of these prayers nowadays do seem less than human to worldwise historians, they definitely are deemed still greater by those who offer them prayers and gifts—at least for the duration of these ritual presentations.

The duration of how long a person retains his or her religious posture is of no consequence for the basic perspective of this approach. Not even the mightiest among deities is responded to religiously by everyone, or all the time, as if he or she was unquestionably greater. This is to say, that a *Homo religiosus* in this world practices his or her religion neither one hundred percent nor all the time. Every living *Homo religiosus* is always more than that. He or she is a *Homo ludens* and, as such, a bundle of playfulness, oscillating between being a *Homo sapiens* aggressor and a *Homo religiosus* engaged in commonsense religious retreats. I am prepared to classify a human response to reality as "religious" whenever there are clear

Copyrighted Material

behavioral indications that the responding person, as far as he or she is concerned, acknowledges and defers to a greater reality.

So for instance, it is possible to observe a person's religious responses even at the mild intensity level of "fascination." Expressions of fascination are religious, because during an initial encounter an object that fascinates, ontologically considered, ipso facto, is not a less-than-human "object." Its effects on the human experiencer are inflicted, at least momentarily, by what looms as being potentially greater. But being only a mild borderline religious response, a state of simple "fascination" is impermanent and may quickly be deflected in one of two opposite directions.

An experience of "fascination" may be pushed, by the defensive ego of an experiencing individual, toward a desire for greater egalitarian "familiarity." It may be pushed beyond that point even toward a desire of gaining experimental control; that is, control over the reality that initially has stimulated fascination. This is the time-worn path over which myriads of predators' fascinations have deteriorated, under analysis, into curiosities and have been thereby reduced to the status of victims.

But then in the other direction, whenever confronted by a tenaciously fascinating reality configuration, an experiencer's ego may as well retreat further. A retreating ego may allow itself to be transported into an even more intense mode of religious experience or retreat. Inasmuch as a gradation of intensity is involved, the entire range of ontology, experiences and responses from total "control" to total "surrender," can be plotted quantitatively along a graduated scale that indicates degrees of experiential intensity.

The Teeter-Totter Scale

Any subject matter, which human minds are capable to submit to academic scrutiny, must be capable of delimitation. Thus, "religion" as a subject matter of study must be identifiable not only in terms of its content but also in contrast to whatever is not religion. That is to say, such general designations of religion as a "life-style" or as a "way of life," although they may be broad enough to embrace all religious behavior, do not delimit it sufficiently. To conceptualize a contrast between what is and what is not religion, it is necessary to begin with the simplest and most concrete ontology imaginable: a

Copyrighted Material

threefold ranking of creatures or entities relative to one another and as belonging within the larger food chain or environmental process.

All living beings on earth survive by feeding on lesser, conquerable things. For comfort they socialize with potential equals, to procreate offspring and provide nurture. And at some point in the larger hierarchy or "food chain"—by means of which organisms on earth are woven into a single fabric of life—everything and everyone eventually surrenders to greater realities. Thus, a fully conscious creature not only moves about to survive between earth and sky, but also discovers itself as caught up in threefold proportional ontology. This ontology includes the entire known dimension of a creature's realm of experiences (see Figure 1). Categories such as the greater Food Chain, Environment, or the Fabric of Life have all been recognized in recent anthropological literature, rather "religiously," as greater-than-human realities.

Of course, in the case of a superior species whose members are capable of doing a lot of mental reflection, such superiority as humankind recognizes in itself, consideration of one's finitude within an objectified almighty Food Chain or Environment does not necessarily also lead to a subjective religious awareness of one's own finitude. Aggressive nonreligious "wrestling" with modern larger reality configurations tends to be at least as serious as, in earlier mythological contexts, human bouts with gods, angels, devils,

So-perceived configurations of reality

less-than-human realities	potential equals	greater-than-human realities

Experiences and responses

control	experimentation	hypothet. rearrangement	analysis	familiarity	fascination	awe	fear, trembling	surrender

Figure 1. Human experiences of, and responses to, so-perceived configurations of reality.

Copyrighted Material

demons, or dragons. Ontologically our scientific quests are no better grounded than were the struggles of our antecedents in earlier culture strata.

The multitude of causes in nature that together determine our lives and eventually will do us in can be approached in opposing ways. They can be accepted religiously as divinities, and after analyzing these deities into smaller quanta, they can be ignored or hidden under heaps of abstract philosophical principles and symbols; that is, under the indigestible excrement of analytic aggression and digestion. If all of Nature together appears threatening and hostile, then a composite of many lesser natural forces, or even a chaotic array of such, may to a playful analytic mind seem less intimidating. The human penchant for analysis makes it possible to kill, dissect, digest, or disperse larger ontological threats. It also enables us to think and dispose of threatening entities in the abstract, as lesser epistemological "problems" rather than entities. This general need for physical as well as mental victory underlies all human endeavors, theologies, philosophies, and sciences alike.

Systematic theologies accomplish such human victories with the abstract treatment of their respective God or gods. It is obvious that large gods are more fearsome than smaller ones. It is obvious, too, that gods of whatever size, who are systematically analyzed into sacred aspects or attributes become less frightening than those who still loom over humankind as virile and whole personages.

Accordingly, our scale of experiential intensities is threefold. From left to right it plots human responses to so-perceived reality configurations of increasing size or greatness. And thereby it measures degrees of religiosity, or intensities of religious experience. Human behavior toward less-than-human realities not only is different from religious behavior, it differs also from behavior directed toward potential equals at the midpoint of the scale.

Less-than-Human Realities

Lesser realities can be manipulated, experimented with, conquered and controlled. The quest for food, aggression and progress, the sciences, technology and the arts, all score heavily as involvements in this dimension of so-conceived realities.

Copyrighted Material

The first step in the scientific approach, analysis, initially breaks down targeted reality configurations into smaller, manageable portions. Only less-than-human realities subsequently can be rearranged hypothetically, can so be experimented with, and can be manipulated and controlled. When potential equals are targeted to become food or scientific subject matter, they will either put up a fight or submit only smaller or unessential portions of themselves for analysis or experimental modification. For example, I personally have never permitted a surgeon to operate beyond a clearly defined trouble spot, such as the vicinity of a hernia. What I have surrendered was never my complete self.

Moreover, there is nothing particularly new or modern about our celebrated "scientific" experimental method. It is the same method by which all creatures with alimentary canals happen to survive. It is also the same method by which many an ancient greater-than-human or potentially equal configuration of reality—such as a formidable animal, a god, or a fellow humanoid—has been confronted, captured, killed, or eaten. All latter-day mental, physical, or chemical analyses have been anticipated as concrete prototypes at the animal level. They have been anticipated by the basic activities of claws, teeth, and digestive juices, as well as by the mental-analytic reflections that early hominids have applied during their still simple tasks of hunting, tool making, butchering, and eating. Latter-day scientific analysis by hominid hunters—the breakdown of reality configurations into lesser portions—represents essentially no more than an intellectual elaboration on such simple and primitive activities as tearing, biting, chewing, and digesting. All rational creatures in the animal kingdom are still caught up in these same basic activities.

It follows that an excessive glorification of teeth, even of advanced humanoid scientific "brain-tipped teeth," sooner or later will leave us marooned in a world littered by our own chewed-dry cut reduced to excrements. Termites that have reduced their woody residences to sawdust, by their natural method of physical analysis, are forced to move on. Where will humanoids with their mentally advanced termite skills hope to move? To some other planet? Or to some nirvana or heaven—after all! Or, perchance, to that other more progressive place of eternal purging and analysis by fire—after all that!

Copyrighted Material

Potential Equals

At the middle of the spectrum of experiences and responses, potential equals do share, communicate, or compete with one another. Social cooperation and humanistic learning together thrive best when focused on this balance point for potential equality. They thrive in accordance with the Golden Rule.

Inasmuch as one recognizes that a *Homo sapiens* and a *Homo religiosus* taken together add up to a *Homo ludens*, the metaphor of contemplating a teeter-totter plank seems somewhat appropriate. This metaphor even brings out the fact that all along the biological and social playground dynamic has enticed our minds to extract the subject matter "religion," as well as all commentary presented in this book, from the plethora of ordinary life, space, and time.

Encounters with potential equals, around the middle of the spectrum, can be studied as oscillations from that point toward either end of the scale. In the course of a day, between rising, eating, and falling asleep, and certainly during the course of a year, all living creatures on earth do oscillate from one extremity on this scale to the other. Inasmuch as hominids on that teeter-totter plank apply their intellect in their quest for nourishment and survival, analytically, they are indeed *Homines sapientes*. But they are also *Homines religiosi* when they move in the other direction and when they retreat from aggression. In fact, they are involved around the middle and toward both sides of the spectrum, most of the time. Over the course of a lifetime, experiential positions are finalized and come to rest, willingly or unwillingly, at the extreme point of surrender at the right end of the spectrum. Willingly or unwillingly, every creature's existential teeter-totter balances the totality of aggressive behavior, religiously in the end, by virtue of that creature's inherent weakness and mortality.

A measure of humane balance is necessary for coexistence even in science laboratories and in technological workshops. Experiences of "fascination," mild religious experiences, are cultivated there to entice newcomers into the cults of business, management, technology, scientific experimentation, as well as militarism. However, such mild religious experiences are appreciated only up to a point. No sooner has an excess of fascination been sensed by masters who preside over modern organizations of science, industrial production, and conquest,

Copyrighted Material

than all available didactic knowhow is being mobilized to bring a fascinating subject matter within range of "familiarity." Fascination is thus eclipsed, and the targeted familiarized subject matter is further reduced by systematic "analysis" to the status of "objects." Less-than-human objects can be subjected to hypothetical rearrangement, experimentation, and thereafter to full human control. A creature who intermittently has been a *Homo religiosus* on retreat becomes hungry again, namely, a fullfledged *Homo sapiens-necans*. Of course, not only innocent inferior species are victimized and endangered by the wide swing of human pendulums and teeter-totters. The human species as a whole, with all its lofty visions of egalitarian coexistence and self-realization, has put itself in jeopardy by its collective imbalances as well.

Greater-than-Human Realities

In turn, by so-conceived greater-than-human configurations of reality a human being is fascinated, awed, scared, experimented with or dealt with in some other fashion, tranquilized, and eventually done in. Moving toward the right along the experience-response spectrum, mild religious "fascination" registers more intensely when it is upgraded to a state of "awe." Enraptured in a state of awe the human being, as a *Homo religiosus*, rests poised at a temporary happy equilibrium. The human creature stands frozen perhaps, after the manner of the prophet Muhammad when he saw the angel Gabriel appear to him everywhere along the horizon. He could move "neither backwards nor forwards." In a similar manner, the three disciples of Jesus, who accompanied their master to his mountain of trans-figuration, insisted on prolonging such a state of awe and happy equilibrium.[1]

Much of religious ceremonialism aims at achieving, and stabiliz-ing, the level of temporarily feasible bliss, as close as possible to the point of "awe" on our scale. All the fine and not-so-fine arts of humankind, at various points in history, have attempted to concretize and stabilize some such fleeting whiffs, or sounds, or glimpses of

---

[1]Ibn Ishak died in 768 C.E. He is quoted in Thor Andrae, *Mohammed, the Man and His Faith* (New York, 1960), p. 44. Transfiguration accounts about Jesus are given in *Matthew* 17, *Mark* 9, and *Luke* 9.

Copyrighted Material

paradise. The music of Bach, Händel, and Mozart among others, along with pipe organs in European cathedrals, orchestras, and large brass choirs, or painters like Michelangelo, Rembrandt, and Dürer, have accomplished this feat to some degree for this writer.

Nevertheless, human attempts at structuring and fixing experiential modes of awe, inevitably, have compromised the religious pacifity and quality of these same experiences. Artistically mediated ecstasies compare to pure religious ones as canned edibles compare to fresh food. No denigration is here intended. Canned rations certainly are preferable for human nourishment than the alternative of starvation.

Leaning then, from the point of "awe," still farther toward passive experience, "fear and trembling" become definitive modes. In religions where the ontological *mysterium tremendum* has been avoided, as for instance in much of Buddhism, this point of fear and trembling might better be designated as a state of transitional "tranquility." Had this book been written primarily for Buddhist monks, the right half of our teeter-totter spectrum could have been marked off, as well, with the eight steps from the Buddha's Eightfold or Middle Path. For discourse with less devout philosophical schools, methods for "knowing oneself"—that is, ritualized introspection and self-criticism—may as well serve the purpose of selfless retreat, for balance and tranquility. All the while, even in the philosophical exercise of introspection the human self is contrasted with some greater-than-human standard of truth.

The endpoint to which all life on earth moves, in a variety of ever-changing combinations of aggressive and retreat responses, is ultimate surrender in death. In the course of every organism's life, death is prefigured by cycles of fatigue, a need for rest, and falling asleep. Ritualized or organized religious paths often do recommend to their followers "submission" or "surrender" as a fact already accomplished in its essentials during life, or else at least as something soon to be perfected. Nevertheless, all of humankind's organized religious paths in one form or other do differentiate certain "degrees" of surrender, or levels of seeing and knowing. They carefully distinguish between temporary and less intense surrenders—or states of awareness—on the one hand, and the intensity of surrendering one's ego unreservedly with the finality of death, on the other. So for instance, the baptism of Christians means initiation into preliminary dying and rising with Christ (*Romans* 6:3-4), whereas for Buddhists the nirvanic experience of moksha is the prefiguration of pari-nirvana.

Copyrighted Material

Religious responses are gestures and patterns of retreat behavior, always evoked implicitly by the experienced presence of greater-than-human realities. Such retreat behavior affects modes of conscious activity as well as mere tremors of emotion. It delimits the scope of perception as well as the range of subject matter deemed safe for objective thinking, for killing, eating, or for scientific manipulation. On the other hand, the acknowledged presence of greater realities enables an aggressor who finds himself "in over his head" to retreat honorably. This means one is able, religiously, to explain one's retreat behavior as something "reasonable." In communication with others, who also express their "will to live" by way of retreat, the desire to escape from greater-than-human dangers will always seem reasonable. Thus religious behavior, in this context, may be understood as the business of making honorable and rational retreats from greater-than-human odds.

Therefore, ranging from "fascination," which is the mildest form of religious experience, to mystic "surrender" in death, which constitutes the most intense, religion does extend over half of the spectrum of possible human experiences, that is, over half of the available range of ontological involvements. The opposite half on that spectrum is defined by modes of aggression.

Social balance among potential equals, near the middle of the spectrum, may be allegorized as a bird in flight; aggressiveness is represented by one wing, and religious retreat by the other. During flight the two wings must balance each other's movements, and they must compensate for each other's adjustments during gliding.

The fact that most so-conceived greater-than-human configurations of reality have been encountered, traditionally, as personal deities also is a very rational happenstance. A *Homo sapiens* who defines his own existence in terms of intelligent personhood cannot help—upon prolonged reflection on the puzzle of his own finitude and upon being caught up in a biological food chain—but postulate the superiority of some external greater intelligence or personage. He recognizes personality status in anything that reveals itself effectively as greater—at least up to the level of, and a little beyond, his own ego and personality awareness. To deny one's own finitude in relation to the forementioned threefold proportionality, that is, to deny the common sense need of thriving near the middle of one's experiential spectrum—somewhere between the extreme points of "eating" and of "being devoured"—would be tantamount to insisting in relation to
Copyrighted Material

others on divine status for oneself. A reflective mind cannot escape this query. If the ontological substratum that has given birth to me as self-reflective ego is not personal, if that ground of being is not personal, then what is this "I"? Then, what does it mean to be a person? And then, what is human dignity?

Although I attribute the religious discovery of personal attributes among so-encountered greater-than-human configurations of reality to keen human intelligence, I must insist on one more point in this regard. "Reason" or "reasonableness" transcends the narrow limits of mere analytic reasoning.

To confront less-than-human things analytically and to manipulate them scientifically can be deemed a reasonable undertaking, provided the things to be controlled are indeed less-than-human. Our short-term survival depends on the success of such "rational" pursuits. However, being confronted by greater-than-human beings, and responding with fascination, awe, fear, tranquility, or surrender, may be equally realistic and rational. For instance, running in fear from a dangerous predator may be the most rational thing a person can do under certain circumstances. And moreover, to surrender and face death with poetry on one's lips may be the most rational behavior under slightly more severe conditions. Religious behavior is irrational only when it is expressed in relation to less-than-human things or idols, or toward equals.

All the while, meeting potential equals and discovering ways to coexist with equals in accordance with the Golden Rule count among the most rational lessons a human mind can learn. Acts of idolizing fellow human beings, from the perspective of the Golden Rule, are religious irrationalities; and acts of manipulating fellow human beings, from that same vantage point, are aggressive or scientific irrationalities. Either extremity threatens balance and humane survival.

Human rationality cannot be evaluated by either the presence or the absence of analytic hunger, greed, or cunning; nor can it be judged by the presence or absence of momentary happiness or mystic bliss. The acid test for human intelligence, in the end, always will be the degree of realistic balance achieved in relation to one's own private threefold ontology, that is, in full awareness of all factors and options that make for balance. Thus, a narrow analytic or scientific application of human reason, at the neglect of greater reality configurations and contexts, will always boomerang and result in

Copyrighted Material

foolish self-destruction as soon as the larger context begins to reassert itself.

Religion and Culture

Religious responses, or religious retreat behavior, generally speaking, always are the behavior of individuals. If I coerce someone to retreat as I do, I do not act religiously toward that person but aggressively. However, if that person retreats by way of imitating my example, both of us act religiously. Managed or culturally organized retreat behavior therefore never is completely religious for all involved.

A similar ambiguity exists at the culture building or aggression side of the continuum. A soldier, for example, who obeys a commanding officer to attack an enemy position acts aggressively toward the enemy; he or she acts religiously toward the commander and toward the entire superior chain of command. Each superior in that chain acts religiously toward his or her respective superior and aggressively toward his or her inferiors—unless he or she decides to disobey an order and suffer the consequences. In that case the subsequent sufferings of punishment tend to absorb into themselves all the religious behavior that otherwise would have been evoked down the line, all the way to the soldier and the enemy.

Then, reaching for another analogy farther back in time, latter-day cultural struggles may be regarded as having been prefigured already in a primitive hunter's simple quest for food. His aggressive scavenging, hunting, killing, and eating are followed inevitably by religious retreat behavior, by inactivity occasionally associated with remorse and fasting, and by other restrictions imposed on him during his quest and consumption of food. Such restrictions usually are explained by primitive hunters religiously, as having been imposed on them by some greater-than-human hunter deity. In the modern atheistic idiom, the effect that such greater-than-human obstacles have had on the human soul continues to register as conscience; that is, "con-science" in the sense of being con or contra to progress-oriented science.

Inasmuch as religious retreats generally do imply a confession of weakness, the political enforcement of religious behavior among groups of people may evoke embarrassment or even shame. It

Copyrighted Material

eventually also may generate resentment at being bullied. Or it may evoke defensive-aggressive reactions. If left to themselves, people ordinarily do engage in religious retreat behavior together, and they do think religious thoughts naturally and voluntarily. They ordinarily do so within the safe context of mutuality. They withdraw and retreat together for comfort and encouragement. They share religious retreat behavior with other people who happen to be on a similar path of retreat.

In shared states of weakness lies comfort, and also the potential and the strength for a joint comeback. Together, religious folk tend to acknowledge and submit to benevolent greater-than-human realities that in some way endorse, sustain, or at least tolerate their survival.

Every surviving individual lives by balancing his or her life, embedded in collective modes of cultural aggression and religious retreat. Likewise, every social group, every culture and civilization, survives by achieving a similar balance—by cultivating a balance somewhere between states of predatorial aggression and mystic surrender.

Collective imbalances in the direction of either extreme, aggression or retreat, sooner or later will result in reactionary movements in the opposite direction that, in turn, tend to overshoot their points of balance. Aggressive military campaigns and penitential religious pilgrimages therefore tend to alternate in the ebb and flow of tribes and nations. A necessity for balance determines the fate of all strata of society, even in situations where at one or the other behavioral extreme, control or surrender, an elite stretches its theatrical high wires to perform upon.

Aggressive heroes provoke regressive and gentle saints; pious folk stimulate haughty scoffers; and scoffers in turn provoke humble pious folk into becoming first defensively proud—and later aggressively proud. Aggressive grand domesticators drive sensitive people to a point where they identify with doves; stubborn martyrs suffer in hope of shaming their killers into repentance.[2] And finally, kings on horseback have at one point in the history of Near Eastern civilization generated a political climate, of popular disdain, that even a poor man

---

[2] *Grand domestication* refers to the era in human evolution that follows simple "domestication." See the section on "Reorientation in the History and Evolution of Religion," later in this chapter.

Copyrighted Material

on a donkey could be acclaimed the next and better eternal King of kings.

Religious soteriologies—gospels of salvation—are initially always predicament-specific. They are invoked in response to specific socio-cultural imbalances. Religious gospels are designed to neutralize specific aggressive excesses; they exist to balance specific cultural emphases or sins.

Religion and culture together, up to this point, have been delineated behavioristically, as opposites, and in terms of directional movement toward one or the other extreme. A closer look at socio-political dynamics is now called for. Deliberations in this book categorically place "retreat" in opposition to "aggression." The essential behavior that builds and supports culture is aggression; its outer limit is conquest, killing, and imposition of absolute "control." In contrast, the essential religious behavior is marked by retreat that at its extreme limit culminates in the total surrender of egos.

In the course of a person's struggle for survival, full religious retreat is compromised in the form of "structured retreat"—analysis and hypothetical rearrangement are imported from the aggression side to impose rational communicational structure on greater-than-human reality. Structured retreat behavior may be compromised further by folding it over onto the general realm of aggression, thus establishing the subcategory of "justified aggression." Aggressive behavior, for the sake of cultural balance and survival, must derive its justification from structured retreat at the other side; whereas, inversely, structured retreat was obliged to obtain its tools and skills of organization and communication from the aggressive side. And finally, the category of justified aggression may be compromised further by unchecked aggressive behavior.

As to our definitions of *Culture* and *Religion*, and their interrelatedness, the matter may be summarized as follows: Culture is anchored first in its realm of Aggression, then is fortified by its own subregion of Justified Aggression, and contemporaneously is inspired in dialogue or tension with its most remote dimension, Structured Retreat. Religion is complementary to Culture and anchored first in its realm of Retreat; it is conceptualized and communicated in its subregion of Structured Retreat, and finally is organized or institutionalized in culture, more or less aggressively, in the dimension of Justified Aggression. (This is illustrated in Figure 2.)

Copyrighted Material

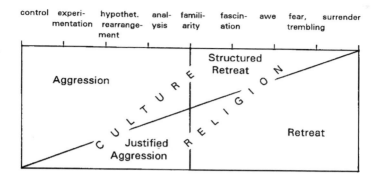

Figure 2. Religious experiences and responses in relation to "culture" building and organized "religion."

An emphasis on Justified Aggression, however, which is no longer anchored in Pure Retreat and Structured Retreat, ceases to be religious. By the same token, Pure Retreat behavior by itself contributes nothing tangible to Culture as such.

Religious retreat behavior and culturally aggressive behavior are expressed by all living beings. However, among higher and rational animals there is copresent a heightened sense of self-awareness, namely, an awareness of one's own habits of analytic aggression (science) as well as of one's own habits of religious retreat (conscience). Aggressions or progressions on one side, and religious retreats on the other, therefore interplay with one another as checks and balances. Near the midpoint of the existential scale, delineated in Figures 1 and 2, all these realms and subrealms may contribute together, as checks and balances, to a favorable balance for societal survival, supported by rites that embody the Golden Rule. There, in the vicinity of that egalitarian point of balance, amidst culture and religion, equals do share, compete, coexist, and multiply.

Copyrighted Material

Reorientation in the
History and Evolution of Religions

The process of "evolution," as it has been refined by anthropological theories during past decades, no longer means what it meant in the nineteenth century: progress from lower to higher levels of existence. Modern anthropological evolutionists, nevertheless, may recognize a gradual increase in the complexity of human cultures over the long haul, to the extent that archaeological data support their conclusions.

Inasmuch as in this chapter we already have carefully delineated the reciprocal relationship between "culture" and "religion," there exists no longer a need for holding evolutionary thinking in the history of religions hostage to the old ghosts of our progress-oriented founding fathers. Religion defined as retreat behavior never can mean "progress." Religion may entail not only physical retreat behavior in environment and space, but include retreat nostalgia and remembrance rites in the dimension of time. There is not a single religious founder, recorded in the annals of our discipline, who has not in some way returned his followers to an earlier simpler relationship with greater-than-human reality. These founders did so in the hope of persuading not only their immediate followers, but whole cultures and nations unto a return path as well.

Another common misconception about "evolution" must be dispelled at the outset. The evolutionary eras suggested here are not successive stretches of time where each has been replaced, progressively, by a next; rather, they are accumulated strata. All may be visualized together as interfused strata representing overlapping time sequences. For example, hunter-gatherer cultures and religions are still with us and in some parts of the world still are alive and exposed to sunlight. I myself have lived and participated in all the evolutionary culture strata mentioned in this book. While doing so I became existentially involved in the aggressiveness, the sins, the guilt, and the atonement retreats of people whose struggles for existence have left them stranded in more specialized cultures and religiosity than my own happens to be. The general evolutionary eras given here and illustrated in Figure 3 can be harmonized with most current anthropological theories on evolution. They are presented here tentatively.

Copyrighted Material

ca. 2,500,000 years ago: gathering, scavenging, hunting— — — — — — — — — — — —

ca. 12,000 years ago: domestication— — — — — — — — — — — —

ca. 5,000 years ago: grand domestication— — — — — — — —

ca. 3,000 years ago: religions of universal salvation—

ca. 300 years ago: democratic revolts—

Figure 3. Eras in the Evolution of Cultures and Religions

Gathering, Scavenging, Hunting

The span of time in humanoid evolution identified here with the activities of gathering, scavenging, and hunting may be estimated in excess of 2 million years, as having begun with the manufacture of stone tools. In isolated regions of our globe this culture stratum survives to this very day. Subsistence in this culture depends on the ability to forage and on the ability and the courage to kill animals. Hunters and gatherers interfere at the ends of their victims' life cycles. They inflict that end and assume full control over their victims' remains by way of consuming them.

With an increase in intelligence, driven by the desire to have better weapons, there also increased the possibility for discerning responsibility, guilt, and suitable paths of justification. Hunting is trickery par excellence. Hunter gods therefore were mostly greater-than-humanoid hunters who, accordingly, appeared mostly in the form of predators. Some hunters paid share offerings from the carcasses of victims they killed. For their sins of killing, primitive hunters developed and performed religious retreat rituals—primarily to alleviate feelings of guilt. They atoned for their trespasses.

Domestication

The cultures of domesticators are marked by the activity of taking control over entire life cycles of plants and animals, from fertilization to consumption. They claimed ownership of seeds, plants, and livestock, and they paid their gods with sacrifices in kind—often

Copyrighted Material

whole specimens of animals and sheaves. Creator gods vouched and bestowed titles to these properties. Domesticators also claimed ownership to dwellings and land; they roamed as less than nomadic hunters and built more permanent houses, especially where agriculture had become their primary basis for subsistence.

In tropical areas the earliest practice of horticulture was probably dominated by women while the men continued to specialize on hunting. Success in horticulture produced for these people an increase in population; this, in turn, gave the men fewer animals to hunt and subsequently saddled them with an identity crisis. Secret warrior societies, and cults of headhunting and cannibalism, were some of the men's religio-cultural adaptations to that ego crisis. Subsequent aristocratic warrior societies and priesthoods, together, have drawn much of their ethos and mythos from this crisis of readjustment among men—the transition from hunting to domestication.

On prairie lands where hunters gradually adapted to shadowing remnant herds, where they claimed and guarded these herds as their own, the men remained the chief providers. Women in these situations rose in status only with great difficulty. This adaptation was typical on the semiarid prairies of northern Africa, the Near East, and Central Asia. On the other hand, cultures that came to practice a mixture of gardening, animal husbandry, and simple mechanized cultivation with draft animals were able to distribute labor and gender roles more evenly.

Grand Domestication

The grand domestication phase in human evolution is important for understanding this book. Egypt has been a grand domestication system par excellence. The Hebrew "Exodus" tradition defined itself as a reaction against it. Greek philosophers, who also reacted to the problems of grand domestication, have themselves drawn much basic ontology from Egyptian grand domestication religion. Subsequently Christendom, from the moment of its conception, has inherited the Hebrew reaction against Egyptian grand domestication; but it also has taken up into itself some of Egypt's own ontology and theological structures.

Grand domestication began wherever ambitious domesticators, very often men of a herder tradition, have pushed beyond the limit of merely controlling the life cycles of plants and animals. They

Copyrighted Material

proceeded to also control groups of people, as human herds, together with those people's gods. Their most conspicuous methods for over-domesticating humankind were militarism, slavery, castration, and human sacrifice.[3] Methods for domesticating the gods of subjected peoples included the building of stately barns or temples, setting up their gods in form of statues, feeding them on altars, and organizing the life of their subjected people by means of sacred calendars and festivals, thereby fixing the visiting and feeding hours for successfully sequestered gods.

Many of these grand or overdomestication schemes began innocently enough with the full collaboration of their subjects. Efforts of defense against other grand domesticator hordes required strict organization under some kind of King of kings and God of gods. This is to say, that such great divine beings functioned in a real way as saviors of the people who, in turn, worshiped them and organized, who allied themselves and survived, under their sponsorship. Whereas warrior, headhunter, and cannibal societies already may be seen as primitive forms of grand domestication, human sacrifice, as such, represents an elaboration on advanced domesticator logic—to pay original divine owners.[4] Human sacrifice demonstrated and symbol-ized the grand domesticator's claim for absolute power over the life and death of his subjects—thus his divine right to ownership.

A history of religions approach, in the larger perspective of human evolution, need not follow slavishly the valuations of field historians who, since time immemorial, have been singing the praises of empires and other kinds of grand domestication schemes. Kept on the payroll of grand domesticators, many repaid their sponsors with valuing and glorifying grandiose aggressiveness as "civilization." Let the historians of grand domestication continue to glorify the battle-

---

[3]When contemplating the atrocities of glorious grand domesticators, I occasionally feel obligated, in this book, to apply the judgmental term *overdomesticators*—lest I be perceived as endorsing them.

[4]Priesthoods and aristocracies in Middle American civilization, from Olmec to Aztec, appear to have developed directly from the lower hunter-domesticator level of democratized overdomestication. Their bouts of headhunting and cannibalism developed directly into grand domestication, with massive human sacrifices. They have not had the benefit of the herder experience with its matching checks and balances, involving ecology and the "Good Shepherd" ideal.

Copyrighted Material

fronts and victories of empires, it remains the task of historians of religions to understand types of religious retreat behavior as opposites. Historians of religions are interested foremostly in the histories of commonsense retreat movements—in movements away from aggression and culture building.

Universal Salvation Religions

These are movements on behalf of ordinary people, which attempted to liberate them from the clasp of grand domestication systems that had become unbearable. They are popular patterns of religious retreat behavior that claim universal dignity for all people, regardless of imperial boundaries, wealth, or inherited privileges. Theologically they may deny or claim as their own the privileged relationships of grand domesticators to their supreme sources of authority. Universal salvation religions spread beyond imperial boundaries and became international movements.

Approximately during the thirteenth century B.C.E., Moses is said to have led a group of slaves to freedom under the auspices of a God (Yahweh) who in all respects was equal to the God of gods of the Egyptian empire (Amun). That escapee religion has survived partially in Judaism and Samaritanism. Strong traces of its prophetic theological impulse continue also in Christianity and Islam.

Some time before two and a half millennia ago, in Iran, the man remembered as Zoroaster effected a religio-political reform against a herder priesthood that thrived on performing animal sacrifices. He enlisted the help of a benign grand domesticator and introduced worship of a universal deity, Ahura Mazda.

During the fifth century B.C.E., in India, the founder of Buddhism ignored the authority of the traditional Aryan priesthood and nobility, whose powers were amplified regularly with the performance of spectacular sacrificial festivities that mediated the blessings of the gods and the endorsement of acquired prosperity and wealth. Gotama dropped out from his aristocratic social class and became a mendicant hippie-monk, bent on finding an escape route from samsara and the effects of karma and on making available to all a universal path to happiness and nirvana.

Soon thereafter, in China, the sage Lao Tzu recorded his philosophy in a little book that gave prominence to the need of living in

Copyrighted Material

harmony with the universal Dao. He gave his readers the mental tools with which they could ignore the mongering warlords and ambitious overdomesticators of his time. Some Daoist faithful, as at the White Cloud Temple in Beijing, still revere this ancient hippie-philosopher as Lord Most High—a similar status that, for similar reasons, has been attributed in the West to Jesus, as Christ the Lord.

About that same time, in China, the sage Kung Futzu (Confucius) taught a doctrine of universal ethics for decent political behavior that imposed Heaven and formal etiquette upon people's relationships toward one another. His ethical teachings eventually put ambitious grand domesticators on the defensive; he prescribed for them a gentlemen's code of behavior, under the tutelage of Heaven and of ancient Sage Kings. When his behavioral and ethical prescriptions gradually took hold, and when they were adopted by farsighted grand domesticators, they helped stabilize China for over two thousand years.

The many "heavenly emperors" of Chinese religious Daoism—rising in popularity again today—do constitute a multiplicity of religious hopes similar to the "kingdom of heaven" that Jesus gave to Christendom. Chinese Daoist priests balanced their traditional problem, of having an earthly grand domesticator rule the Middle Kingdom as the Son of Heaven, with a number of heavenly emperors and their generals.[5] This multiplicity of heavenly saviors may reflect prior knowledge of hosts of Buddhist bodhisattvas. In part, their problems with overdomestication resulted from the generous endorsement Confucians rendered to the office of the Son of Heaven. Still, Confucius should not be blamed for the exaggeration of imperial power that resulted in his name. Confucius lived and taught during times of war when the emperor was powerless, and he was convinced that the imperial office was necessary to restore a semblance of peace and order.

During the first century C.E., in Palestine, a man named Jesus lived the role of a Son of God—a title that in the Near East for three thousand years had signified "heir of a divine emperor." He acted this role so obstinately that the masses of people followed him even after he had been crucified. They proclaimed his resurrection from

---

[5]The Daoist White Cloud Temple, in Beijing, has recently published the portraits of sixty heavenly generals. Copyrighted Material

death as their salvation, and in the religious movement that ensued they became all brothers and sisters of this heavenly Son of God. The hereditary kings and emperors of the region gradually lost their following to this "king of heaven."

During the seventh century, in Arabia, Muhammad the prophet organized a nomadic people who had been dwarfed in the shadows of two re-overdomesticated universalisms: Zoroastrian Persia and Christian Byzantium. His universalism, of inviting all people to submit to Allah's will together, as equals, has quickly arrived at a synthesis for the religion of Islam—by way of grand domestication ambitions and competitive warfare with Byzantium and Persia. Whereas it took the Christian universal salvation religion three centuries to revert to grand domestication, it happened with Islam during the lifetime of its founder.

Democratic Revolts

Revolutions in recent centuries, which in Europe deposed hereditary kings and instituted democratic forms of government, drew their sanctions from a long history of ideological conditioning. For nearly two millennia Christians in Western civilization have become accustomed to think of themselves as brothers and sisters of Christ, the new King of kings. They have lived to reign some day with him in his heavenly kingdom. That faith may have been a "pie in the sky" notion, as Marxist ideologists have perceived it; but that hope also has depreciated the status of hereditary kings to a point where their god-fearing subjects could depose them.

Karl Marx came out of Judaism, and Friedrich Engels came from conservative Christian Pietism. Their communism need not surprise us in light of the fact that primitive Christianity itself, a Jewish sect, began as a communism. Moreover, the "commune" ideal is recorded as a historical datum in Christendom's most sacred book; it is still practiced in the modern state of Israel today. Dissatisfied with organized religion during the Industrial Revolution and blessed with the prophetic conviction that a Judeo-Christian God who sponsors organized injustices cannot be real, they both chose for their platform an ontology of reactionary atheism.

The Communist liberation armies, of Russia and China and beyond, have themselves spread the Judeo-Christian ethos—minus its

Copyrighted Material

theology. They spread it unknowingly, like a heron's legs carry the eggs of fish from one pond to another. To the extent that nowadays, in lands where Communist systems are being restructured, the Christian religion acquires many new followers, it results not only from the lure of wealth that emanates from Christianized lands. Latter-day followers of Communism have been drilled for decades on a radical version of Judeo-Christian ethics, minus God. They now simply are trying to find their own theological-ontological soul.

Revisiting Near Eastern Religions

Perhaps the thought of no other geographical area of the world, in the history of religions field, has been studied and restudied as much as the religious traditions that originated in the ancient Near East. Why, then, is another book and a fresh look necessary? What can a general historian of religions hope to contribute to an area of study already researched by thousands of specialists? Obviously, such a contribution cannot hope to provide greater detail or precision. Rather, it can offer a wideangle overview with glimpses of four distinct academic fields in their interrelatedness: ancient Egyptian religion, the Hebrew tradition, Greek philosophy, and early Christianity.

Individual religious traditions ordinarily are studied by specialists, beginning at moments of their inception or with the biographies of their founders. The histories of these chosen religions then are traced forward in time as far as records will carry. For an extraordinary broad scope, specialized historians occasionally will look sideways, at parallel traditions, that happen to have been thriving nearby; or they will apply a variety of perspectives borrowed from auxiliary academic disciplines. But rarely do specialist historians position themselves at the beginning of their favorite tradition to seriously look back in time, to see the full depth of the evolutionary process surging toward them—and watch that process as it saddles religious founders with the necessity of having to institute reforms.

The ancient Egyptian civilization and its concomitant religiosity provided Hebrew religious tradition with its raison d'être. Egyptian theology furnished Greek philosophers, beginning with the Ionians and concluding with the Neoplatonists, with their ontological

Copyrighted Material

presuppositions. And Hebrew and Egyptian religion, assisted by Neoplatonism, contributed content and structure to orthodox Christian theology.

As far as Christianity is concerned it may now be argued that, supported by the broader historical background, it had fiery Hebrew religion as its father. Yes, indeed! This book will not detract anything from that well-documented paternal heritage, nor will it depreciate the general Semitic context of Judaism in Mesopotamia. But with that same historical honesty one now must also acknowledge the fact that ancient Egyptian religion has been Christendom's more quiet mother. In any case, post-Jamnian Judaism was not the father of Christendom. It was a sibling born alongside and, apparently, from the same parents.[6]

Christianity is a religion that began with a Jewish founder and a dozen apostles whom he inspired. The sacred scriptures of Christendom are of Hebrew origin as well, and they are composed of two major strata. The Hebrew canon was adopted as "old testament," a covenant between God and humankind subsequently superseded or fulfilled by Christ. In many ways the Old Testament serves as a foil for the new gospel, which is the Christian "new testament." This second layer of scripture was first written in Greek, which was the dominant literary language in the eastern Mediterranean realm during the Hellenistic period when Christianity began.

From a Jewish perspective the Christian New Testament reflects sectarian Jewish experience at the periphery of first century C.E. Judaism; certain intrusions from the diaspora are acknowledged for good measure. In a larger historical context, however, the teachings contained in the New Testament have provided a bridge that led away from Jewish tradition toward what gradually has become a distinct Christian theology—including soteriology, christology, numenology, and mariology. All the while, the distinct "Christian" strain of fresh theological awareness, of fresh revelation, mostly has been a revival of time-tested ancient Egyptian theological truths.

---

[6]In light of the Egyptian dimension explored by this book, the popular historical category of a "Judeo-Christian Tradition" may remain more useful for balancing the religio-social dimension of life in America than for illuminating the actual history of Near Eastern religions.

Copyrighted Material

With historical hindsight the christological, mariological, and numenological controversies, during the early Christian centuries, may now be understood as birth pains for the emergence of Christendom. These birth pangs, while they are now almost forgotten by the offspring, were nevertheless real labor pains on the part of Christendom's mother, the expiring religion of ancient Egypt. Our old Egyptian mother died in the centuries during which her vigorous offspring emerged and began prospering in the Mediterranean world. Her labor pains were her death pangs.

Throughout her life of almost two millennia, this Christian daughter born of Mother Egypt has remained relatively well informed about her ancient Hebrew paternal tradition—being reminded of it constantly by the Hebrew origins of its early layer of sacred scriptures. At the same time the mature daughter, Christendom, to this day has not been told about the identity of her deceased mother religion—whose theological and soteriological temperament she closely resembles.

Beginners' Questions

All updated perspectives and new insights require that fresh questions be asked. When new questions are asked and focused on a revised historical screen, then frequently, new and more satisfactory answers snap into focus as if on their own accord. To assist the readers of this volume in their general task of reorientation, a few preliminary questions shall be mentioned at the outset. While no attempt will be made here to answer these questions systematically, their resolution should gradually become apparent to all who survey the full length of the book.

1. How has the Christian gospel, of God "begetting" a Son, ever made sense to Jewish minds who previously had been living under the spell of traditional Yahweh theology? Is it really conceivable that the apostles of Christ, Jews, were favorably impressed by Greek mythological models—as for instance by the lewd affairs attributed to Father Zeus that resulted in a variety of inter-species "begettings"? Or must one look for logical antecedents elsewhere in the Near East?

Copyrighted Material

2. When and where has the *logos* concept, the creative Word of God, been recognized first? Was it in the *Genesis* creation account? Or has it sprung part and parcel from the orthodox tradition of Egyptian monotheism, monism, and emanationalism?

3. How has Christianity gotten its trinitarian theology? Were Indo-European tripartite systems really the basic models, as has sometimes been postulated? Or, should one rather look for its antecedent in the first trinity of the Heliopolitan Ennead? Has the early Christian debate concerning the Holy Spirit, as proceeding from the Father and/or the Son, been provoked by Egyptian or Greek theology and logic? Or by both?

4. Upon what Jewish logical basis could the pharisaic faith in the resurrection of the dead have evolved? It seems obvious that it could not have sprung from Greek dualistic reasoning, according to which only souls can survive human death. Was it derived from Iranian Mazdaism as many scholars think? Or, is it possible that ancient Egyptian funerary orientations have furnished it with initial credence?

5. Why in the early history of Christendom has the "kingdom of heaven" gospel been converted so quickly to a personal "death and resurrection" eschatology? Could that personal dimension have received its logical structure from ancient Egyptian funerary perspectives as well?

6. The "kingdom of heaven" proclaimed by John the Baptizer and Jesus as an antithesis to kingdoms of this world—was it based only on sentiments anticipated by ancient Hebrew prophets? And if so, how was the entire prophetic Hebrew tradition of "kingdom" criticism affected by the threat and temptation of Egyptian imperialism?

7. How Jewish or non-Jewish was the pantheistic theological accommodation that, according to *Acts* 17:28, the apostle Paul has submitted to an Athenian audience? The "in him we live and move and have our being" is generally traced by scholars to Epimenides of Crete; and the "for we are indeed his offspring" has been derived from the earlier *Phaenomena* by Aratus. Both of these quotations certainly do harmonize much better with ancient Egyptian theological common sense than either of them does with Jewish or Greek notions.

Copyrighted Material

8. And then, how Roman or how Egyptian was the "restless heart" of Saint Augustine as he hoped for eternal "rest in God"? Augustine came from Hippo, in northern Africa, and it is conceivable that already early in life he has been touched by some basic Egyptian theological sentiments.

9. At Alexandria, how extensive was the seepage of Egyptian religion into Hellenistic ways and thinking? How extensive was the influence of anonymous extant Egyptian priests, who refrained from writing and whose cults continued to flourish throughout the Hellenistic period? What has been their influence on Greek philosophy, Judaism, Christianity, Christian monasticism, and on various Gnosis movements?

All these questions touch only the tip of the Near Eastern proverbial iceberg. As some of these questions will be studied, and answered better by specialists during the decades ahead, surely, many more related puzzles and their solutions will float to the surface of our vast murky sea of evolutionary unknowing. This book pretends to be no more than a preliminary sketch of probable "prenatal" inheritances of Christendom, from ancient Near Eastern ontologies. It is an attempt at envisioning again some of those ancient religious fascinations by which Western religion and civilization were engendered. It is a humble fresh beginning.

The task of envisioning the evolution of several ancient cultures and religions together, and sketching the larger panorama of the Near Eastern history of religions, is not unlike the artist's task of sketching a larger than average mural. Miniature paintings and precise smaller-than-life representations are legitimate human endeavors as well. But the overall history of drawing and painting would definitely be the poorer, were the grandiose murals of a Michelangelo and the bolder dabbings of a Van Gogh not also extant, as well as the intentional economy of brush strokes practiced by Chinese or Japanese landscape painters and calligraphers.

To some extent, the style of this book will correspond to the scarce brush strokes of the latter (see Figure 4). A small number of fresh strokes and emphases, depicting here and there the ancient Egyptian theological heritage, will have to suffice as primary subject matter for Part One. A similar economy of sketchy lines, regarding

Copyrighted Material

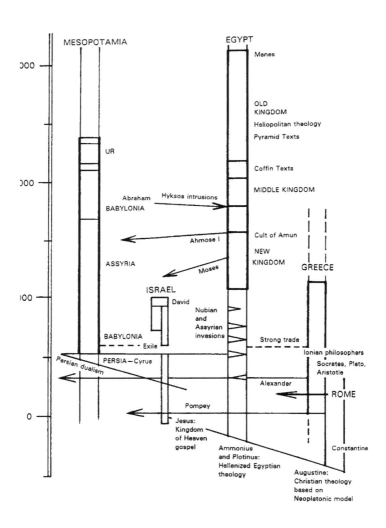

Figure 4. Schematic drawing, depicting the ancestry and birth of Christendom among Near Eastern civilizations: Judaism was its father; Egypt was its mother; Mesopotamia stood as godparent; Hellenism served as midwife.

Copyrighted Material

Hebrew and Greek responses to their respective Egyptian inheritances, will be adhered to while rounding out the larger pre-Christian
mural (Parts Two and Three). And then, inasmuch as the beginnings
of Christianity have been explained extensively in textbooks already
available, an even more terse list of fresh glimpses will be offered in
Part Four to sketch the birth process or emanation of Christian
theology from Egypt.

In all likelihood, readers who already are familiar with the
outlines of Neoplatonic philosophy and Augustinian theology, both
being territories not frequented by historians of religions, will have
an easier entry into this book.

All the while it is acknowledged that the actual rewriting of
history books in light of this new perspective eventually will become
the task of those with "miniature painter" temperaments. Their tasks
will demand many lives and, by munching them between the molars
of boredom, will devour many a mind that otherwise could have
enjoyed the luxury of greater creativity.

I have no illusions about the impermanence of my contribution in
the larger drift of discoveries, knowledge, time, space, and shifting
sands. Although I expect to communicate a few historical insights,
and I am confident that some of these will outlive the wrath of my
immediate critics, I am also reconciled to the prospect that the larger
world picture of which I have seen fresh glimpses can be recognized
only slowly, through the combined efforts of a large number of
scholars. It can be brought into focus only piecemeal and with help
from many others. To that effect I hope that my few brush strokes
will serve a next generation of historians, if not as guidelines then as
creative aggravations—as stimuli for fresh inspirations.

Copyrighted Material

Copyrighted Material

PART ONE:
EGYPTIAN LIGHT

Copyrighted Material

Copyrighted Material

Preface to
Egyptian Light

Our historical quest for better understanding the roots of Christendom in the Near East must begin, quite logically, at the oldest written source materials containing religious information. These sources we find in the royal pyramids of the Egyptian Old Kingdom and in patrician coffins reaching into the First Intermediary that followed.

This is not to say that Semitic Mesopotamian materials are unimportant for a comprehensive history of Near Eastern religions. They are important. But with all its claims to a wider angle of view, this book will have to draw a boundary line somewhere. Its limited aim is to emphasize, albeit onesidedly, what hitherto has been neglected. It skips what all along has been sufficiently accentated—practically by all scholars who have labored in the shadows of Judeo-Christian traditions.

Therefore, this book focuses on a few primary rivulets of theological structure, philosophical abstraction, and political accommodation. After flowing through three millennia these rivulets have swelled to the size of great rivers. They have caused a few inundations along the historical paths of cultures and religions. We still can recognize the ancient river beds in the living geography of world ideologies today.

Our grasp of ancient Egyptian religion is patchy at best; but then, timidity and willful insistence on faddish impossibilities would probably be worse than incomplete grasping. In ancient Egypt, as anywhere else in the world, the first strata of written religious texts have belonged to an elite—to royalty, to their priestly and aristocratic collaborators, to their entourage of retainers and officials. In the absence of written data, the religion of the common people, in ancient Egypt, generally has not fared very well in historical reconstructions. Most of what has been inferred about the lives of the common people still had to be based on extant information from the tip of imperial

Copyrighted Material

hierarchy, and then mostly from the funerary cult by which royalty and aristocracy memorialized itself for subsequent scrutiny.

The lacuna in our knowledge of popular ancient Egyptian religion becomes especially painful as we move into the first millennium B.C.E. Below the ruling classes Egyptian religion, by and large, has remained silent throughout the ancient history. Only at the apex of the hierarchy were sufficient central tenets of faith expressed in writing, or were memorialized in monuments bold enough for survival. When, during the last millennium B.C.E., foreign armies periodically clipped the Egyptian apex, records concerning the Egyptian mysteries of gods and life after death necessarily slowed to a trickle. Only later, in the broader Hellenistic ferment, have some Egyptian cults erupted and spread forth into Mediterranean daylight. The imperialistic nations who were the keepers of books during the centuries of Egypt's decline, who produced the books of which some were destined to survive, were not interested in the "superstitions" of colonized Egyptian natives.

The critical reader will surely demand: "Show us the late Egyptian sources that pharisees in Judah could have read and from which they could have learned about resurrection! Show us the books that Ammonius Saccas and Plotinus studied before they inflicted their Egyptian outlook on philosophers in Alexandria!" My reply to these requests is doomed to a more or less haughty silence.

Personal predisposition and common sense must prevail even along a trail were documents and ruins of past cultures have been obliterated. At points where inscribed certainties end, commonsense probabilities may be contemplated a little ways farther.

* * *

Life experiences sometimes speak louder than academic theories. I dedicated a decade of my life to collecting Navajo Indian oral religious traditions, four bundles total. Each unit of materials I was able to collect and see published, earlier had been declared extinct by scholars. And in spite of my successes in fieldwork, my recordings amount to only a small portion of what is still on the Navajo reservation. I have insisted on finding some of these oral traditions because I have found old traces of them in the scientific literature of the dominant Anglo-American culture.

Copyrighted Material

As I now view the matter, a similar relationship existed between Egypt and what became the Judeo-Christian tradition—in relation to Hellenic philosophy and Gnosticism. In these traditions I have found unmistakable traces of the ancient Egyptian central theology that, as historians concede, has flourished most conspicuously at Heliopolis. In post-Egyptian religious traditions and philosophies these ancient Egyptian traces determine central existential axioms. They explain the origin and evolution of the cosmos, of God and gods, life, death, and visions regarding the destiny of humankind. Axiomatic notions of this sort ordinarily do not disappear from human minds until they are dislodged by more plausible substitutes.

Thus, unless I am shown the process or the "mechanism," along with the axioms that supposedly have been substituted—to the effect that Egyptians actually became Hellenized dualists during those problematic centuries—I am obliged to regard Egyptians as having remained within the general drift of their Heliopolitan heritage. Egypt appears to have endured in the shadow of its own theological tradition until strong new religious movements swept over it. Only two great religions, first Christianity and later Islam, can be seen as having had the power to obliterate Egypt's ancient ontology. But even with regard of these conquering waves the question might be asked how thorough or how superficial, how permanent or how temporary, these obliterations could have been.

There is another reason why a historical reconstruction may be attempted—the evidence regarding a backlash effect. Elitist philosophies and popular universal salvation religions rarely affect more than the phenotype of a culture's ontology. In superficial historiography it may seem as though Hellenic philosophers had indeed converted the Egyptian elite, and that beginning with the first century C.E. Christian theology and a variety of Gnostic soteriologies converted the masses. This is how philosophers and Christian historians have interpreted the events, of course.

But the ontologies of these conquering waves tell a different story. Christians, gnostics, and philosophers can be seen as having rationalized, all the while, their own gospels in terms of Heliopolitan emanational ontology. In hindsight their teachings appear as the scatter from a single ancient Heliopolitan fireworks explosion. This theological scattering of ancient Egyptian ontology happened during the centuries when ancient Egyptian culture and religion were aging, while Egypt's colonized thinkers nevertheless managed to pass on

Copyrighted Material

traditional ontology to their foreign masters, quietly and for the most part anonymously.

The purpose of Part One of this book therefore is to delineate what still can be seen of the ancient Heliopolitan ontological vision, of the glory and light of Ra, the Sun deity, during moments before its unitary radiance exploded, before much of it was scattered and spread abroad.

Copyrighted Material

2

Heliopolitan Theology:
A Reconstruction

The ancient Egyptian cult center Junu, named *On* in the Hebrew Bible, was renamed *Heliopolis* by the Greeks in recognition of the fact that the sun god Ra (Helios in Greek) presided there.[1] Junu is mentioned in the Pyramid Texts as the "House of Ra." Nevertheless, there was another and more mysterious dimension to Heliopolitan Ra theology; it was Atum.

Many basic Egyptian notions, of thinking about gods, animals, and humankind together, definitely do date back to a most ancient hunter-gatherer stratum of mythology. However, the basic Heliopolitan theological notions themselves belong later in the evolutionary sequence of Egyptian culture and religion. They correspond to pursuits of domestication and grand domestication. Nevertheless, the basic Heliopolitan theological notions could have been formulated as early as Menes, the founder of the First Dynasty (ca. 3,100 B.C.E.). Overall, the theology of Junu was well suited for the justification of imperial grand domestication by which, specifically, the lower and upper Egyptian realms have been united and a great variety of regional cults accommodated.

---

[1] Discussion of ancient Egyptian religion, in this book, is indebted to the works of a large number of Egyptologists, especially to Hans Bonnet, *Reallexikon der Ägyptischen Religionsgeschichte* (Berlin, 1952); R. T. Rundle Clark, *Myth and Symbol in Ancient Egypt* (London, 1959); Adolf Erman, *Die Religion der Ägypter* (Berlin and Leipzig, 1934); Henri Frankfort, *Ancient Egyptian Religion* (New York, 1948); J. H. Breasted, *Development of Religion and Thought in Ancient Egypt* (New York, 1912); Siegfried Morenz, *Ägyptische Religion* (Stuttgart, 1960); and Erik Hornung, *Geist der Pharaonenzeit* (Zürich, 1989).

Copyrighted Material

As a system of thought, the theology of Heliopolis has been put on record during the Fifth and Sixth Dynasties (2494–2181 B.C.E.) on interior walls of seven large pyramids. This theology thereby survived in the masonry afterworlds of divinized pharaohs. Together their inscriptions have been published as the "Pyramid Texts."

Pyramid inscriptions reflect a time when Heliopolis was the major cult center of the united kingdom. *Atum* was the name given to the God of gods who was the source and essence of all other Egyptian gods, and of everything else. Atum's dynamic self-manifestation through the modalities of his lesser divinities, of his world, and even of his distant human progeny—especially through those divinities who gave birth to pharaohs as legitimate representatives of the godhead—that is what Egyptian high theology has been all about.

The Helipolitan version is the clearest formulation of any Old Kingdom theology we have; though, by modern standards it could scarcely be praised as "systematic." Somehow it became the dominant orthodox strain of thought by which subsequent Egyptian religious notions and rites were oriented. Generally in Egyptian religion, later theological formulations showed a need to embrace their antecedents, to accommodate them as well as they could. It has been precisely this tolerant and endless incorporation of older theological statements that, to this day, has held our understanding of Egyptian royal religion in suspense.

Western minds who are accustomed to disjunctive logic may see in ancient Egyptian religion only an irrational conglomeration of magico-theological notions. Pronouncements made about any one Egyptian god apply to other gods as well. Yet, this apparent theoretical untidiness is not the result of faulty Egyptian logic. Such an impression derives mostly from the fact that Western scholars hitherto have read the Egyptian theological statements as explaining "gods of polytheism," or more precisely, as an incoherent collage of idols that had to be defamed in opposition to what has become Hebrew monotheism and Greek rationalism.

All the while, however, the blending of divine natures and functions could have been understood easily by the simple fact that, for learned ancient Egyptians, there has persistently been a single God who has staged the entire combined polytheistic show. No less than nine divine names were fused at Heliopolis into a single Ennead, a Ninefoldness. On what basis could a Christian scholar classify his own theological "Trinity" as monotheism and keep insisting that the

Copyrighted Material

Heliopolitan "Ennead" belongs to polytheism? The "monotheism" of the pharaohs had no difficulty sponsoring, embracing, and absorbing lesser provincial deities throughout Egypt as additional members or offspring of the divine Ennead. Lesser cults, in turn, were supported by imperial Horus descendants of that same ninefold divinity.

* * *

The political dimension of the Heliopolitan theological system has been the subject matter of frequent academic discussions that need not be belabored here in their entirety. A single such commentary suffices to make a preliminary point. Rudolf Anthes has concluded that the theologians at Heliopolis postulated a genealogy of five generations of gods, and that they did so to establish the divine and primeval character of the ruling king. Accordingly, the lineage of Horus, of the god with whom ruling kings of Egypt were identified, "encompasses cultivated land and desert, heaven and earth and whatever is in between, as well as the ocean out of which Atum arose." The Heliopolitan theogony therefore may be understood as a "systematic demonstration that all the world was identified with, or belonged to the realm of, Horus."[2]

As reasonable as such an explanation of political divine claims may appear by standards of modern political theory or Greek mythic genealogies, it is also a fact that Heliopolitan priests have included in this realm of Horus all conceivable aspects of their cosmos. They pursued this habit of inclusion far in excess of what an Egyptian king actually could hope to rule. This happenstance invites us to examine the larger cosmic dimension specifically with regard to its religious comprehensiveness.

Our Western preoccupation with the metaphor of a divine "genealogy," after the manner in which kings used to keep track of their authoritarian ancestors, thus far has unduly hindered our understanding of the larger Egyptian cosmo-political order. A discussion of the Heliopolitan theogony ought never lose sight of the fact that an Egyptian deity, a greater-than-human reality confronting humankind, although he or she may alter his or her manifestation from time to

[2]Rudolf Anthes, "Mythology in Ancient Egypt," in *Mythologies of the Ancient World*, S. M. Kramer ed. (Garden City, N.Y., 1961), p. 42.
Copyrighted Material

time, or even may prefer invisibility, will never really cease to exist during all these transformations. As soon as this simple fact is recognized, the Heliopolitan "sequential genealogy" that Anthes has postulated evaporates from view. The supposed "generations" of gods thereby are rediscovered as an ongoing process that "generates" a multitude of *ba* mutations that, in turn, are all expressions of one timeless eternal God or *ka* essence.

The Egyptians called the invisible life force, that spark of life which energetically manifests itself from within, the *ka*. They named outward manifestations, which in human awareness and epistemology register as phenomena or as phenotypal mutations of that life force, the *ba*. Both *ka* and *ba* are what we might call *soul*. A *ba*, appearing along the outer reaches of divine *ka* emanation, is a visible, shadow-tainted, and estranged unit of *ka*, whereas a *ka* unit by itself may be characterized as a relatively pure participant within the original plethora of divine essence. The *ka* represents divine essence, and as such it exists in and emanates from the divine source of all being.

True to the ancient "prehuman flux" mythology of hunters and gatherers, the gods of Egypt continued to appear in any garb or *ba* they desired—of any animal, fish, bird, plant, or other natural phenomenon—as well as in the human figure of a ruling pharaoh.[3] They also could appear in prehuman flux "twilight," in half-dress, as half-animals or half-humans. In contrast to the gods, humans were enabled substantially to transform their *ba* only by way of dying. In this manner Egyptian ghosts in animal or half-animal form, who have gotten caught up in the condition of prehuman flux alongside the gods, lingered in Egyptian memory throughout the ancient period. They were known to appear in the shape of animals or half-animals in accordance with the ancient mysticism typical of hunter-gatherer religiosity.

The entire plethora of Atum's generative emission or flux does mean, therefore, that within the larger Egyptian cosmic scheme of

---

[3]*Prehuman flux*, in hunter mythology, refers to mythical conditions or a time when gods, humans, animals, plants, and other natural phenomena were still one kind of "people." These primeval people exchanged their skins and appearances after a manner in which humanoids change masks and clothes. Participating thus in the life-styles of all imaginable species, they lived together in harmony and still spoke a common language. For an introduction to hunter-gatherers' prehuman flux mythology, see Karl W. Luckert, *The Navajo Hunter Tradition* (Tucson, 1975), pp. 133ff.

Copyrighted Material

things we are not contemplating five "generations" of divine person-ages. Nor are we faced with an assembled pantheon of separate individual deities. Instead, we behold with our very human eyes the manifestations of a single godhead along his more or less visible periphery—a periphery that, as far as can be perceived at our low level of existence, is an ever-evolving play of light and shadows. But all the while the one God of gods remains, within and in himself, eternally the same source of all being.

Heliopolitan theology, or ancient Egyptian orthodoxy, is best approached from its two oldest strata of extant data; namely, the funerary literatures that have survived as pyramid and coffin inscriptions. Excerpts and phrases from funerary liturgies, comprising spells for good fortune in the hereafter, were inscribed on royal pyramid walls and on patrician coffins. The oldest among these texts, in the pyramids, were intended to establish a hallowed intellectual context for the return of a deceased pharaoh to his new state of fulfilled godhood. Thus, by and large the Pyramid Texts delineate the royal soteriology of returning from an estranged human condition to a more unified and divine mode of existence.

The road "thither" corresponds exactly to the road that has led a human *ka* portion or life-soul "hither."[4] This is to say that soter-iology, in accordance with Heliopolitan theology, traces the cosmo-gony in reverse. And inasmuch as the greater-than-human cosmos in ancient Egypt was deemed personal and divine, cosmogony equalled theogony—and soteriology was the theistic theory of salvation.

The entire theological system can be visualized as a flow of creative vitality, emanating outward from the godhead, thinning out as it flows farther from its source. Along its outer periphery this plethora of divine emanation becomes fragmented into what begins to appear as the light and shadow realm of our material world. It becomes visible. Next, beyond this periphery of visible matter lies the realm of nonbeing that, in Egyptian mythology, was conceptualized as watery chaos, or Nun. Thus, the boundary realm between divinely generated being and nonbeing is what contains our apparently

---

[4]Our procedure of rendering *ka* as life-soul may seem unduly redundant. The word *soul* by itself would signify as much. But in Egypt we also have the *ba* to consider, a conception of soul that may be specified as "apparition," as "visible soul," or as "shadow soul."

Copyrighted Material

concrete experiences of life and death. From a Western point of view this ontology could be called a *philosophical idealism,* were it not for the fact that the dichotomies of "ideas and things" and "mind and matter" are not applicable here.

Along its outer periphery the plethora of divine existence, of generation, of emanation, of being, and of life—the divine current of *ka* radiation—becomes visible as a multitude of *ba* apparitions. Along that outer periphery it meets with nonbeing, is stunned by nonbeing, and as a result curls inward on itself. Individualized and estranged *ka* units, that is, *ka* sparks in *ba* manifestations confronting nonbeing, may swirl for a while about, along that outer periphery of divinity, as ghostly apparitions in lostness and confusion. But these *ka* souls also may be meaningfully reoriented to again travel homeward to the source of their being, the godhead.

While the sole and hidden deity has thus been generating and giving birth to its self-emanations, in external visibility as if it were an ongoing process of "exhaling," this same sole divine source has also continually been "reinhaling" its own life essences. Along the outer edge of human ontology and epistemology these essences, perceived as finite manifestations, have been stunned by the kiss of death and nonbeing. They are thereby purified, turned around, or "resurrected" with the help of religious funerary rites. Divine generation and emanation from the godhead, and the nostalgic return of estranged individual life-souls to their former source, therefore happens along a busy two way dimension.

The creative descending emanation ends in the cul-de-sac of life made manifest, as if being caught up in the curve of a U-turn. The entire road of creation leads hither from God to finitude; the road of resurrection and salvation leads home again toward the heart of God.

The First Hypostasis (Level 1)

At the starting point of generational flow one may, in Heliopolitan manner, visualize the source of all being as manifesting itself concretely in the form of a phallic primeval hill, Atum, on the rise. His creative emission or emanation may be visualized, more aptly perhaps, as Ra who is the rising, radiating, and life-evoking phoenix or sun deity. For a still clearer ancient perception, one may visualize our world from the vantage point of the sun god, or even from the

Copyrighted Material

vantage points of descending sun rays. At the turbulent terminals of their emanational paths, at their points of impact on nonbeing, these sun rays evoke for us here on earth certain sensations that cause the phenomenal or material world around us appear with substantiality and with color—even us to ourselves.

The notion, of Atum as a hill rising from the chaotic waters of Nun, was sublimated to account as well for the presence of theriomorphic as well as anthropomorphic generation or procreation within this world. The rising hill of Atum was a rising phallus. As such it was replicated on consequent masculine hypostases like Shu, Geb, and Osiris. Atum's fondling hand itself became the prolific vagina of Tefnut, Nut, and Isis without ever ceasing to be Atum's own hand.

All these generative divine "organs" in successive hypostases, male as well as female, could be contemplated in singular androgynous as well as in plural form. The Heliopolitan Ennead in its entirety was nine as well as one. It also manifested itself in any number between one and nine—and beyond those.

In the beginning Atum arose from Nun, the chaotic primeval waters (see Figure 5). Nun is the inconceivable and chaotic nothing, a moist void which at best can only be described as being "potentially" there. By contrast, when Atum arose as primeval Hill amidst Nun, he was the first solid someone or somebody. Not unexpectedly, this rising Hill was visualized by male priestly storytellers as being principally a masculine generative deity. And again not unexpectedly, it turned out that Atum's sanctuary at Junu had been built exactly on this primal and cosmic hill.[5] Many scholars have alerted to the fact that the recessions of floodwaters from the Nile valley bottom land, annual events before the Ashwān Dam was built, have displayed through millennia the reemergence of hills and land for Egyptian cultivators.

Although the exact experiential moment when Atum became identified with the sun god Ra can no longer be determined, it already was standard practice in the Old Kingdom to refer to these polar manifestations together as a single Atum-Ra. Cosmologically, one can visualize the two together, as Sun rising above the primeval Hill. In time the hidden Atum was contrasted with the radiant Ra of daytime visibility. That is to say, Atum in his original hidden form corre-

---

[5]Cf. especially Pyramid Text 1652, later in Chapter 3.
Copyrighted Material

sponded then to the sun god who has just set to hide again in darkness. Politically, the upward and sunward orientation of Egyptian kings as Horuses (see Levels 4 and 5 later), as falcon deities soaring toward the sun, provided an easy directional association of royalty with the rising Ra. By logical extension this orientation accomplished a fusion of the rising Hill with the ensuing Ennead. Being Horus-Ra, and being assisted by the solid masculine hill-power of Atum, the Egyptian god-king hoped to survive death and to rise in solar glory and splendor.

The Second Hypostasis (Level 2)

Heliopolitan mythology and theory of evolution begins with an androgynous conceptualization of the divine generative process, it develops from there in the direction of a sexual process of generation. Shu and Tefnut, male and female together, are the second hypostasis

Figure 5. In the beginning, within chaotic Nun, Atum arose as primeval hill. Ra emerged as phoenix or sunburst above Atum. Together they comprise Atum-Ra, the total godhead of Heliopolitan theology.

Copyrighted Material

Figure 6. Atum spat forth Shu and Tefnut, Life and Order, to expand himself and to prepare the realm for life and offspring. Their invisible union, which defies illustration, has generated Geb and Nut.

in the emanation and manifestation of Atum's pleasure (see Figure 6). Shu and Tefnut sometimes are mentioned together as Ruti, a pair of divinities who become visible in the *ba* apparitions of a male and a female lion. Thus, though Heliopolitan theology is basically monotheistic, at the second hypostasis it may be characterized as being ditheistic or dualistic. Any single "One" being contemplated by an analytic human mind, sooner or later, will reveal its two, three, or more aspects.

Whereas the "Ruti" dualism represents a convenient accommodation to the local cult of Leontopolis, Shu and Tefnut in their indigenous Heliopolitan context still were thought of as forming a trinity, together with Atum, from whom they both proceed.[6] Within this trinitarian frame of reference, Shu personifies the masculine "phallus-semen-life-breath" extension of Atum, whereas Tefnut personifies the

---

[6]See Pyramid Text 447, below in Chapter Three.

Copyrighted Material

feminine hand-womb-mouth-order dimension. Both dimensions together continue the creative activity of Atum's original "spitting," which had generated and brought them forth in the first place. And in this manner they, in turn, generate a next hypostasis, one that would exhibit slightly more visible (or more easily imaginable) contours.

Atum in the form of High Hill created Shu and Tefnut, a brother and sister pair of twins. In terms of cosmographic visualization, Shu pushed forth from the solid Hill as a force of life—as a soul-charged divine breath of air. Within Shu, and to the limits of Shu, there arched together with him a kind of feminine "order" or "firmament." In the Hebrew creation story this firmament was established by God for the orderly purpose of separating the waters above from those below (*Genesis* 1:6–7). Theologians at Heliopolis knew this firmament or "order" as Lady Tefnut, or Lady Mahet. It was she, now, who delimited and held back the all-enveloping domain of chaotic Nun.

This entire trinitarian portion of the Ninefoldness and All-God, Atum together with Shu and Tefnut, at the demise of ancient Egyptian culture was transposed by Plotinus into Greek-looking philosophy: into One Father (Atum), Mind (Mahet), and Soul (Shu). Around that time it was also transposed by Christian theologians into Father (Atum), Son (Shu), and Holy Spirit (Mahet).

Modern connoisseurs of origin stories may be baffled by the very basic anthropomorphic demeanor of Egypt's high god, Atum. Egyptian theologians were no Indo-European dualists; their material world was not hopelessly severed from a qualitatively separate and superior spiritual realm. Much less were they dualists subscribing to later Zoroastrian or Manichean conceptualizations that distinguished sharply between personal Good and Evil.

These ancient Egyptians felt only slightly uneasy about cultivating a masturbation metaphor in their high theology. Their uneasiness stemmed not from a realization that sexual prowess was unbecoming of a God of gods. On the contrary; it stemmed rather from the fact that God's sexuality could be imitated somewhat at the lowest human level, at a scale far too small to be kept lastingly in reverential focus. They therefore broadened their sexual metaphor in light of analogous emission processes—spitting and expectoration—which, it turned out, were scarcely more endearing to later Indo-European dualistic theological sensibilities.

Copyrighted Material

The Third Hypostasis (Level 3)

Geb and Nut are the manifest divinities at this level (see Figure 7). Together they represent a hypostasis in which anthropomorphic conceptualization and cosmological visualization have come together. Ancient Egyptian artists themselves have drawn our illustration for this hypostasis. They were in the habit of drawing the contours of Geb and Nut in various degrees of anthropomorphism and sexual explicitness. The preceding illustrations in this book, depicting more elementary hypostases, were drawn as backward projections based on descriptive statements.

Geb as Father Earth and Nut as Mother Sky, nevertheless, constitute an anomaly among the mythologies of humankind. In most other cosmogonies the Sky is Father and the everbearing Earth is recognized as Mother. But Egyptian royalty has identified itself

Figure 7. Geb as Father Earth is represented in person and by his emblem, the Great Cackler, on the left. He rises to meet Mother Sky, Nut, who arches above him. Their father Shu, on the right, proceeds to separate them. Together they illustrate the Egyptian cosmology-theology in the anthropomorphic mode. Twenty-first Dynasty Papyrus of Tameniu, British Museum. Drawn after Ions.

Copyrighted Material

unambiguously with the life-evoking splendor of the sun. Kings preferred to be born from on high, "trailing clouds of glory" as William Wordsworth would have said.

The geofocal myth that describes the emergence of Atum as a rising hill, or a rising phallus, has given direction to the generative nature of all subsequent hypostases. It has established the primacy of the masculine dimension of Atum-Ra as godhead in the personae of Shu, Geb, and Osiris. It has kept Egyptian royal masculinity anchored solidly on earth and has bestowed upon pharaohs the authority to administer and to rule "the heritage of Geb"; that is, the visible earth. The pharaoh as a divine predator and Horus-falcon, having been born from on high, thus was empowered to rule all that lived or grew on earth. By extension, he also ruled everything that was mummified and buried in it.

From Level 2 onward in the creative process, the texts read as though the deity is emanating by way of perpetual sexual union between its Shu and its Tefnut aspects. Cosmographically speaking, from the perspective of an earthling observing Level 3, it also would have been difficult to perceive how far the body of Geb, the male, reached and where the body of Nut, the female, began.[7] Some descriptions given in Pyramid and Coffin Texts nevertheless are very explicit theography—pornographic theography in fact.[8] That such a very intimate engagement has lead to pregnancy and offspring in another hypostasis should come as no surprise.

All the while, no negative valuations have been intended by these stark depictions. The visible world, which was the subject matter of graphic, sculpted, and scribal depictions, was never more than low-intensity divine reality. Our low-intensity material world is perceived

---

[7]Cf. especially Coffin Texts, Spell 80, in Chapter 4.

[8]Some among our Western readers may have felt disgust on account of the pornographic theophany depicted in Figure 7. Their response, of course, is no solution to the ancient problem but merely a symptom of the five-millennia-plus conflict between herder and planter cultures and their concomitant religious rationalizations. A patient reader who continues this line of study to its completion, at least through Chapter 11, will discover that many obscenities in Near Eastern and Western civilization, including wars in the name of religion, have been aggravated by this inheritance of conflict between northern dualism and Egyptian monism or mysticism. Our monastic and Puritan scruples have evolved somewhere in between these two.

Copyrighted Material

by human eyes as being generated, by *ka* energies, from shadow contrasts over against what ontologically speaking amounts to even less—chaotic Nun or nonbeing.

Atum, that is, Shu and Tefnut together, procreated Geb and Nut. These two offspring together constitute the more or less "visible" Father Earth and Mother Sky. Cosmographically, it may be said that the creative emissions of Atum, by which Shu and Tefnut have come to occupy a joint visible realm of life and order, have with the appearance of Geb and Nut come into sharper focus. Father Geb can be felt, seen, and understood much more easily than his still invisible father Shu. His concrete outlines can clearly be discerned and can even be modified by human hands and skill. Mother Nut can be visualized as well. In the azure sky she can be seen as being there. Though, everyone will admit that seeing her, and her attempts at concealing her nudity, requires a healthy dose of masculine imagination—which, we may safely assume, presented no real obstacle to Egyptian priests.[9]

In this manner the godhead Atum displays his otherwise hidden nature, channeled through the still invisible personae of Shu and Tefnut. His essence is diluted, of course, as it is made visible in the *ba* modes of Geb and Nut. But all such light-and-shadow apparitions happen for the benefit of human eyes whose ability to perceive is limited to that outer boundary of Nun-tainted reality.

The Fourth Hypostasis (Level 4)

With Mother Sky and Father Earth now having come into better focus, the Egyptian world was ready to have still more specific divine births occur. From Geb and Nut were born two brother and sister pairs of twin gods: Osiris with Isis, and Nephthys with Seth (see Figure 8). These twin pairs were envisioned anthropomorphically or, sometimes, were seen as existing in a twilight condition of prehuman

---

[9]I readily admit that, up to a few years ago, this visualization of sky as Lady Nut presented to me some difficulties—until, somewhere in Xinjiang, while explaining a waterfall, a Kazakh old wise man interpreted the falling curtain of water as a nude maiden. When the girl discovered that she was being observed, by men like us, she started diving into the creek below. She is still diving there, now. As a result it has become easier to see a diving maiden in a waterfall, and to behold Mother Sky in the azure.

Copyrighted Material

Figure 8. Seth and Nephthys, Osiris and Isis. These children of Geb and Nut occupy the lowest rank in the Heliopolitan Ennead, at Level 4; they exist low enough to participate more intimately in the human experience of life and death, at Level 5. Drawn after Bonnet, and Erman (1934).

flux. As gods at Level 4 they appeared and operated understandably on a smaller and more visible scale than their great parent(s). At this level of specificity the Egyptian godhead sponsored and renewed divine-human kingship in the world of Egyptian planters and domesticators—in the visible realm that was the lowest visible level of his emanation.

Gods of this fourth hypostasis, or "generation," function primarily along the outer edge, the turnaround curve and perimeter of divine emanation. Nephthys, as goddess of the home fire, was credited with having suckled and nurtured young Horus kings. Seth, as god of desert heat and of enemy lands, has been saddled with the blame and responsibility for having death occur. He was the one who stopped living Horus kings dead in their tracks; and he transformed them into corpses, that is, into Osiris natures. Because this involves a bonafide male member of the Ennead, one can assume that Atum's phallus

Copyrighted Material

somehow was also present for Seth—but the "sexual" distinguishing mark of Seth happens to be a hunter's or a warrior's phallic aberration: a deadly weapon with which to stab and to kill. By contrast, Osiris is the real phallus bearer of this generation of Enneadean gods. He procreated all subsequent Horus-kings of Egypt while Isis, as divine mother, gave fresh birth and nurtured the offspring of Osiris.

The Turnaround Realm (Level 5)

The gods who may be mentioned together with the outermost generation of the Ennead, and in association with the "turnaround realm," played major roles in Egyptian funerary proceedings, at least in so far as these proceedings were overshadowed by Helipolitan theology. Foremost among these lesser gods may be mentioned Horus, Thoth, and Anubis (see Figure 9). Horus represented any duly installed Egyptian king—a divine falcon-king. The ibis-headed Thoth was scribe and keeper of the divine words; he was later in Memphite theology rediscovered as tongue of the All-God, Ptah. The ibis-headed Thoth and the jackal-headed Anubis belonged to some kind of

Figure 9. Left to right: Horus, Thoth, and Anubis. Drawn after Erman (1934).

Copyrighted Material

lower or "lesser Ennead." At the same time, Horus in the "turn-around realm" became associated more personally and intimately with the "great" Ennead. As the son of Isis and Osiris he seems to have functioned at times almost as the Ennead's "tenth" member.

Of course, in the Heliopolitan perspective these lesser gods are created, like everything else in the cosmos, by that same emanation that also generates the primary hypostases of the Ennead itself. Everything that now exists comes into existence as Atum. In Atum's emanation all creatures live and move and have their being.

The cosmos was generated by Atum alone, first; and from that point on simultaneously by the trinity composed of Atum, Shu, and Tefnut. By the same divine breath of Shu and presence of Tefnut was generated the visible cosmos—by Atum himself or by his trinity simultaneously—for the All-God to become increasingly more apparent to humankind as Geb and Nut (see Figure 10).

It just so happened that various Egyptian local traditions cultivated additional divine manifestations and saviors who had to be reckoned

Theogony: Generation and Emanation		Soteriology: Journey Homeward to the Godhead
Atum — — —	1 _____	9
Shu and Tefnut — — —	2 _____	8
Geb and Nut — — —	3 _____	7
Osiris and Isis Seth and Nephthys — — —	4 _____	6
Turnaround Realm — — —	__ 5 __	

Figure 10. Directionality and levels in Heliopolitan theogony and funerary soteriology.

Copyrighted Material

with. The wise theologians of Junu knew how to accommodate them all in their system. Some of these divinities found new roles to play along the lower end of an already variegated Enneadean emanation. They found new ways "to surf," as it were, on the waves that rolled along the outer perimeter of Atum's emanation. They helped reverse the fates and redirect the movement of *ka* sparks, of life-souls, who had become estranged from their source and gotten caught up in the shadow play and confusion that exists in the vicinity of moribund bodies.

Some such lower gods were called upon to serve as preparers, guides, and conveyors of life souls during funerary proceedings. Anubis was undertaker; and Thoth officiated as priestly scribe. In performing their saving tasks these extra gods interacted with some of the lower among the divinities of the Greater Ennead. Turnaround assistance also frequently was provided by Nephthys and Isis. The significance of Horus to Egyptian soteriology and the funerary cult increased during the Intermediary Period (2181–2040 B.C.E.), when patricians availed themselves of royal Heliopolitan soteriology. In Coffin Texts the god Horus is recognized as a living savior symbol unto whom, on his way home to the godhead, a deceased's soul could attach itself for easier travel. For some returning souls Horus even had become the focus of mystic reidentification with divinity.

The ability of Horus to function as a son of God and savior of humankind is underwritten by Heliopolitan imperial mythology. Horus, the divine falcon-king of United Egypt, was a son of the god Osiris and of his mother Isis who, for the purpose of enthronement rites, embodied the Egyptian throne. Every divinely installed Egyptian king was ceremonially reborn from her—upon that throne. Then, when a ruling god-king of Egypt came to the end of his career, he was transformed. First his pulsating human body was transformed by Seth into an Osiris kind of *ba*, a corpse apparition. His *ka* was thereby liberated from its own shadow. He was "reborn" from his human appearance or *ba* to return to the godhead and live purer.

When a deceased pharaoh was put into his coffin he represented the potentially creative and masculine Atum-Shu-Geb-Osiris "phallus" dimension. Isis—and we may refer to her as representing the feminine Atum-Tefnut-Nut-Isis "hand" dimension—hovered over the entombed

Copyrighted Material

royal body of Osiris to be impregnated by him.[10] As a result she gave birth later, as throne, to the new Horus falcon-king. That these combined wedding-burial and enthronement rites still represent Atum's selfsame emanation becomes evident when one contemplates the Heliopolitan system in its entirety.

Repeatable cycles, of God begetting a son to rule the human realm of Egypt and returning this son again unto himself, are what gave to the Egyptian grand domestication system an enduring rhythm through the millennia of its known history. An offshoot version of this Egyptian stability, enveloped by a slightly modified version of Helipolitan trinitarian theology, took shape in subsequent Western history—it stabilized Christendom and the Holy Roman Empire.

The Journey Home

In Pyramid Texts, as well as in the Coffin Texts later on, Helipolitan "theogony" or "cosmogony" are explained only incidentally. The primary concern of all ancient Egyptian funerary texts is, necessarily, the journey of *ka* souls homeward to the godhead. Therefore it has become necessary for us to discuss "generation and emanation," and even the "turnaround realm" as preliminary and as derived conceptualizations.

Levels 6 through 9 can be understood more easily by turning directly to the textual data. Excerpts from Pyramid and Coffin Texts, which will be presented in Chapters 3 and 4, will provide direct imagery and samples from Egyptian soteriology. Materials that are as foreign to modern minds as the funerary utterances of several millennia ago are best understood when they are left to speak for themselves. Extensive commentaries tend to obscure what in the original context might seem only quaint.

The commentary in the next two chapters will be kept to a minimum. It can be abbreviated further with the help of the reference numbers introduced in Figure 10. These numbers will help link

---

[10]Inside on many ancient Egyptian coffin lids was painted an image of Isis. This practice obviously refers to the Osiris-Isis myth involving Osiris's sexual resuscitation, Isis's conception, and the expected birth of Horus. As will be shown later in Chapter 4 (Coffin Text Spell 84), the soul of a deceased person may be expected to issue forth from Isis anew as her son Horus and then journey homeward.

Copyrighted Material

theogonic hypostases (Levels 1 through 4) with "way stations" along the soul's journey homeward to the godhead (Levels 6 through 9).

All the while, it will be good to keep in mind that reference numbers for hypostases, along the generative flow of divine life force, correspond to numbers assigned along the homeward path in the following manner: 1 corresponds to 9, 2 to 8, 3 to 7, and 4 to 6. The number 5 is left to represent the Turnaround Realm in which the material world, life, and death are experienced physically and to some extent visibly. The use of these numerical codes in the next chapters will make our exposition of Pyramid Texts and Coffin Texts considerably easier.

Copyrighted Material

Copyrighted Material

3

Heliopolitan Theology in the Pyramid Texts

This chapter focuses on a small selection of pyramid texts that may be useful for sketching Heliopolitan theology logically and coherently. Critics of our present approach to ancient Egyptian religion, who hitherto may have prejudged Egyptian "polytheism" vis-à-vis Hebrew "monotheism," probably will want to insist on the absolute individuality of each and every Egyptian divinity. But, be that as it may, this writer is saddled with the historical and human obligation to visualize ancient peoples in light of how they themselves might have lived out their finitude vis-à-vis greater-than-human realities—or might have accepted their temporality in light of their own glimpses of eternity. Hebrew religion, Greek philosophy, and Christian theology are latecomers. From their respective places in history they have no parental claims over early Egyptian religion.

Logic is not abandoned when one tries to understand human existence the ancient Egyptian way; namely, from the perspective of divinely radiated energy and life, from within emanations of divine purpose and pleasure, or from sun rays which in turn engender what we, nowadays, regard as being more "substantial" protoplasm and genes. The ancient stream of a godhead's conscious emanations will surely outlive our finite spans of memory, our schizophrenias and mental traumas. Eternity itself will arbitrate between moribund analytic and disjunctive reasoning, on one hand, and the type of holistic reasoning which was cherished by Heliopolitan priests on the other.

Copyrighted Material

Pyramid Texts 1248-49

The portion of liturgical utterance that follows affirms the self-createdness of Atum and suggests a method by which the godhead might reasonably have generated or given birth to his next hypostasis, Shu and Tefnut. Concerning Levels 1 and 2 we are given an anthropomorphic explanation of the theogonic and emanational dimension of Egyptian mythology.[1]

Atum is he who [gave pleasure to himself] in On. He took his phallus in his grasp that he might create orgasm by means of it, and so were born the twins Shu and Tefnut. May they put the King between them.[2]

Kurt Sethe's translation suggests the primeval givenness of the phallus-in-hand situation, a creative process, rather than the volition of God to create in that manner:

Atum ist der [von selbst] entstand, der mit sich onanierte in Heliopolis. Dem sein Phallus in seine Faust gelegt wurde, damit er sich geschlechtlich vergnüge mit ihm, und geboren wurden zwei Kinder verschiedenen Geschlechtes, Shu und Tefnut. Setzen sich nun den N. zwischen sich.[3]

This soteriological utterance delivers the returning king directly into the arms of the godhead, at Levels 8 and 9, which, of course,

---

[1]For Level numbers see Figure 10, in Chapter 2.

[2]All English translations of Pyramid Texts quoted in this chapter, except this one, are kept in line with R. O. Faulkner's translation, *The Ancient Egyptian Pyramid Texts* (Oxford, 1969), and are quoted by permission of Oxford University Press. Although Faulkner's translation "Atum . . . who masturbated in On" may be literally correct, his rendition appears nevertheless banal and distorted—at least in as far as the original statement has surely originated in a liturgical setting. Our modified rendition of "Atum. . .who gave pleasure to himself" seems sufficiently precise and more fitting in the ritual context. In addition, Faulkner's renditions of *Tefenet* have been adjusted to the more commonly used *Tefnut*.

[3]Kurt Sethe, *Übersetzung und Kommentar zu den Ägyptischen Pyramidentexten*, Vol. 5 (Hamburg, 1962), p. 147.

Copyrighted Material

correspond to Levels 2 and 1 along the path of emanation. More precisely, the king is placed smack between Shu and Tefnut. He has returned to the primeval moment, or to the primeval condition, at which and in which all subsequent gods and life-souls have had prior existence. Atum's emanation as Shu and Tefnut constitutes a trinity. One must keep in mind that both aspects of the deceased, his Shu and Tefnut relatedness, are subsequently engaged in creative sexual union and that between these two is no empty space for a separate royal personage to coexist. The king therefore is mentioned here as being "set among the gods" after the manner in which all gods and hypostases blend into one another. Being an Osiris spark of *ka*, the deceased king henceforth is contained in the All-God and participates in his creative self-emanation, more intimately now than prior to having suffered death. In the final analysis, the king who is "set among the gods" is situated "within the godhead." He returns home to the source of all being, at Level 1 and 9.

Pyramid Texts 1652-55

The royal pyramid dedicated by the words that follow here has been built in the realm of ontological turnaround, at Level 5. All the while, the theogony is invoked along its entire dimension. The entire creative Ennead is mentioned in its full spacial presence (Levels 1-4). This is done to arrange a mystic primeval union of the king's pyramid with Atum himself. It was understood that, by dying, the ruler will have achieved a mystic union of sorts, with the edifice he had built. In it he was to rest as an Osirian corpse. It is Atum's own embrace that bridges or collapses the distance from Level 5 through 9:

O Atum-Khoprer, you became high on the height, you rose up as the *bnbn*-stone in the Mansion of the "Phoenix" in On, you spat out Shu, you expectorated Tefnut, and you set your arms about them as the arms of a *ka* symbol, that your essence might be in them. O Atum, set your arms about the King, about this construction, and about this pyramid as the arms of a *ka* symbol, that the King's essence may be in it, enduring forever.

O Atum, set your protection over this King, over this pyramid of his, and over this construction of the King, prevent anything from happening evilly against it for ever, just as your protection was set

Copyrighted Material

over Shu and Tefnut. O you Great Ennead which is in On—Atum, Shu, Tefnut, Geb, Nut, Osiris, Isis, Seth, Nephthys; O you children of Atum, extend his goodwill to his child in your name of Nine Bows . . .

Pyramid Texts 167–78

Defeated by Seth at Level 5, the Egyptian Horus-king was transformed into the condition of Osiris who exists at Level 4 and 6. It is noteworthy regarding the liturgical utterance that follows that its writers have not found it necessary to acknowledge the god Osiris— apart from the presence of the mummified body of the king. Had they done so, Osiris would have been invoked between the lines that address Nut and Isis. This means that the presence of a dead king, in his funerary rite, was deemed sufficient recognition of the presence of the god Osiris. It also suggests that during his funeral the deceased king was already firmly counted as having been fused with a member of the Great Ennead.

> O Atum, this one here is your son Osiris whom you
> have caused to be restored that he may live . . .
> O Shu, this one here is your son Osiris . . .
> O Tefnut, this one here is your son Osiris . . .
> O Geb, this one here is your son Osiris . . .
> O Nut, this one here is your son Osiris . . .
> O Isis, this one here is your brother Osiris . . .
> O Seth, this one here is your brother Osiris . . .
> O Nephthys, this one here is your brother Osiris . . .
> O Thoth, this one here is your brother Osiris . . .
> O Horus, this one here is your father Osiris . . .
> O Great Ennead, this one here is Osiris . . .
> O Lesser Ennead, this one here is Osiris . . .[4]

---

[4]Sethe (1962, Vol. 1, p. 87) explains the Lesser Ennead as having been postulated in contrast to the honorific appellation *Great Ennead*, which was misunderstood in a numerical sense. This may be so. But I suspect that, in this prayer sequence, the addition of Thoth and Horus adds up to an extended Ninefoldness. The *Lesser Ennead* therefore may refer to the inclusion of lesser gods—that is, to the extension or thinning out of the Great Ennead—in the realm of human kings, humankind in general, and the shadow realm of mortality.

Copyrighted Material

Pyramid Texts 1660-62

Inasmuch as the temple compound at Junu contained two sanctuaries, one for Atum and another for Ra-Herachte, the duality of the godhead as "rising Ra" and "setting Atum" seems to have been an early aspect of the Heliopolitan cult. Therefore, even at its cultic core has the theological oneness of the godhead contained this dual dimension. The exact path of reasoning along which the one dual God, Atum-Ra, first was perceived as a Shu and Tefnut duality perhaps no longer is traceable. In the text quoted next it appears as though, initially at Heliopolis, Shu and Tefnut also had distinct cultic realms assigned to them. Significant is the fact that, in the case of Shu and Tefnut, the theologians of Junu adhered to their Two-as-One formula—as all along they had been doing while contemplating Atum-Ra. They continued doing so, still, with regard to Geb and Nut.

O you Great Ennead which is in On [Heliopolis], make the King's [name] endure, make this pyramid for this King and this construction of his endure forever, just as the name of Atum who presides over the Great Ennead endures. As the name of Shu, Lord of Upper *Mnst* in On, endures, so may the king's name endure, and so may this pyramid of his and this construction of his endure likewise for ever. As the name of Tefnut, Mistress of Lower *Mnst* in On, endures.

Pyramid Texts 447-49

The soteriology expressed in the next selection focuses on Levels 8 and 9, thus on Ruti and Atum. Shu and Tefnut as lion pair, or Ruti, are implored to grant to the deceased king safe passage past their own divine presences along the horizon. This implies that the deceased is now on his way home to the first and eternal One, Atum.

You have your offering-bread, O Atum and Ruti,
Who yourself created your godheads and your persons.
O Shu and Tefnut who made the gods,
Who begot the gods and established the gods:
Tell your father
That the King has propitiated you with your dues.

Copyrighted Material

> You shall not hinder the King
> When he crosses to him at the horizon,
> For the King knows him and knows his name;
> "Eternal" is his name;
> "The Eternal Lord of the Year" is his name.

In support of Level 8 and 9 soteriology, this passage also makes reference to Levels 1 and 2 at the generative or theogonic side. Atum is acknowledged as the original godhead who created his own masks, personae, duality or plurality of gods. Shu and Tefnut are credited with having subsequently begotten other gods. And, as everywhere in the Heliopolitan system, soteriology in this passage is based on the trinitarian theogony-theology of Atum, Shu, and Tefnut.

Pyramid Texts 552–53

The deceased king's identification with Shu and Tefnut, at Level 8, explains his new mode of existence. His hunger and thirst are satisfied after the manner in which gods satisfy theirs. The "morning-bread which comes in due season" seems to provide a cosmological hint: Shu as air, and Tefnut—as sunlight that introduces order, perhaps—appear themselves to be nourished when together they consume the morning dew:

> I will not be thirsty by reason of Shu, I will not be hungry by reason of Tefnut...

> My hunger is from the hand of Shu, my thirst is from the hand of Tefnut, but I live on the morning-bread which comes in due season. I live on that whereon Shu lives, I eat of that whereof Tefnut eats.

Pyramid Texts 1817–18

Although the syntax of the next text is somewhat problematic, it nevertheless is clear enough to provide a hint about the interrelatedness of Shu and Atum. Atum's phallus is on Shu. By extension, in light of the importance of the phallus for Osiris-Isis mythology and

Copyrighted Material

coronation mythology, one might surmise that subsequently it is thought to be also on Geb and Osiris.

O Shu, you enclose for yourself all things within your embrace [.] this Osiris the King; may you prevent him from escaping [from you...] of Atum, whose phallus is on you, that you may be [...] his *ka*; may you protect him...

Pyramid Texts 2065-67

The various hypostases of the godhead are in the course of a funerary washing rite visualized as a flow of pure water that originates with Atum the father or with Shu and Tefnut. Immersed in this "baptismal" flow of living water the king is made divine for his return journey to the Father:

Behold this King, his feet are kissed by the pure waters which exist through Atum, which the phallus of Shu makes and which the vagina of Tefnut creates. They have come and have brought to you the pure waters with their father; they cleanse you and make you divine, O King. You shall support the sky with your hand, you shall lay down the earth with your foot...

Inasmuch as in Egyptian iconography Shu frequently is depicted as the one who lifts up Mother Sky with his hands, the last phrase in this statement may provide a cosmogonic hint about Tefnut. By contrast, she seems to be the one who laid down Father Earth, with her foot—with the force of her light that introduces order, perhaps.[5]

Pyramid Text 1405

An invocation addressed to Tefnut provides a further hint about her place in theogony and cosmology:

---

[5]It is obvious that the "foot" of the mother of the sky goddess must be explained, somehow, to fit the larger Egyptian experience of Tefnut as a cosmic being. I am reminded of Navajo Indian "roots or feet of sunlight"—spectacular streaks of sun rays breaking through billowy clouds that visibly touch the earth. Tefnut's activity of "shining" is better expressed later in some Coffin Texts, such as in Spell 78.

Copyrighted Material

The earth is raised on high under the sky by your arms, O Tefnut, and you have taken the hands of Ra...

Thus, Tefnut's function is complementary to that of her brother Shu. As masculine manifestation of the divine life force, Shu supports the arching sky goddess, Nut, for Geb. Tefnut as female life force is found balancing the Heliopolitan ontology on a larger scale than Nut. Her presence delimits the masculine earth god, Geb, and also sustains his passion and his masculinity to arch skyward.

Pyramid Text 1443

The deceased king presents himself to the sun god, Ra, in hope of being given conveyance across the sky. The sun deity here is acknowledged as born from Nut, upon the arms of Shu and Tefnut. No contradiction between this and earlier Pyramid Text selections is implied. As cosmic mother, the sky goddess Nut manifests herself from within Tefnut as well as participates in the function of the prior "hand" of Atum. The daily birth of Ra, from Nut, repeats the primordial sunburst of light that has issued from Atum's phallic hill.

The face of the sky is washed, the celestial expanse is bright, the god is given birth by the sky upon the arms of Shu and Tefnut, upon my arms.

Apparently the deceased king, though he introduces himself a little later in Pyramid Text 1448 merely as a son of Geb and Osiris (Levels 3 and 4), nevertheless identifies here his own arms with the primeval arms of Shu and Tefnut (Level 2), to obligate the sun god toward him as a brother, perhaps.

Pyramid Text 1066

This formation in which the soul returns to Atum may have been determined by the theogonic sequence. The emanation Tefnut

Copyrighted Material

emerged from Atum "behind" her brother Shu.[6] It would follow, therefore, that, on a corresponding return journey of souls to Atum, at Levels 8 and 9, the order of these divinities is reversed:

I am a man of Dendera, I have come from Dendera with Shu behind me, Tefnut before me, and Wepwawet clad[?] at my right hand.

Pyramid Texts 1466–69

Egyptian priests were capable of reasoning at various ontological levels. This much is demonstrated by the text given next. Indeed, everyone knew how Egyptian kings were born first of human mothers, bodily, onto this earth. And surely, many people also knew that during coronation rites their kings were reborn as Horus gods, from the womb of Isis who was present as throne. Being a member of the lowest Enneadean hypostasis, Isis therefore dwelt conveniently "in the Lower Sky." All the same, the king existed in Atum from the beginning of creation as a spark of *ka*—an Imperishable Star. Or, shall we say "he existed as a gleam in the All-Father's eye"?

The King's mother was pregnant with him, [even he] who was in the Lower Sky, the King was fashioned by his father Atum before the sky existed, before earth existed, before men existed, before the gods were born, before death existed. . . .the King will not die because of any dead, for the King is an Imperishable Star, son of the sky-goddess who dwells in the Mansion of Selket. Ra has taken this King to himself to the sky so that this King may live, just as he who enters in the west of the sky lives when he goes up in the east of the sky.

Truly, this text resonates in harmony with such famous post-Egyptian statements as "before Abraham was I am," or, "the child is father of the man." In any case, the deceased king returned to his point of origin. He participated in the eternity of the sun god Ra as well as in the total godhead, Atum-Ra.

---

[6]This question of sequence in the emergence of Shu and Tefnut is developed more seriously in the Coffin Texts; see especially Spell 76.

Copyrighted Material

Pyramid Text 841–43

The liturgical context of the next statements is not difficult to surmise. They belonged to a purification rite that was performed during funerary proceedings.

O King, stand up, that you may be pure and that your *ka* may be pure, for Horus has cleansed you with cold water. Your purity is the purity of Shu; your purity is the purity of Tefnut; your purity is the purity of the four house spirits when they rejoice in Pe.

Be pure! Your mother Nut the great Protectress purifies you, she protects you. "Take your head, gather your bones together," says Geb. "The evil which is on this King is destroyed, the evil which was on him is brought to an end," says Atum.

The exhortation to the deceased king begins here in the turnaround realm at Level 5 and it covers the entire distance from there back to Atum, at Level 9. The purity that is achieved provides the rising and returning king with an affinity to all major hypostases or divinities along the way—to four house spirits, to Nut and Geb, and to Shu and Tefnut—guaranteed and decreed all along by the eternal godhead himself.[7]

Pyramid Texts 2051–53

Many commentaries on Egyptian religion fail to recognize the unity of the Ennead as constituting a single godhead. The English rendition of the following text provides an occasion to address this issue:

If the King be caused to be embalmed, the [female] Great One will fall before the King, for the King's mother is Nut, the King's (grand)father is Shu, the King's (grand)mother is Tefnut, they take the King to the sky, to the sky, on the smoke of incense.

[7]The four house spirits at Pe, or Buto, may be the four "children of Horus" or "sons of Osiris." They were Amset, Hapi, Duamutef, and Kebehsenuf. See Hans Bonnet, *Reallexikon der Ägyptischen Religionsgeschichte* (Berlin, 1952), pp. 129, 315f.

Copyrighted Material

As a meticulous translator, R. O. Faulkner has added the parenthetical generational indicators (grand)father Shu and (grand)mother Tefnut. That would definitely be an improvement if, in an absolute specific sense, the goddess Nut could be identified as the King's mother. But divine relationships in ancient Egypt were never that static or specific. While the king still ruled as Horus divinity on the throne of Egypt, the proper "generation" of his mother would have been Isis; and that designation would have rendered Nut to be his grandmother, and Shu and Tefnut to be his greatgrandparents.

However, now that the king is dead and being contemplated in his Osirian condition, Nut indeed is his proper mother and, generationally speaking, his (grand)parents are those whom Faulkner has designated. Nevertheless, theologically speaking no family tree with specific branches need be concocted in this case. Heliopolitan theology regards all masculine manifestations in the Enneadean godhead as one Father. Likewise, it regards all feminine manifestations as one Mother.

It makes little sense to speak here of specific generations of gods as if their family tree had become known, as is the case with mortals, in linear time. Family trees with fixed and immutable branches make sense only in the realm of mortals among whom sequence and death are significant existential boundaries. All along in this presentation, the term *generation* must be understood in its gerundial sense—of the godhead "generating" or "procreating" his own hypostases. Enneadean theology collapses the divine "family tree" into a single process of emanation. Divine "generations" that precede the human level of existence do not die. Atum is godhead, he lives as Shu and Tefnut, he lives as Geb and Nut, and he lives as the remainder of the Ennead combined.

Thus, the deceased king in this instance is carried as *ka* or divine Osiris-soul to the sky, ritually on the smoke of incense but ontologically by Shu and Tefnut. He is carried by these parental deities past the hypostasis of Geb and Nut, all the way home to Atum.

Pyramid Texts 1687–95

The deceased king has traveled in the barque of the sun god toward the western horizon, as though he were the very son of Nut, the sun god Ra himself. Before he died, the king had lived in human

Copyrighted Material

flesh, temporarily, for the worthy purpose of ruling Egypt. When he died he returned to the gods to continue ruling among them. Boys will be boys, and kings will be kings! It stands to reason that, to enable an Egyptian pharaoh to retain his identity as a ruler, the gods graciously assembled to play a game of "monarchy" with the newly arrived. A freshly deceased king, still saddled with imperial ambitions, was thereby given an opportunity to play-act his royal skills a while longer. Concurrently, of course, he is also expected to provide moral support for his royal successor on the throne of Egypt, as follows:

> Go aboard this bark of Ra...in which Ra rows to the horizon, that you may go aboard it as Ra; sit on this throne of Ra that you may give orders to the gods, because you are Ra who came forth from Nut who bears Ra daily, and you are born daily like Ra... "Who is like him?" say the two great and mighty Enneads who preside over the Souls of On. These two great and mighty gods who preside over the Field of Rushes install you upon the throne of Horus as their firstborn; they set Shu for you on your east side and Tefnut on your west side, Nu on your south side and Nenet on your north side; they guide you to these fair and pure seats of theirs which they made for Ra when they set him on their thrones.... Do not be far removed from the gods, so that they may make for you this utterance which they made for Ra-Atum who shines every day. They will install you upon their thrones at the head of all the Ennead(s) as Ra and as his representative. They will bring you into being like Ra in this his name of Khoprer; you will draw near to them like Ra in this his name of Ra; you will turn aside from their faces like Ra in this his name of Atum.

In the second portion of this important text the individual gods gather to make enabling utterances—of the kind they made when they empowered Ra-Atum, the one who shines every day. Of course, this is bloated poetry that reverses orthodox cosmic causality. Originally Atum-Ra himself empowered everyone and everything else. Such ambitious poetry was concocted to lend credence to priestcraft and statecraft in the lower visible regions. So it may seem from an outsider's perspective. But what if these gods have all along been no more than *ka* manifestations of the All-God?

Copyrighted Material

Be that as it may, Ra, like Khoprer the cosmic dung beetle, brings forth the visible sun. When he shines from on high as sun, Ra is godhead in his manifest mode; after he sets as sun and hides in darkness this same godhead is more appropriately named *Atum*. While a deceased Egyptian king traveled so in the company of Ra, he participated for a while longer in the administration of the cosmos. But he went his way, just the same, to fuse again his *ka* with Atum-Ra, the total godhead.

Noteworthy in all these texts is the ease with which the plurality of the Ennead(s) is made to blend into a single godhead. The difference between polytheism and monotheism, or pantheism for that matter, generally is one of perspective and focus. And this perspective, or focus, ordinarily is a function of a mortal person's degree of ego-assertion or ego-surrender vis-à-vis the gods or God. It is a question of whether human wills can be pious enough to permit their God to show a single face or more than one—or to show no specific face at all—at any given moment in time. Pantheistic revelations generally reflect a condition of mystic surrender, wherein the human ego has surrendered to a single God as an "All-God." Pantheism is no more and no less than a mystic's maximum version of monotheism.

Pyramid Texts 1773–74

Here again the king ascends as Ra to shine back upon Egypt, as essence of the sun god. His rays, however, descend upon the land as Mahet (order and righteousness); namely, as the divinity who somehow happens to be copresent with natural sunlight. As such she is copresent with visibility and order. In this manner, deceased Egyptian kings supposedly have continued to bless their land, especially at the occasion when the people celebrated New Year—the advent of another round of sunlight:

The King passes the night, having daily mounted up to Ra, and the shrine is opened for him when Ra shines. The King has ascended on a cloud, he has descended [. . .] Mahet in the presence of Ra on that day of the Festival of the First of the year.

Copyrighted Material

Pyramid Texts 1582–83

As in the preceding text, so too in the following one, the king is destined to shine Mahet (the divinity of order and righteousness) that represses wrongdoing. This is considered an extension of his royal duties which he performed while ruling Egypt. This righteousness is meant to be radiated on Egypt every day, along with Ra's sunlight.

May you shine as Ra; repress wrongdoing, cause Mahet to stand behind Ra, shine every day for him who is in the horizon of the sky. Open the gates which are in the Abyss.

It appears as though Mahet is envisioned here as a form of Tefnut who, in cosmogonic sequence, emerged from Atum "behind" Shu. This possibility must be considered again later, in relation to Coffin Texts, Spells 76 and 80.

Pyramid Text 5

The deceased king is loved by the gods, especially by the sky goddess, Nut (Level 3). According to divine gossip, which somehow had reached the ears of knowledgeable priests in Heliopolis, Nut as sky goddess was more lovingly disposed toward this particular deceased pharaoh than toward her own mother—or more than Tefnut was. In either case, Enneadean divine love flows outward—flows downward in the direction of king and humankind.

Recitation by Nut the great:...The King is my son of my desire....All the gods say: Your father Shu knows that you love the King more than your mother Tefnut.

Pyramid Texts 1353–54

Cosmologically speaking, the realm of Shu and Tefnut is situated in the upward direction. Hence, the deceased's soul is "raised aloft" on the hands of these divinities. Moving in the upward direction, the homeward bound soul arrives where Nut arches as firmament (Level

Copyrighted Material

7), as celestial manifestation of Atum. We are told that previously, at Level 5, Nephthys sustained the king:

Your water jar is firm...you are raised aloft on the hands of Shu and Tefnut in the Mansion of Her who provides, O King, because you are a spirit whom Nephthys suckled with her left breast.

Pyramid Texts 2097-99

The embalmed and wrapped corpse of the king participates in the nature of Osiris, his face wears a jackal mask, and his *ka* is now wrapped in Atum's own divine flesh, which, of course, is not "flesh." The return of a king to the primordial condition is indicated by allusion to very archaic "prehuman flux" hunter mythology.[8] Thus begins the king's homeward journey at Level 5. Inasmuch as Shu and Tefnut themselves are his primary guides, his full return to the godhead is assured.

This King comes provided as a god, his bones knit together as Osiris. . . . Your face is that of a jackal, your flesh is that of Atum, your soul is within you, your power is about you, Isis is before you and Nephthys is behind you, you encompass the Horite Mounds and you go round about the Sethite Mounds, it is Shu and Tefnut who guide you when you go forth from On.

Pyramid Texts 1984-85

The deceased king's destination once again is the source of all being, Atum. He is the "great god" as long as oneness is considered (Level 9). Shu and Tefnut are his designation when he is contemplated as twofold hypostasis (Level 8). To invoke the assistance of Shu and Tefnut as ferry gods who "row," as considered within the trinitarian logic of Junu, implies nothing less than that the great godhead himself conveys the deceased king unto himself.

---

[8]For a discussion and samples of prehuman flux mythology, see Luckert, *The Navajo Hunter Tradition*, pp. 133ff.

Copyrighted Material

... you go forth that you may go up to the broad hall of Atum, travel to the Field of Rushes, and traverse the places of the great god. The sky is given to you; [it is] the good great gods who row you, (even) Shu and Tefnut, the two great gods of On.

Pyramid Text 1739

The king's progress is assured because he is carried homeward by Ra, or Atum-Ra. The divine and royal status of the god, as carrier of the sun, does not permit him to weaken or to turn back on his path. In addition, the king's progress during his journey is guaranteed because he is being carried along not only by the self-conscious and dependable sun god, but also by Tefnut and Shu:

... Tefnut seizes you, Shu grips you; the Majesty of Ra will not turn back in the horizon, for every god sees him.

Copyrighted Material

4

Heliopolitan Theology in the Coffin Texts

The second stratum of literary sources for Heliopolitan theology are Coffin Texts from the First Intermediary Period and the Middle Kingdom (2133–1786 B.C.E.). These were written on inside surfaces of wooden coffins on behalf of patrician owners who had status and wealth. Their material possessions afforded these mortals not only more elaborate funerals and prestigious burial facilities but also higher status in relation to the gods, thus, a better entry into afterlife.

Like the Pyramid Texts after which they were modeled, Coffin Texts are spells or "strong prayers" that, in the obvious presence of death, affirm and insist on more life. Generally these affirmations proceed on the assumption that the deceased person will be able to achieve a special mystic relationship with a great deity. The divinities on whom Middle Kingdom patricians depended were not low-ranking gods at Level 5 who could, just possibly, be persuaded to serve as guides to realms beyond. Rather, a dying person of rank identified himself or herself in the manner of superior pharaohs during the Old Kingdom, thus, with the greatest divine presences whom he or she dared approach.

Among the various theologies quoted for existential reinforcement in Middle Kingdom coffin spells, the Heliopolitan theology still appears the most coherent. This state of affairs attests to the fact that the Old Kingdom priests of Junu, who composed spells for inscription in royal pyramids, were able to perpetuate their theological tradition throughout the period of Egypt's first major political crisis, the Intermediary Period, which lasted from 2181 to 2040 B.C.E.

The Heliopolitan Ennead or "Ninefoldness" was understood by orthodox Egyptian theologians as one All-God; that is, as a single

Copyrighted Material

divine reality or process that has manifested itself in causal succession, contemporaneously, as nine divine personae in four pairs.

Heliopolitan mythology assured that, on the death or Osirization of a Horus-king, his ceremonial offspring would be born as the next new Horus-king unto the throne of Egypt. This ritualization of the political process allowed for a measure of flexibility in the choice of royal successors; it also made the rare changeovers to other dynasties less traumatic than otherwise they could have been. Isis represented the feminine divine throne on whose lap a duly installed king was ceremonially reborn.

Nevertheless, even in the context of idealistic mythology, this royal "soteriology" has produced its own bout of fighting between Horus and Seth. Only the intervention of a third god, Thoth, who was known as a god of wisdom, could return this ritualized defense of Osiris's honor on the part of his successor Horus—or, could whitewash a new dynasty's violent takeover—to a state of normalcy. Thoth himself healed the wounds of the divine combatants, and thereby the new king was endorsed to rule Egypt henceforth in peace.

All the while, the decisive battle fought against Seth as the cause of death, and fought on behalf of mortal humankind as much as it was for the continuity of the empire, was thereby repeatedly postponed. That battle had to be remembered by each succeeding generation and dealt with anew.

Alongside this dynamic monotheistic theology and soteriology, the divine status of an Egyptian pharaoh was also anchored in the sure fact and foil of his de facto human mortality. Whereas a living pharaoh, as a divine Horus-falcon, represented the first and highest human rank that emanated from the Ennead, a dying pharaoh returned toward the Ennead, and the godhead, by virtue of being immediately transformed into Osiris. Egyptian royalty thereby oscillated between membership in the Ennead, on the one hand, and being anthropomorphically reborn as Horus-falcon divinity, on the other.

Dying is the birth process in reverse. Therefore, getting saved in the face of death required the homeward movement of the human ka, swimming against the original procreative flow of divine emission and emanation. Theologically this meant that any mortal king who wished to preserve his royal status, or any king who had just suffered the misfortunes of death, was able to view himself as someone caught up in the original mythic "turnaround struggle" perpetually being waged between Osiris and Seth. Any mortal king thereby could also

Copyrighted Material

participate in Osiris' moment of truth—in his triumphant journey through death and in his regenerative collaboration with Isis.

During the Intermediate Period nobles of lesser rank usurped royal authority. They continued doing so, still, during the Middle Kingdom by way of insisting on equal burial status in relation to the ancient deified royalty. The cult that served to save dead pharaohs during the Old Kingdom was expanded, during the Middle Kingdom, to also include patricians. And then it was only a matter of time before, during the New Kingdom, a democratization of afterworld status was being claimed piecemeal by plebeians as well. Numerous papyri, found in New Kingdom coffins of commoners, bear inscriptions of ancient spells that have precedents on earlier coffin and pyramid walls. Their very existence attests to a massive trend of democratization concerning status in the afterlife.

The insistence among Egyptian common folk on royal status after death was internationalized and universalized later in the wider Greco-Roman world, under the guise of Hellenistic philosophy and various branches of gnosticism. It also was given new form by the Kingdom of Heaven movement founded by John the Baptizer and continued by Jesus of Nazareth. All these trends of democratization and universalization have undercut the divine status which hitherto was claimed by human emperors and kings. So, for example, Jesus undertook to distribute this divinely bestowed royal status as evenly as he could among those commoners who followed in his footsteps as his brothers and sisters.

Freedom from grand domestication systems—this our Western modern reformers should not forget—was achieved by commoners in ancient Egypt first on behalf of their dead. It was derived by the living later on from the status of privileged ghosts. Still later, in the course of Christian history, egalitarian rights could be derived from the royalty status that could be assumed by faith in a "kingdom of heaven," another kind of world, which was open to all people. Equality and freedom could and has been claimed, in each instance, by living folk who would labor to accumulate sufficient merit and status for their personal postexistence. Equality and freedom could be derived by modern democratic revolutions from that greater-than-human dimension and extended, on "afterlife credit," one might say, to all those who were willing to die or to dedicate their dying to the cause of a more egalitarian democratic order.

Copyrighted Material

The selections from among Coffin Texts in this chapter have been made on the basis of certain emphases and themes in Heliopolitan theology, which are present in this second stratum of Egyptian literature. These selections pertain (1) to general theogony and the emergence of trinitarian theology as Atum, Shu, and Tefnut; (2) to the soteriological functions of Isis and Horus proceeding at Level 5; and (3) to the ensuing process of overt theologizing and latent philosophizing.

In conjunction with our previous exposition of selected Pyramid Texts, the present selections from among later Coffin Texts will add to our understanding of the larger ancient Egyptian background. They will enable us to revise our historical understanding of Hellenic philosophy, of Neoplatonism, and of the origins of Christendom and Gnosticism.

Theogony and Cosmogony

Some of the most informative sentences concerning Heliopolitan theogony and cosmogony, in the published Coffin Texts, can be found among Spells 75, 76, 78 and 80. Spell 80 is the most explicit and deserves to be quoted at the outset in larger than ordinary install-ments. The method to be followed for its exposition calls for presentation and discussion of paragraph-size quotations, followed by commentary on those excerpts.[1]

> O you eight Chaos-gods, being truly Chaos-god of the two Chaos-gods, who encircle the sky with your arms, who gather together sky and earth for Geb, Shu fashioned you in chaos, in the Abyss, in darkness and in gloom, and he allots you to Geb and Nut, while Shu is everlasting and Tefnut is eternity. I am the soul of Shu at the head of the celestial kine, who ascends to heaven at his desire,

---

[1]Unless otherwise indicated, English quotations of Coffin Texts are from R. O. Faulkner's translation, *The Ancient Egyptian Coffin Texts*, Vol. 1 (Warminster, England, 1973), by permission of Aris and Phillips Ltd. In quoting from his translation only his rendition of *Tefenet* has been changed to the more widely used *Tefnut*, and *Ma'et* has been adjusted to *Mahet*.

Copyrighted Material

who descends to earth at his wish. Come joyfully at meeting the god in me, for I am Shu whom Atum fashioned, and this garment of mine is the air of life. A cry for me went forth from the mouth of Atum, the air opened up upon my ways. It is I who make the sky lighten after darkness, my pleasant [azure] colour is due to the air which goes forth after me from the mouth of Atum, and the storm-cloud of the sky is my efflux; hail-storms and dusk are my sweat. (Spell 80)

These opening words are put in the mouth of Atum, the "soul of Shu." He addresses the remaining Chaos-gods contained in his ninefoldness. The entire Heliopolitan Ennead consists of Chaos-gods inasmuch as, together with Atum, the remaining eight gods of the Ennead also have risen from chaos or Nun.

The second phrase still addresses all the remaining gods, but it acknowledges that they are one in number, at Level 1, and that there are two of them at Level 2. Together Shu and Tefnut form a triune unity with Atum, the All-Father. As such their arms embrace sky and earth and hold them together as the next explicit unit in which life was to be generated and made possible. Shu, the masculine manifestation of Atum, has fashioned the other gods in chaos inasmuch as, at Level 2 symbolism, he represents the creative hill or phallus of Atum that, it is said, rose from chaos or Nun.

We also learn that the tenures of Shu and Tefnut are everlastingness and eternity. Accordingly, in hope of its own eternity, the soul of a deceased person identifies with these divinities who, initially, have contained all the primeval stirrings and all the energies of life. Mystic identification with Shu makes sense, indeed, because this god is air and life. To the extent that the god Shu is air, it follows that he embodies the very life breath of Atum. The living breeze of Shu also brings light after darkness, the dawn, and while doing so he radiates a pleasant color. His masculine temper occasionally erupts in hail storms whereas morning and evening dew, it would seem, are his own gentle sweat.

The portion from Spell 80 that follows next is central to understanding the dawning of Tefnut's manifestation as Mahet. Atum has generated Shu and Tefnut and, in all likelihood, Mahet is here identical with Tefnut.

Copyrighted Material

Atum said: Tefnut is my living daughter;
she is (will be) with (her) brother Shu.[2]
His name is Living One; her name is Mahet (Order).
I live with my two children; I live with my two fledglings.
For I am before them; they are behind my body to lift (me) up.[3]
I live with my daughter Mahet:
One (fem.) is within me; one (fem.) is behind me.[4]
I have raised up upon because of them;
their two arms are behind me.
It is Geb who will live, (he) whom I begat in my name...
(Spell 80)

I have obtained a fresh translation for this passage because
Faulkner's rendition assumed, erroneously I suspect, that the text
refers to two goddesses, Tefnut and Mahet. To achieve his desired
degree of separation between these two divine names, Faulkner was
obliged to disregard the predicated use of *Mahet* earlier—as in "her
(Tefnut's) name is Mahet." Concerning Tefnut he therefore translated
"righteousness is her name." In our next installment from Spell 80,
it will become clear that Mahet indeed is identical with Tefnut.

Also, quite clearly, in the beginning Atum himself decreed creative
togetherness for his twin offspring, Shu and Tefnut. Shu is air,
breath, and life whereas Tefnut is containment and order (Mahet). But
no sooner than the creative union of Life and Order has been
determined by the godhead, than he reflects on his continued intimacy
with his twin children—as a union and expression of himself. The

---

[2]Retranslation of this section of Spell 80, by Professor Garth Alford, is gratefully
acknowledged.

[3]*Translator's Note:* sdr means "lift up" when used with ▭▭▭▭ sky determina-
tive. May also read "(to) lift (me) up! So that I may live with my daughter Mahet."

[4]*Author's Note:* The two "feminine ones," who are given in all the extant texts,
appear nevertheless to refer only to a single "one." This text appears to present a case
of synonymous parallelism; for example, "she is within me; (as) she is behind me."
Within me seems to refer to Tefnut being within Atum prior to her emergence and birth.
Behind me seems to refer to her two arms embracing, as lover, Atum in the form of
Shu. This much is suggested by the sentence that follows.

Copyrighted Material

goal of this self-union of Atum as primal trinity is the procreation of
Geb and Nut—Father Earth and Mother Sky.

Faulkner's note 15, in his published translation, suggests that two
documents "erroneously" have named the son of Atum as Geb. He
insists that mythologically this son should be Shu. It is precisely this
sort of disjunctive reasoning, about ancient Egyptian theology, that
has obscured for modern minds the ancient Heliopolitan "riddle of
life." In the larger scope of Enneadean theology, Geb is not born as
an estranged or separate entity; he is never seen as being less than an
emanation or manifestation of Atum. Geb is only somewhat more
distant from the All-Father than is his immediate father Shu. As
Father Earth, Geb simply is made to appear a little more specific and
concrete, that is, more visible than his immediate sire Shu who
represents Life or the invisible breath-soul of Life. We must realize
that in the Heliopolitan scheme of things, where generations of divine
creative phalluses are fused as manifestations of a single primeval
rising hill, a "grandson" remains always a son, and a son in turn
continues to emit the essence of his father(s) through his son(s).

So, who is within? Who is behind? Who rises? And who embraces?

We are faced here with a splendidly convoluted puzzle; namely,
the Heliopolitan riddle of cosmos and life. As one might expect, this
puzzle of creation had to be stated in an inverse mode from the
familiar puzzle that all along has been attributed to the Sphinx. The
Sphinx, an afterworld guardian caught up between human and
mysterious animal existence, between the realms of the living and of
those who continue to exist in a state of twilight beyond prehuman
and postmortem flux, naturally belongs to the turnaround realm of
Level 5. Accordingly, the riddle of the Sphinx to King Oedipus
pertained to aging and mortality. And, true to her station in the
scheme of things, the Sphinx traditionally has killed her victims and
therefore also had to be defeated, somehow.

But this, here, is the much greater riddle about Atum as the source
of all life and being. It pertains to the secret of the All-God's mode
of creation, to his generation and his love, and to the intelligence he
inspires. How does one go about searching for an answer to this
riddle? What, ontologically speaking, is the creative dynamic within
the first trinity of the Heliopolitan Ennead—within Atum, Shu, and
Tefnut? Can there, perchance, be found in the Kama Sutra an
analogous posture or relationship? Or perchance in the Perfumed

Copyrighted Material

Garden? There is no need to make this ancient Egyptian riddle of divine life and existence more complicated than it really is. There is no need to scavenge extravagances from among the life-styles of mortals.

First, the phrase "I have raised up upon because of them" surely links up, as do all risings in Atum's realm, with the original rising of Atum as primeval hill and creative phallus. However, in the present symbolic mode, the "hand" of Atum, which served to give him creative pleasure in the context of Level 1 symbology (see Pyramid Text 1248), here is transposed appropriately to Level 2. The All-God's "hand" thereby has become the "arms" or embrace of Shu and Tefnut. Shu is the life-energy that issued forth; and Tefnut is the containment, order, and firmament, an emanation of "hand," which Faulkner hedgingly has translated as "righteousness." Indeed, *righteousness* in the sense of containment and order is what is meant when Tefnut is referred to as Mahet.

It must be obvious that this entire passage narrates a single event, the procreation or generation of Geb and Nut by Atum. However, for that purpose Atum has appeared in the mode of his Father-Son-Daughter (Atum-Shu-Tefnut) trinity. It should also be obvious that both Shu and Tefnut are manifestations of Atum on a smaller scale. The generative Atum contains and, in turn, is lovingly embraced by both of them. It is equally obvious that the existential scopes of Geb and Nut are made manifest, accordingly, in a still more specific and more visible manner than the scopes of Shu and Tefnut. In turn, the specific offspring of Geb and Nut have become manifest on a still smaller scale; they have become much more visible at the lower existential frequencies of Level 4.

The answer to our riddle lies at hand. Indeed, in this primeval embrace of one, two, and three divine personae, the arms—and with confidence one could even add the legs—embraced the primeval Atum who as primeval hill and phallus was contained within that self-same embrace; namely, within a single unit of divine creative pleasure. Atum's phallus, and that much we have learned already from the Pyramid Texts, for the purpose of creation was on Shu as well.

Nu(n) said to Atum: Kiss your daughter Mahet, put her at your nose, that your heart may live, for she [they] will not be far from you; Mahet is your daughter and your son is Shu whose name

Copyrighted Material

lives. Eat of your daughter Mahet; it is your son Shu who will
raise you up.

I indeed am one who lives, son of Atum; he has fashioned me with
his nose, I have gone forth from his nostrils; I have put myself on
his neck and he kisses me with my sister Mahet. He rises daily
when he issues from his egg which the god who went up shining
fashioned. . . .

My father Atum kisses me when he goes forth from the eastern
horizon, and his heart is at peace at seeing me; he proceeds in
peace to the western horizon, and he finds me in his path.
(Spell 80)

One Coffin Text variation of Spell 80 contains the plural form
they—indicated parenthetically in the first sentence—which Faulkner
judges to be an error. However, *they* appears to be correct because
the statement forthrightly continues to tell about Mahet and Shu. In
the preceding discussions we already have shown what the closeness
of these two divinities, in relation to Atum, has been all about. Moreover, we have learned from the present selection that Atum has not
only kissed his daughter with his kiss of life, but he has done so as
well to his son Shu. At this point in the reading there should no
longer be any doubt that Mahet indeed is identical with Tefnut. Other
coffin inscriptions, such as Spell 121, support this conclusion as well.

The deceased, whose death has been the occasion for having
inscribed in his coffin this most complete of all theogonic spells, Spell
80, should not be faulted for having contemplated Tefnut with an
emphasis on her order-righteousness-wisdom or her Mahet dimension.
After chaotic moments of death, the ordering efforts of Mahet were
expected to produce order and life.

But whence came Atum's idea, to the effect that he should kiss his
daughter, or to the effect that his Shu and his Tefnut should be
united? This notion, we are told here, originated already while he was
still hidden in Nun, in chaos. The latter, Nun, somehow "knew" a
thing or two about the chaotic potentiality of Atum's breath and about
the potency of his rising. But then, whence did Chaos "know" all
these things? Perhaps it would have been wiser for our ancient author
not to have attempted an explanation of this deepest creative mystery
of Atum. At some point during ontological learning and speculation
all human questions and answers must cease. Divinely given life is

Copyrighted Material

destined to discern and find delight within its own inherent chaos and order.

Life or *ka* essences rising, resurrected *ka* essences soaring homeward and trailing their temporarily visible "comet tails" or *ba* appearances, that is what Coffin Texts are all about. Atum still rises daily; his emissions of *ka*, as light of the sun god Ra, demonstrate that fact. The dead look up to that divine manifestation for conveyance to travel homeward in the direction of Atum. In contrast to his own Ra manifestation, the hidden aspect of Atum is suggested by his daily retreating, into darkness and gloom. The Ra-rays of Atum simply continue to give the primeval kisses that the godhead began giving while he was still coiled unto himself in gloom. These rays are intended for those among his offspring who have come forth to live for a while in sunlight.

* * *

Our excerpts and exposition of Spell 80, pertaining to theogony and cosmogony, may be supplemented with quotations from Spells 75, 76, and 78. In various coffin texts the god Shu is mentioned as though he were more important than his father Atum. This, of course, is due to the fact that Shu is the god of life and breath. During funerary proceedings, whereby the effects of death are to be checked and undone, he is in great demand in that mode. This practical funerary concern has spilled over into theogony when, as an answer to the demands of mortal minds, the generative role of Atum increasingly became associated with Shu. The mythological basis for this transposition, naturally, has been the credo about Shu's continuation of Atum's emission or his spitting.

> I am the soul of Shu the self-created god, I have come into being from the flesh of the self-created god. I am the soul of Shu, the god invisible in shape. . . . I am merged in the god, I have become he. (Spell 75)

The unique status of Shu is based on his parthenogenetic origin. He issued directly from his father. Atum conceived him by himself, with his own mouth. He spat out Shu and Tefnut together to be born. Shu's primacy is established by the fact that Tefnut emerged after him. In addition, Shu's attributes are clearly identified as being breath

Copyrighted Material

of life or, more anthropomorphically, as being the breath of life that
has come from Atum's throat. The eye of Atum once sought Shu and
his sister Tefnut. This hint probably refers to the mythic moment
when the two began mating as a pair:

> I [the deceased] indeed am Shu whom Atum created, whereby Ra
> came into being; I was not built up in the womb, I was not knit
> together in the egg, I was not conceived, but Atum spat me out in
> the spittle of his mouth together with my sister Tefnut.[5] She went
> up after me, and I was covered with the breath of the throat. The
> phoenix of Ra was that whereby Atum came into being in chaos,
> in the Abyss, in darkness and in gloom. I am Shu, father of the
> gods, and Atum once sent his Sole Eye seeking me and my sister
> Tefnut. (Spell 76)

The two action metaphors, of seminal emission and spitting, were
used separately in the Pyramid Texts (see 1248 and 1652). From that
point on each metaphor appears to have engendered its own train of
mythic conceptualizations and ritual responses. And so Atum's hand
and phallus led the myth makers to imagine the discovery of a series
of mating twins. On the other hand, Atum's spitting mouth has
encouraged speculation about air and breath; and eventually that line
of speculation has evolved to mean the spoken divine command or
logos. Spoken words are but breath made audible. This we shall find
expressed by Memphite theology, in the next chapter.

From the point of view of a dead person, Shu as god of life is
understandably the most significant divine personage mentioned in
these funerary spells. On that account he also is the one most clearly
introduced. He is air, breath, and life. By contrast, the naturalistic
equivalents of Tefnut are a little more difficult to determine. Spell 78
is significant because it supports what we already have learned about
Shu, and in addition, it gives us a new hint about the nature of Tefnut
and her destiny to become the mother of Atum's creation. As her

---

[5]Western readers who have difficulty appreciating these mystic identifications of
Egyptian souls with their saving deity, and of the gods with one another, are advised
to recall a saying of Jesus: "Before Abraham was, I am" (*John* 8:58), or "I and the
Father are one" (*John* 10:30). These claims of Jesus, whether they were his own or
have later been ascribed to him, sound completely reasonable in the context of Egyptian
ontology and logic. Copyrighted Material

brother Shu elsewhere (as in Spell 80), so here Tefnut also "shines on the gods."

It appears as though Shu's ability to shine has been a direct extension of Atum-Ra's "phoenix in Heliopolis" (Pyramid Texts 1652). For Shu it is the "flame of the fiery blast" and is his radiant emission, whereas the shine on the countenance of Tefnut, mentioned subsequently, appears more like an afterglow in the feminine experience of that same event.

> I am this soul of Shu which is in the flame of the fiery blast which Atum kindled with his own hand. He created orgasm and fluid (?) fell from his mouth. He spat me out as Shu together with Tefnut, who came forth after me as the great Ennead, the daughter of Atum, who shines on the gods. (Spell 78)

The priestly mind that composed this spell has been well in tune with combined Shu and Tefnut mysticism; but, obviously, it was out of touch with the original metaphors that applied to Atum specifically. The priest who composed this particular spell was plagued by conscientious literalism. He no longer understood that *phallus* and *mouth* were alternate expressions for phallus and hand. His was a mind that hoped to eliminate ambiguity by way of rationalizing and combining the separate "ejaculation" and "spitting" metaphors. The result was a third metaphor, of masturbation culminating in auto-oralism, a theological symbology that begins to approach the grotesque.

Soteriology in the Turnaround Realm

In Coffin Text Spells 131 and 335, and at other places, the god Seth is mentioned as the one who causes death. This attribution is based on the fact that, mythologically, Seth is known to have been the killer of Osiris. By extension he also is the one who slew every moribund Egyptian pharaoh since that formative mythic event. And, by further extension from the royal cult, through the usurpation of royal status by lower ranking folk during the Middle Kingdom and later, Seth has become the cause of death for other ranks of human-kind as well. Accordingly, the twin sister of Osiris who was Isis, and

Copyrighted Material

for good measure even Nephthys who was the twin sister of Seth, provide encouragement:

> "Raise yourself, O my brother, so that your heart may live and that Seth may not exalt over you." (Spell 74)

The homeward-bound ancient Egyptian soul could identify with the great soul of Osiris. This soul, as the sexual opposite of Osiris, continues to enact the role of Isis true to orthodox mythological perspective. Formerly the gods commanded Osiris to copulate with his twin sister as with his soul. The theogonic background certifies this soteriological option:

> "Go forth and copulate with your soul" say all the gods. (Spell 96)

By virtue of Osiris's primeval copulation, a latter-day deceased, for whom this spell was inscribed, was remade "into his (i.e., Osiris's) living soul according to the word of the gods."

It may be surmised that most ordinary Egyptian folk, later on, had no ambitions of being reborn as actual Horuses, as if coming forth from Isis and destined to sit upon the throne of Egypt. They therefore also had no need to identify specifically with Osiris's emission of seed that, ceremonially, has been transmitting a concentrated divine spark of life to Horus-king successors. Ordinary people therefore focused their mysticism on the process of copulation itself. They interpreted the union of Osiris and Isis mystically as the God's loving embrace of their own souls, as though their souls were somehow feminine partners in that relationship.

Of course, it is possible, too, that Spell 96 was first intended and inscribed on behalf of a deceased woman. In that case the contrary identification with the male offspring of Isis, with Horus (as in Spell 84 and elsewhere), could be interpreted as a "masculine" variety of spells. However, it appears far more likely that the Enneadean sexual union between Isis and Osiris itself has furnished an existential model for the human soul's surrender to, and union with, the godhead.

Nevertheless, reasoning in Egypt about the mystic-sexual union of Osiris and Isis, in accordance with Heliopolitan coronation theology, produced real offspring. Moribund human minds could hurry to a quick conclusion and thereby think of liberated *ka* sparks as having

Copyrighted Material

been subsequently, as well as momentarily, reborn from Isis. Joyously they could exclaim:

"I have issued from between the thighs of Isis as Horus."
(Spell 84)

Then, being sent on its way by the birth waters of Isis, the returning soul could analogously be seen as "going out into daylight"; it could be envisioned as swimming homeward. This swimming home after being reborn constitutes, cosmo-biologically, a reversal of direction from the original generative seminal emissions of Atum. In the lower turnaround realm, at Level 5, Seth stopped Horus; by killing him he returned him to the condition of Osiris.

The role of Isis accomplishes similar results. By way of giving birth to Horus she stopped and reversed the flow of seminal emissions that had come her way from the masculine Atum-Shu-Geb-Osiris lineage. Birth from a female is a process of swimming against the current of masculine emission—also against the larger current of Atum's generation. These mythico-biological facts have brought the reborn and homeward-bound Egyptian souls to a point where they began swimming in Isis' birth waters.

O Horus of the Netherworld, you have swum to Pe [the cult city of Horus], and the gods who were given to you by Atum have swum after you, the men who are among them have followed you, the women who are among them have turned back faint through you and through your seed, O Osiris... (Spell 74)

Although this passage remains opaque at some points, several interesting notions can still be gleaned from it. Those who swum after Horus were given and sent by Atum—and, whatever Atum sends corresponds, cosmo-biologically, to his emission and the procreation of his divine offspring. Of course, a Horus who enters the Netherworld is no longer a Horus; he has been promoted to the full Enneadean rank of Osiris. Then, by identifying with the virility of Osiris, as is suggested by the effect he has had on the women mentioned in Spell 74, the deceased person implicitly identifies with the general procreative activity of the godhead. It therefore can be

Copyrighted Material

argued that the "swimming" metaphor of rebirth has remained a close parallel, all the while, to the initial mystic-sexual union of Osiris and Isis.

Even the best of swimmers in Egypt, along the river Nile in which crocodiles are plentiful, is tempted to dream of a safer alternative to swimming. Human salvation and the journey home to God were not immune to temptations from technology. There is an alternative to salvation by swimming: it requires rowing a boat. Accordingly, in Spell 181 Isis no longer gives birth or only reverses the water-of-life current in her old-fashioned feminine way of feminine secretions, birth water, and giving birth. Isis actually is portrayed as rowing a boat.

Engaging Isis as a ferry lady seemed a little farfetched to another wayward soul; its coffin spell preferred to seek salvation in traditional Osiris-Isis mysticism. But a mystic union with Osiris, on the part of a human soul who had learned to identify with Isis, needed to be properly augmented with assistance from her offspring. Salvation for souls who knew themselves as Isis, and who needed help with rowing across the waters of death and rebirth, was better left to the divine son whom the friendly goddess was able to persuade:

"I am Isis; I have gone forth from my house and my boat is at the mooring-rope; Horus ferries me over, Horus brings me to land." (Spell 182)

Our data are insufficient for telling whether the change-over between ferry personages, between Isis and Horus, stood in some kind of relationship to the gender of the deceased. Perhaps it does not really matter. Being ferried by either Isis or Horus is a euphemism. It is a way of claiming salvation by virtue of being "sired by Osiris" and "born of Isis" into the larger family of God.

There is an inherent difficulty in the soteriology of rowing yonder. Mythologically considered, Horus is either a king or a falcon. Egyptian kings, that is, Horus falcons existing in prehuman flux twilight, occasionally would avail themselves of boats and the services of oarsmen, but falcons preferred to fly and soar. Therefore, another coffin spell begins to reason afresh, at the point of traditional Osiris-Isis mysticism:

Copyrighted Material

Isis wakes pregnant with the seed of her brother Osiris. She is uplifted, (even she) the widow, and her heart is glad with the seed of her brother Osiris. (Spell 148)

A time later Isis "goes down to the Releaser who brings Horus," who apparently is releasing Isis by way of hastening Horus to be born. The soul of a dying person that is about to emerge from its bodily containment now experiences being born of Isis, as a consequence of experiencing death—that is, birth pangs. The proud Horus-soul promptly introduces itself as a "leader of eternity," with confident words like these:

"See Horus, you gods! I am Horus, the Falcon who is on the battlements of the Mansion of Him whose name is hidden.... my place is far from Seth, the enemy of my father Osiris. I have used the roads of eternity to the dawn, I go up in my flight."
(Spell 148)

The one "whose name is hidden," in this passage, is the single godhead of the Ennead who later in the history of Egyptian religion has become known specifically as Amun, the Hidden One. The ontological home, or the mansion of this source of all being, is located far from his distant Sethian hypostasis; that is, far from the lesser god of death who roams along the outermost perimeter of the Enneadean emanation.

Sooner or later the god Seth has wounded every Horus-king who ruled over ancient Egypt, and invariably he has transformed these kings into Osiris corpses. But then, this act in Heliopolitan turnaround mythology was followed by the miraculous impregnation of Isis, by Osiris. And Isis, in turn, has given birth to a new Horus-falcon king. In royal religion this mythology and ritual has facilitated succession on the throne of Egypt and also helped establish new dynasties. At the level of democratized personal soteriology, during the Middle and New Kingdoms, this same turnaround mythology has been invoked to stop and reverse the outward flow of the All-God's creative emanation among ordinary folk as well. On having encountered Seth, somewhere along the lower and outer edge of the divine Enneadean emanation, all human souls or *ka* sparks could be reborn, freed, and returned. They could be liberated to swim or fly homeward against the currents and swirls of Enneadean generation.

Copyrighted Material

A number of spells inscribed in Middle Kingdom coffins insist emphatically that their inhabitants refuse the naturalistic demands that traditionally the gods have placed on dead humankind. So for instance, some mortals have expressly put their foot down and have refused to accept the consequences of mortality regarding their appetites. Doing so they insisted on an older and more primitive version of salvation, salvation from mortality's reversals. They refused to walk upside down or eat excrement—even if these be the excrement of the god Osiris himself!

> "Eat this excrement which issued from the hinder parts of Osiris; what (else) can you live on?" say the gods to me. "What have you come to eat?" (Spell 173)

Reversal of living space and alimentary processes are common-place in primitive eschatologies. And indeed, such a limited and primitive victory could seem sufficient if one's homeward journey led only to an afterworld in horizontal space. Was it really necessary for the human soul to immerse itself mystically in the entire Enneadean stream of life? Flying and soaring in the air certainly seemed preferable to the person who selected Spell 173. He or she continued to eat the food of the living, as well as the habit of flying aloft—and thereby watched Egypt from on high. Impossible? No, not if you are the divine Horus-falcon:

> "I eat of bread and of white emmer..."
> "Be off!" say they to me. "Who pray are you?"
> "I am Horus [on] his tall perch(?)." (Spell 173)

From Theology to Philosophy

The priestly rites and activities that dealt with human mortality, and with prospects for eternal life, have inspired confidence in dealing with the gods directly. Some priests relied on methods of bureaucratic bluffing; that is, on the methods that had served them well in the environs of the Egyptian royal court. Vis-à-vis humans and gods they learned how to function as skillful politicians, theologians, and magicians. Not many Egyptian mortals would have dared

Copyrighted Material

to boast in their coffins with ambitious spells such as the next one. But this particular chief magician knew all too well how Egyptian theology had been put together through the ages:

> I am indeed the son of Her who bore Atum, I am the protection of what the Sole Lord commanded, I am he who caused the Ennead to live, I am "If-he-wishes-he-does," the father of the gods....
>
> I have come that I may take possession of my throne and that I may receive my dignity, for to me belonged all before you came into being, you gods; go down and come upon the hinder parts, for I am a [chief] magician. (Spell 261)

These words constitute the ultimate in a mystic's daring among Egyptian coffin spells. This homeward-bound *ka* did not even think to bother with lesser gods like Horus, Isis, Seth, or even Osiris. He went straight home to identify with the source of all being: He identified with the very power that generated Atum's first appearance and emanation. This chief magician—or shall we call him a chief systematic theologian?—knew how imperial theology was reasoned and how it was amended and expanded through time. He understood the process by which greater gods absorb smaller ones. He even understood the secret of how to transpose theology into psychology.

This magician was an If-he-wishes-he-does kind of "father of the gods." He knew that if one wished to influence, control, or usurp a present divine power one either had to be, or one had to identify with, the next greater power on whom such a present power depended. She who bore Atum—if such an All-Mother was ever thinkable in ancient Egypt—must have been the chaotic and indefinable Nun herself. Thus, from his exalted point of self-esteem this headstrong returning theologian's soul, this coequal partner of Atum, has commanded all gods to "go down and come upon the hinder parts"; thus, to approach him on their haunches.

Fortunately for Atum's primordial status, this haughty magician and systematic theologian remained humble enough not to also claim identity with "Mother Nun" herself. Looking at the positive side, it may be said that with this man's passing the godhead Atum has received back a confident collaborator in his work of generation. In his own wise Egyptian way, this chief magician either became divine

Copyrighted Material

himself or else he helped humanize the Egyptian cosmic All with help from Heliopolitan theology. His exaggerated mysticism may sound like blasphemy. But if that is what it was, then his spell differed only in degree from others in ancient Egypt, who also sought salvation through identification with Atum.

Daring and selfish priests turn into magicians. Doomed as they are to perform labors of the mind, being *homines sapientes*, they perform, react to, and put in question inherited rites of passage. But then, it is also a fact that the contributions to human life made by boisterous challengers are often of a negative sort. Great ideas that can sustain human balance and survival are hatched more often than not from common embryos, nearer to the heart of an orthodox ontology. Clothed in orthodox garb some great new ideas can be adopted without resistance, for a time, as simply representing common sense. Here is such an instance:

> Oh you eight Chaos-gods whom I created from the efflux of my flesh, whose names Atum made when the Abyss was created, on that day when Atum spoke in it with Nu(n) in chaos, in darkness and in gloom. (Spell 76)

Spoken from the point of view of the self-created first God, Atum, the other members of the Ennead can be designated properly as the remaining "eight Chaos-gods." But then, a rational adjustment had to be made in these funerary spells in light of the fact that Shu, the Son, was frequently honored as the god of "life" in place of Atum the All-Father.

Inasmuch as all life known to humankind could be traced through Shu, it seems significant to learn from Spell 76 that the "names" of all gods—thus also human "ideas" about them—were created first by the one and only Atum while he was still alone in Nun. The ancient Egyptian wise man who composed these lines has concluded that divine ideas and intelligence, in the Enneadean process, must have preceded the throbbing creative commotion of Shu, must have preceded life and his breathing. In the contemplative efforts of some Egyptian *homines sapientes* intellect thereby has been given precedence over physical emotions. Rational thinking demanded this self-oriented perspective, for the welfare of its own process.

Copyrighted Material

In Spell 76 can therefore be found the important seed concept that, well over a millennium later in Greece, blossomed out into Platonic philosophy, into Plato's theory of preexistent and eternal "ideas." Still later, switching homeward again in the direction of Egypt, it ripened and gave birth in Alexandria to a genuine fruit of Egyptian intellect, the so-called Neoplatonic philosophy—philosophized Egyptian theology.

Copyrighted Material

5

Other Ancient Egyptian Theologies

In this chapter we will introduce four additional ancient Egyptian theological systems, those of Hermopolis, Memphis, and Thebes. Included in our discussion of the Theban system, as the primary New Kingdom theology, will be a brief digression into the Amarna episode.

Amarna theology here will be mentioned intentionally in a subordinate fashion. Of all the ancient Egyptian monotheisms referred to in this book, the Atonism of Akhenaton is perhaps the least significant. It has been included here for consideration, because Western scholars have propelled it into prominence for the wrong reasons—and to the detriment of our overall understanding of ancient Egyptian religion.

The Theology of Hermopolis

The ancient city of Unet in Upper Egypt, Hermopolis in Greek, is known as the home of an Ogdoad of gods. This Eightfoldness of divine creative personages, apparently in competition with Heliopolitan theology, has come to be structured into four pairs of male gods with female counterparts. First is Nun, the primeval water who coexists with Naunet. Second, Huh or spacial infinity is matched by Hauhet. Third, Kuk or darkness has for its partner Kauket. And

EGYPTIAN LIGHT

fourth, Amun as hiddenness is accompanied by Amaunet. Some sources mention Niau and Niaut as the fourth pair instead.[1]

At some point in time the priests of Hermopolis must have felt significant enough to challenge the Memphite as well as the Theban theology. As a result, the Memphite theologians have incorporated the names of Nun and Naunet into their understanding of the godhead, Ptah. The Thebans on the other hand claimed Amun, and by implication also absorbed his spouse, the Amaunet.

Early Hermopolitan documentation is scarce, and the personages of the Ogdoad are mentioned first in a Coffin Text.[2] In any case it is difficult to tell which of the three cults—Hermopolis, Memphis, or Thebes—first tried to absorb either one or both of the others. For as little as is now known about the Hermopolitan cult, Memphite and Theban theology could indeed be indebted to it.

The Theology of Memphis

A brief glance at the theological system of Memphis is necessary for a larger perspective on the religious history of ancient Egypt. Our source is the famous Shabaka Stone, an eighth century B.C.E. copy or summary of an alleged older text. For Memphite theologians the name of the God of gods was Ptah. Whatever this Memphite god was before his imperial ambitions became apparent, whether or not he was Lord of Memphis or only of that city's artisans remains unclear. We know only that, at one point in the history of New Kingdom theology, someone contemplated the great Ptah of Memphis and, doing so, beheld again the All-God of Egypt.

---

[1]Most commentators on Hermopolitan theology draw from Sethe, "Amun und die acht Urgötter von Hermopolis," *Abhandlungen der Preussischen Akademie der Wissenschaften* (1929): 4.

[2]Hans Bonnet, *Reallexikon der Ägyptischen Religionsgeschichte* (Berlin, 1952); and Adolf Erman, *Die Religion der Ägypter* (Berlin and Leipzig, 1934), p. 5. Much of the information for this survey chapter has been gleaned from these helpful books, among others mentioned earlier.

Copyrighted Material

Some scholars have tended to project the Shabaka Stone theology back in time to the beginnings of Egyptian history. This leap into the past, beyond 3000 B.C.E., was suggested by the fact that Memphis was Egypt's first capital city. It served as residence for Menes who was the founder of the First Dynasty. But such a generous historical backward projection leaves insufficient room for the Heliopolitan system to develop and become better established by comparison. Heliopolitan theology flourished and dominated at least by the time when the great pyramids were built (2494–2181 B.C.E.). During the reign of the Hyksos kings (1720–1540 B.C.E.) the cult center at Heliopolis was still regarded as primary in Lower Egypt.[3] And still during the reign of Ramses III its budget far exceeded that of temples in the capital city of Memphis; the center finally may have been destroyed by Cambyses, the Persian.[4]

All of this, taken together, may recommend the reign of Tuthmosis I (1494–1482 B.C.E.) as a time for the formulation of the prototype Shabaka Stone theology. This was a time when Memphis again had been made the capital of Egypt; and this would have been a reasonable moment for priests of Ptah to have made their bid for primacy among the cult centers and theologies in the land. Shabaka Stone theology, as it has been preserved, constitutes an obvious usurpation of Heliopolitan theological claims. Nevertheless, even at this present level of historical uncertainty, the Shabaka text may serve as a good indication on the larger Egyptian theological and political process.

Memphite priests introduced their god Ptah as having been prior in time to Atum, as well as greater in scope. Ptah completely absorbed into himself the chaotic mystery of Nun that all along, although undefined, had been containing within itself the entire Heliopolitan process of divine procreation. The duality composed of Ptah-Nun or Ptah-Naunet, it was said, together begat and generated the Heliopolitan Atum. In Memphite perspective the God Ptah was

---

[3]Cyril Aldred. *Akhenaten, King of Egypt* (London, 1988), p. 237.

[4]Hans Bonnet. *Reallexikon der Ägyptischen Religionsgeschichte* (Berlin, 1952), pp. 543ff.

Copyrighted Material

considered to be "the heart and tongue of the Ennead" and the one "who gave birth to the gods."[5]

Whether Memphite or Hermopolitan priests were the first to seize upon the Heliopolitan weakness of an undefined first Nun, that possibility is now difficult to assess. In any case, at Memphis as well as in Hermopolis the category "Nun" was doubled by the method of introducing genders. Nun, which in Heliopolis was known as the chaotic outside wrapping of the cosmos, was invoked here to encapsulate the entire Heliopolitan theological system—and in this process the significance of Nun was increased to absorb within itself every other Egyptian theology as well.

Prior knowledge on the part of Memphite theologians, about the political importance of the Heliopolitan Ennead with Atum as its godhead, may be assumed. That awareness clearly is reflected in the following Shabaka Stone passage:

(53) There came into being as the heart and there came into being as the tongue (something) in the form of Atum.

This sentence must be one of the cleverest theological pronouncements ever devised. It bristles with priestly ambition and soft diplomatic fur. Memphite priests may have wished that the tradition of Heliopolis would disappear from the face of the earth and make room entirely for their own. However, it is significant that on account of such ambitions they never dared to deny the existence of Junu's godhead. They simply told their Memphite story a little bigger; that is, big enough to absorb the Helipolitan theology within their own. The Shabaka Stone text sets the tone for Memphite theologizing. "Something in the form of..." means that Atum is no longer someone mighty enough to be worried about. His "centrality" has not been denied, of course. That would have been un-Egyptian. He merely was absorbed by the prior and apparently larger Ptah-Nun-Naunet trinity.

All creative power in Ptah theology can be traced in terms of concrete symbology, as thought and word, all the way to the heart

---

[5]John A. Wilson, trans., in *Ancient Near Eastern Texts*, ed. James B. Pritchard (Princeton, N.J., 1969), p. 5 (48). Subsequent quotations from the Shabaka Stone are taken from pp. 4–6 of this publication as well.

Copyrighted Material

and tongue of the God. The claims of the Memphite God of gods thereby were expanded to where all living creatures could be included under the variety of Ptah's intimate *ba* manifestations; that is, as thought sparks of his *ka* that have become audible and visible.

The mighty Great One is Ptah, who transmitted [life to all gods], as well as (to) their *ka*'s, through this heart, by which Horus became Ptah, and through this tongue, by which Thoth became Ptah.

(Thus) it happened that the heart and tongue gained control over [every] (other) member of the body, by teaching that he is in every body and in every mouth of all gods, all men, [all] cattle, all creeping things, and (everything) that lives, by thinking and commanding everything that he wishes.

...Indeed, all the divine order (lit., "every word of the god") really came into being through what the heart thought and the tongue commanded. Thus the *ka* spirits were made and the *hemsut* spirits were appointed, they who make all provisions and all nourishment, by this speech.

Those among us within the Hebrew-Christian tradition who have spent some time wondering about creation as a result of divine command—as it is narrated for example in *Genesis* 1—or those who have contemplated the nature of the divine *logos* in *John* 1 will discover in this Memphite text an obvious antecedent.[6] And indeed, this Memphite creation story tells us something about divine behavior we have come to expect:

And so Ptah was satisfied, after he had made everything, as well as the divine order.[7]

---

[6]Even if the most recent date of the Shabaka Stone (eighth century B.C.E.) is assumed, the text is still a few centuries older than the corresponding Hebrew "priestly source" of *Genesis* 1.

[7]Or, "and so Ptah rested, after he had made everything, as well as every word of the god." Paraphrased, "as well as every divine creative command."

Copyrighted Material

But more is implied in this Memphite theology, and some of it shows the less comfortable side of Egyptian religion. That over-plus is the factor of grand domestication. As far as it mattered to his human inferiors, the person and will of an Egyptian pharaoh blended in nicely with the will of the supreme God of gods. Ptah's creative thoughts and words and the judgments of a divinized pharaoh were one and the same thing, even though each of them operated at different levels of divine emanation. As a result, the king's claim to authority over the lives of his subjects was absolute. Memphite theology rationalized the authority and power of its king as follows:

(Thus justice was given to) him who does what is liked, (and injustice to) him who does what is disliked.[8] Thus life was given to him who has peace and death was given to him who has sin. Thus were made all work and all crafts, the action of the arms, the movement of the legs, and the activity of every member, in conformance with (this) command which the heart thought, which came forth from the tongue, and which gives value to everything.

The function of imperial theology, as constitution for Egyptian grand domestication, becomes unmistakingly clear as the catalog of Ptah's founding activities is enlarged upon. A reader of these theological sentences ought to keep in mind that for whatever this creative God of gods is given credit, some reigning Horus-king felt called upon to own and supervise.

(Ptah)...had formed the gods, he had made the cities, he had founded nomes, he had put the gods in their shrines, he had made their bodies like that (with which) their hearts were satisfied. So the gods entered into their bodies of every (kind of) wood, of every (kind of) stone, of every (kind of) clay, or anything which might grow upon him, in which they had taken form. So all the gods, as well as their *ka*'s gathered themselves to him, content and associated with the Lord of the Two Lands.

Shabaka Stone theology is historically significant for two main reasons: (1) for illustrating ancient Egyptian ways of theologizing, of

---

[8]Wilson's injustice could be translated here more freely to read "punishment."

Copyrighted Material

how Atum-oriented theogony was recast into Ptah-oriented theogony, and (2) for showing the transition from an orthodox generative theogony to a cosmogony based on the creative divine word, *logos*, or command of God. The first of these reasons pertains to the history of ancient Egyptian religion, whereas the second affects our understanding of subsequent countercurrents against the Egyptian grand domesticator religion. The second dimension casts new historical light on Hebrew religion and such later universalisms as Judaism, Christendom, and Neoplatonism.

The transition from Atum-oriented theogony to Ptah-oriented theogony most probably has been a concern of city-based schools of priests that vied with one another for the attention of Egypt's religiously contained population. Nothing really new was added by Memphite theology to the conceptualization of Egypt's basic theogonic process; that is, nothing new concerning the godhead who emanates his essence down to an outer level of better visibility. And nothing was really new about the concomitant soteriology either. The primary bone of contention was not the basic structure of Enneadean monotheism and process theology; rather, it concerned the question of whose city deity might be exalted and magnified to lend its name to the unnameable godhead of Egypt—and by extension bestow the godhead's authority on the king as his legitimate Son of God.

The priestly cult center that was able to embrace, rationally, all other Egyptian theologies, could aspire to become the cult center of the empire. Its high priest could become the first cultus minister in the land. In this high priest's divinely favored city, even the nobility could infer from that fact, mythologically and ontologically, their eligibility for divine-royal status—for the eventuality that an older dynasty would be replaced.

However, Heliopolitan theology has been a longstanding tradition that, for centuries and millennia, was able to embrace and contain within itself all rival cults and theological alternatives. To capture the religious life of all of Egypt, the Shabaka document had to make a real effort to absorb first within itself everything that was ever thinkable about Atum.

The primary weakness in the Heliopolitan theogony was that it ascribed the name of Nun to chaos—that it ascribed any name at all to that "nothing." If Nun was really of no consequence whatsoever it should have remained nameless. Names are nesting places for fresh ontological configurations. This is so because it is linguistically

Copyrighted Material

impossible to talk about no-thing, or about Nun, without somehow suggesting its presence as a some-thing. Moreover, a something that also happens to be a first is bound to become significant sooner or later.

Heliopolitan theologians named the Nun and then left it undefined as a next-to-nothing kind of chaos. The Hermopolitan theologians took hold of this weakness; they talked about Nun and then proceeded to pair it off with a Naunet. Memphite theologians, in addition, wrapped up all first manifestations of the All-Father into the divine figure whom in their city they knew as Ptah. These reformulations, on the one hand, claimed cultic and political sovereignty for Memphis; they also reduced the Heliopolitan All-God, his Trinity and his entire Ennead, to a much smaller portion of the larger cosmic scheme.

Mythologically and symbolically the Memphite theology first shifted its emphasis from the ejaculation metaphor to the spitting metaphor, by itself no radical shift. Some Heliopolitan priests had done as much when they contemplated and used the "spitting" alternative. Moreover, Heliopolitan priests even refined their metaphor to mean exhaling forth the essence of Shu—thus of breath, air, and life in general. For good measure they even had Atum emit an audible "cry."

Memphite theologians, in principle, subscribed to all of this. They merely added the specific point that the breath of their godhead, Ptah, resounded with voice and with distinct words. In addition, they insisted that these divine words were first vocalized as creative commands.

Gone was the soothing flow and divine emission of living water, which has been experienced so concretely in Egypt by the presence of the everflowing and overflowing Nile—gone with the stroke of a writer's pen. It was replaced with references to divine commands that coincided with the daily orders issued by reigning pharaohs. All the while royal authority was still being derived, in some fashion or other, from orthodox generative process theology. How else could an Egyptian pharaoh have continued to sit on the throne of Egypt as a real begotten Son of God!

The godhead Ptah has created specifically through his *logos* and that, in accordance with Memphite theology, meant the king's royal command. For all practical purposes, and for the pharaoh's subjects,

Copyrighted Material

the *logos* of the godhead and the *logos* of the ruling God-king were kept indistinguishable.

In breakaway Hebrew tradition, later, the first creation story in the book of *Genesis* was based on divine command or *logos* as well. But this divine command was presented in the context of Yawistic rebel theology, it was introduced without reference to legitimizing a human God-king.

This assessment, of the major difference between Hebrew and Egyptian monotheism, distances itself from commentators like Henri Frankfort who sharply distinguished between theological immanence and transcendence. For instance, Frankfort saw "immanence" as a factor that has reduced the worth of ancient Egyptian religion. Thus, even while he recognized Amun-Ra as an otherwise "supreme and universal god, known within the scope of Egyptian polytheism," Frankfort nevertheless remained more impressed by a divinity that throned as a universal monarch above and beyond earthly phenomena. Still, he noticed a tendency toward theological transcendence in what he called Ptah's "spiritual" creation by thought and word.[9]

Comparisons and evaluations of the kind Frankfort offered obviously are based on a double standard. After all, was the breath blown into Adam's nostrils by the Hebrew God any less material than the Egyptian wind of Shu? Were the creative commands of the Hebrew God, in *Genesis* 1, more spiritual than the commands of Ptah? Or, were the words that resounded from the heart and tongue of Ptah more "spiritual" than Atum-Shu's mostly silent breathing? Then, is a sovereign God any less real if his involvements extend into the human as well as material spheres?

It is high time for historians of religions to become reconciled with this earth and its materiality on which, and by which, we all live and move and have our being. Historians cannot afford to sympathize with only so-called spiritual religions that seem in tune with severe Indo-European dualism—or schizophrenia.

In any case, several centuries after the book of *Genesis* had been edited for the last time—after the "seven days" creation story had been included—Christians broke away from their Hebrew religious environment. One of the major Christian scribes, known as John,

---

[9]Henri Frankfort, *Ancient Egyptian Religion* (New York, 1948), pp. 22f.

Copyrighted Material

began his gospel account with a wonderfully poetic *logos* cosmogony. In his prologue he carefully avoided any allusions to *logoi* that could have been claimed or usurped by human kings. On the contrary, he identified the creative Word of God with a contrary kind of Son of God. That Son of God was sent into this world, specifically to enact a parody on the traditional roles of Horus-falcons, and on all the sons of God who have ruled Egypt and other known civilizations. The Christian understanding of the creative Word of God, although retaining the old *logos* label, implied a radical rejection of imperial or grand domesticator theology. It implied a radical switch from grand domestication theology to "kingdom of heaven" soteriology.

More remains to be told about this Christian modification of Egyptian grand domestication religion in a later portion of this book. But before that history can be told more completely it will be necessary to reexamine outbreaks of Hebrew "fire" and mirror reflections of Hellenic "sophia" from amidst the large Egyptian sea of "light." Only, let it be told already now, that over against the background of Egyptian theology it can no longer be said that the Christian religion was "merely," or even "primarily," an offspring of Semitic religion in general or of Judaism in particular.

The Theology of Thebes

The city of the province Uaset, which was named after that province, is on record since the Middle Kingdom. Occasionally it has been referred to as "Southern City" or as "City of Amun." The historical beginnings of the god Amun cannot be traced farther back in Thebes than the Eleventh Dynasty. But we know that his cult was well established during the Twelfth Dynasty (1991–1786 B.C.E.). Was this god in his first Theban manifestation a modification of the god Min? The headdresses of Amun and Min are similar. Or, did awareness of him begin with Amun-Amauet as a theological branch of the Hermopolitan Ogdoad? Or, has Amun been claimed only spuriously by Hermopolitan politician-theologians?

The resistance and liberation movement against the Hyksos occupation of Egypt proceeded under Ahmoses I, from Upper Egypt and Thebes (Eighteenth Dynasty, 1567 B.C.E.). With this important event the god Amun, manifest in history, has ushered in Egypt's

Copyrighted Material

"New Kingdom" era; in that process the god has fully established himself as Egypt's supreme patron, liberator, and imperial deity. Amun's imperial cult was defined historically, one can safely surmise, by minds who began to think internationally and who were inspired by anti-Hyksos or anti-Semitic national pride.[10]

The Amarna Interlude

Amun's hegemony was interrupted briefly during the Fourteenth Century, by a religious "reform" that the pharaoh Akhenaton (Amenhotep IV) attempted. This king hoped to institutionalize a narrowly defined monotheism that had the solar deity, named Aton, for its focal point of fascination. The name of Aton as a sun deity has been known in Egypt since the beginning of the Twelfth Dynasty; it became frequent during the reign of Amenophis III, Akhenaton's immediate predecessor.[11] At the reform king's new capitol, Amarna, this brand of sun worship was institutionalized. Had this royal devotee of Aton succeeded spreading his reform cult, he would surely have purged most of Egypt's ancient "prehuman flux" transformationalism and much of its monotheistic emanationalism.

Akhenaton's worship of "Aton" featured "Ra" theology in a very restrictive mode. Cyril Aldred, finding fault with Petrie's interpretations of the typical Amarna depictions, has called our attention to the fact that the rays of the Aton "do not give life to each person, but bring its breath only to the nostrils of the king and queen."[12] Amarna hymnody make that same point. Anyone who carefully ponders the king's beautiful hymns, composed specifically for the royal worship of Aton, certainly will discover more than poetic beauty. Had these stanzas been written by someone of low status, their theological shallowness would have remained of little concern. But authored by, or at least ascribed to, an Egyptian king who

---

[10]The Egyptian liberation from Semitic occupation, under Ahmoses I, not only gave rise to anti-Semitic feelings in Egypt. Within a few centuries it echoed in the form of Hebrew anti-Egyptianism, under the leadership of Moses.

[11]Aldred, *Akhenaten, King of Egypt*, p. 239.

[12]Ibid., p. 111.

Copyrighted Material

claimed Son of God status for himself, the narrow scope and selfishness reflected in these psalms indeed does evoke suspicion. That narrowness surely must have raised concerns among all Amun theologians in Egypt at the time.

In none of Akhenaton's hymns is God ever approached as one who would stoop low enough to bless someone other than his chosen and beloved son, the pharaoh Akhenaton himself, together with Nefertete his beautiful spouse. In fact, the entire wonderful world of Aton's creatures is said to have been created for the express pleasure of this jaded king. No allowances were made in Aton liturgy for any problem in the land that the pharaoh himself might be unable to perceive. And there is also no evidence that, preoccupied with the religious legitimation of his royal-divine authority, the king still was capable of recognizing anyone else's needs. The closing stanza of his Great Hymn to Aton is sufficient to expose the narrow vision of this royal would-be reformer:

You are in my heart,
There is no other who knows you,
Only your son, Neferkheprure, Sole-one-of-Ra,
Whom you have taught your ways and your might.
[Those on] earth come from your hand as you made them,
When you have dawned they live,
When you set they die;
You yourself are lifetime, one lives by you.
All eyes are on [your] beauty until you set,
All labor ceases when you rest in the west;
When you rise you stir [everyone] for the King,
Every leg is on the move since you founded the earth.
You rouse them for your son who came from your body,
The King who lives by Maat, the Lord of crowns,
Akhenaten, great in his lifetime;
(And) the great Queen whom he loves, the Lady of the Two Lands.
Nefer-nefru-Aten Nefertiti, living forever.[13]

---

[13]Miriam Lichtheim, *Ancient Egyptian Literature*, Vol. 2 (Berkeley, Calif., 1976), p. 99. *Copyrighted Material*

Akhenaton's "monotheism," if such selfish usurpation of God's created world by a single human ego deserves this appellation, reveals, if nothing else, the loneliness of a hereditary and beleaguered grand domesticator. It exposes the ruler's monotheistic solar theology as a feeble attempt at trying to become an absolute divine Sun-king again. To accomplish his goal he had to rid himself of the religious "checks and balances" that, in the course of Egyptian history, had come to humanize government and safeguard at least some of the interests of common people. Akhenaton wanted to shake off the largest "check and balance" that weighed on him; namely, the Theban cult of Amun. That cult was represented by Amun temples throughout Egypt and beyond, and it had the support of many people. No doubt, Akhenaton would rather have ruled Egypt under a God who created the entire world especially for him.

The Return of Amun

The religion and priesthood of Amun outlived Akhenaton's attempt at royal reintrenchment. And Egypt was probably better off because of it.[14] This is not to say that Amun's Theban-based priesthood was the first of its kind in Egyptian history that stood apart from, or over against, the Egyptian god-king. Already very early, at Heliopolis, Egypt had an imperial cult center that stood in something like a "check and balance" relationship to the royal seat at Memphis. The dichotomy of Thebes and Amarna was only a more recent example of old tensions and conflicting checks and balance arrangements.

The general emphasis ancient Egyptian cult centers placed on funerary proceedings underscores this same dynamic of checks and balances. After all, funerary rites are excellent means to celebrate the balancing of a royal strongman who willfully had pushed too far ahead during his lifetime.

It shall not be suggested here, in any shape or form, that good priests always kept bad kings in check. Check-and-balance institutions all generate their own share of overambitious people. Nevertheless,

---

[14]Donald B. Redford, who in *Akhenaten, the Heretic King* (1984) judged the king's fascination for the sun disk Aton as constituting "atheism," read Horemheb's subsequent "Edict of Reform," too, as an indictment of Akhenaton. It lists what went wrong in Egypt during the reign of Akhenaton (p. 225).
Copyrighted Material

the very fact that a zealous and jaded ruler here was eventually checked by a cult that more broadly appears to have represented the interests of common people—as some of the Amun theology given later will show—in itself is historically significant.

Kings gained leverage and power whenever a neighboring political entity flexed its muscles. Heroic citizen defenders, of necessity, were thereby lured by self-interest into reinforcing their lord's grand domestication scheme for the sake of defence and protection. And then, once a strong leader had dared to raise his head above the limiting norms of religious traditions, he, too, had no other choice but to pursue greater organizational goals. He was obliged to do so for his own personal safety as well as for the fulfillment of his larger grand domestication hopes.

Before Aton and after Aton, in ancient Egypt, there flourished the cult of Amun. During Akhenaton's reform years that cult went underground. However, as seen from the Theban theological perspective, the military and iconoclastic measures of Akhenaton never could inflict real damage on the cult of Amun. The reform king could order that inscriptions of the name Amun be erased from temples and public buildings. But he could not touch the real name of the God who, as all faithful believers knew, kept himself hidden—and who continued to hide his real name behind this cover name *Amun*.

The Leiden Papyrus

Amun theology, after Akhenaton, is beautifully expressed in a document stored at the museum in Leiden.[15] A quick reading will reveal at least one of the heights to which the pseudonym *Amun* has been exalted in Egyptian consciousness, during the New Kingdom era. Not only were priests of Amun active throughout the Egyptian empire, it also appears that their cult of the hidden God responded to some extent to the existential needs of Egypt's people, at least more

---

[15]Subsequent discussion of Amun theology is based primarily on this source. Quotations in English were translated from Adolf Erman, "Der Leidener Amonshymnus," in *Sitzungsberichte der Preussischen Akademie der Wissenschaften* 11 (1923): 66f, 70f, 73. Erman has assigned this document to the restoration period of Amunism, after Akhenaton (p. 81).

Copyrighted Material

than the Aton cult. In contrast to the royal snobbishness inspired by Aton, the general concern of Amun for all status levels of humanity is noteworthy.

Like all imperial gods in Egypt's past, Amun accounted for and embraced all there is. He was the power of growth in vegetation. The God of gods stooped to lower social levels also to save non-aristocratic folk. He stood by them in their hour of need, even while they were dying. Also, this God of gods assisted them while they were still alive. Earlier in Egyptian religious history such lowly functions had been left to lesser and local gods. Now these benign concerns for mortal humanity had become part and parcel of the general grace and demeanor of the Egyptian God of gods.

Amun became known as one who "drives away evil and illness" . "He is Amun who saves whom he will, and be it from the netherworld" ... "He lends his eyes and ears to [protect] the path of anyone he loves" ... "He hears the prayers of those who call on him; he comes momentarily from afar to him who calls out for him" ... "He lengthens and shortens life, and he adds something extra to the destiny of him whom he loves" ... "Amun's name, when called upon, is mighty on the waters; the crocodile has no power when his name is spoken; the wind changes, and the storm subsides when one thinks about him" ... "He is better than millions for him who keeps him in his heart, and with his name a single one is mightier than hundreds of thousands; the truly good protector ... is the irresistible [one in battle]" (pp. 66f).

Amun's indebtedness to earlier imperial theologies is evident in many ways. And yet, earlier Egyptian theologians never have come up with a better description of their All-God:

He who has given shape to himself, his form is unknown, that beautifully shimmering (hue of) color which has become a beautiful but secret form—the one who gave shape to himself and who did create himself. . . . The eight gods were your first manifestations.[16] Before them you alone hast been. Your body was made secret to the ancients, you, who hast hidden yourself as Amun, as the first among the gods. You assumed the form of Tenen (primal

---

[16]The eight gods of Hermopolis, perhaps? They could as well have been the eight subsequent manifestations of the godhead Atum, in Heliopolitan theology.

Copyrighted Material

Hill) to give shape to the first gods of the primeval era.... The Ennead together, (the nine) were in your members, and in your form were all the gods united. Your first form by which you have begun was Amun—namely, he who hides his name from the gods.... When Ra arose in the sky, to rejuvenate himself again, he (Amun) spat forth...to create Shu and Tefnut to be joined. (pp. 70f)

The godhead's hiddenness, together with the obscurity of his name and his general compassionate involvement in human affairs, at every stratum in human history, is highlighted by a number of characteristics that scholars customarily reserved for the Yahweh of the Hebrews. The Israelite "schema" concerning their God's oneness has here been spoken, earlier, by Egyptian worshippers of Amun:

Amun is one! (He) who hides himself from the gods...whose nature is unknown....His nature is not recorded (or displayed) in sacred scriptures; he cannot be described and taught. He is too mysterious for his power to be laid bare; he is too great to be even asked about, too immense to be perceived. One would fall dead suddenly, in fear, if one were to pronounce the god's mysterious name, unknown to everyone. Not even a god can call him by his name, the vital one, because his name is secret. (p. 73)

The most amazing sentence in this passage, in light of historical hindsight, is the one which claims that God's nature has not been adequately recorded or displayed in sacred scriptures. Here the Egyptian theologian-scribe has attained a degree of objectivity and ego-suspension seldom matched again afterward among scribes in reactionary Hebrew, Jewish, Christian, and Islamic traditions. With a larger scope of artistic sacred manifestations still kept constantly before Egyptian eyes, balancing one another—for example, images of gods, the presence of divine kings, and pictorial inscriptions—a wise Egyptian scribe was less prone to fall into idolatry toward a sanctified piece of writing.

Of course, the composite nature of Egyptian official theology, concerning Amun the God of gods, is not difficult to perceive. But this happenstance by itself does not tell very much. All learning by human minds, in any field of knowledge or endeavor, remains piecemeal. Moreover, the composite appearance pertains only to the

Copyrighted Material

human "process" of theologizing. It has not really affected the primeval All-God who is known to be hiding beyond this process of theologizing—hiding even behind the sum total of theologies devised by earlier generations. All Egyptian imperialists have tried to honor, conceptualize, and manipulate the God of gods by governing in his name. Amun theology appears to have been the first contrivance that introduced the "check and balance" of a no-name.

Then, a holy trinity seemed as easily acceptable to Theban priests as an Ennead has been embraced by priests in Heliopolis. The difference between polytheism and monotheism here becomes rather small and insignificant. Human minds understand, what little they do understand, by way of grappling with the pluralities that seem to constitute this world. For finite analytic predator minds, a plurality of ineffable divine manifestations occasionally does appear unified, but only to the extent that such a unity is allowed to overwhelm its beholders religiously.

> Three are all the gods, Amun, Ra, and Ptah. Aside from these is none. He who hides his name behind (the word) "Amun" is Ra at his head, Ptah at his body. His cities on earth are eternal: Thebes, Heliopolis, and Memphis—forever. (p. 73)

Quoted from a religion pronounced dead millennia ago, this trinitarian proclamation still resounds vibrantly alive, mysteriously awesome, magnificent, and to some extent even politically relevant.

Copyrighted Material

Copyrighted Material

PART TWO:
HEBREW FIRE

Copyrighted Material

Copyrighted Material

Preface to Hebrew Fire

Part Two of this book sketches the rivulet of Hebrew religio-political thought and fervor as it flowed through a stretch of historical time. This portion is written from the point of view of someone who, guided still by many positive affections, continues to labor to better understand his Christian heritage. The Christian religion was "conceived" by the seed of kingdom of heaven enthusiasm that issued from Judaism during the first century C.E. It was engendered when that enthusiasm for a new world order was shown forth first by John the Baptizer and then by Jesus of Nazareth. It was anchored in the flow of world history by the messianic role of the latter's style of living and dying.

The notion of God's heavenly kingdom derives from a longstanding Hebrew skepticism toward grand domestication. In Hebrew tradition that skepticism can be traced back, by way of prophetic judgments on ancient imperialistic ambitions. That same antimonarchic sentiment, together with the very instability of attempted Hebrew monarchies, may be traced back to premonarchic priests like Samuel and thence to the Exodus epic told by Levitic priests. The kingdom of heaven idea proclaimed by Jesus, of a kingdom that is not of this world, may be understood as a logical outcome from a long stream of events beginning with the reaction of enslaved Hebrews against Egyptian imperialism.

The ontology that underlies Greek philosophy is another such Egypt-inspired rivulet; it poured from Egypt half a millennium after the formative Hebrew reaction. It will be discussed separately in Part Three.

Of all the parts that compose this book, Part Two proved to be the most difficult to write. Most historians within the larger Judeo-Christian tradition generally write about this subject matter defensively, in smaller-than-life installments. If and when historical overviews are attempted at all, many scholars are prepared to match the expectations of audiences within the larger Judeo-Christian stream.

Copyrighted Material

Historical data in this field therefore often are presented and interpreted at the level of the lowest common denominator. All the while, general historians of religions, who subscribe to the task of seeing all religions in the world together, rarely dare step into the mine field of Judeo-Christian specialties.

Even the attempt of writing for a more limited audience of historians of religions can be perilous. Most historians of religions themselves are refugees from the Judeo-Christian stream and they still work alongside its banks. Some among them have escaped their parental traditions and moved away a little farther than others. Their historical evaluations of biblical texts tend to be either defensive or aggressive, depending on their personal distances. Of course, such defensiveness is never admitted publicly—and perhaps it should not have been mentioned here.

* * *

This historical sketch on Hebrew fire represents a personal inventory throughout. During the years of my youth I was taught to read and believe Bible stories literally and, wherever that was impossible, devotionally. In Sunday school I learned about the universal divine law mostly from *Exodus* 20—during the years of World War II. The ethics pertaining to war and genocide I tried to understand, devoutly, from *Joshua* 7, *Deuteronomy* 7 and 20, and *1 Samuel* 15. Neither I nor my elders understood the absurdity we beheld in our hands, as we were unaware of the holocaust which elsewhere in our homeland actually applied these Bible lessons. I heard about the Holocaust at age eleven, after the war. I noticed the fact of anti-Semitism after I had come to America when, also, I experienced some anti-German backlash. I became aware of the puzzle of Semitic anti-Semitism several years after that.

I served in America's armed forces, and in church I sang along, patriotically, the Battle Hymn of the Republic. I saw glimpses of "the glory of the coming of the Lord" while, at the same time, quietly and increasingly, I began to worry about some of the supposed divine adjurations given in the Bible.

With such sacred scriptures in our hands, how can Jews and Christians ever hope to get along. Our monotheistic faiths supported by idolized holy books, alongside Muslims who brandish their own, we have all become walking contradictions—and ticking time bombs

Copyrighted Material

as well. With specialized divine covenants we have lent our fighting hands to a God whom our ancestors have claimed to understand. Monotheistic and atheistic reactionaries together, fully endowed with their inspired truths, are able to justify on behalf of the world's salvation any amount of destruction. Together these have become our planet's most dangerous creatures.

Such are the questions and worries that led me to the study of the history of religions. These are also the questions that tempted me, at the outset, to omit Part Two and not to write anything pertaining to the Hebrew heritage at all. It is conceivable that my words will generate more strife. But then, for the sake of God's love for humankind, and for human rationality and decency toward one another, our sacred books that we have learned to brandish as weapons need some dulling. The truth shall make us free, perhaps. And doing an honest historical study might contribute a few fresh glimpses to the much-needed larger picture of historical perspective.

Nor is such a study irrelevant in an age when democracy has become a universal beacon of hope. With the confidence that belongs to brothers of Christ the Son of God, with that same confidence secularized ever so gradually, our Western fathers of democratic revolutions have stood up to kings and emperors as their mortal equals. And thus they wrote their Magna Charta, their Declarations of Independence, their Manifestoes. And so they wrote their methodologies for doing history of religions.

Copyrighted Material

Copyrighted Material

6

The Monotheism of Moses

The ancient nation of Israel commemorated its exodus from Egypt as the moment of its birth—and that exodus was inspired by and accomplished with visions of fire. First there was the fire of God's holy presence that Moses saw when he faced a bush aflame in the desert. Then, concerning Israel's exodus from Egypt itself, we are told that

The Lord went before them by day in a pillar of cloud to lead them along the way, and by night in a pillar of fire to give them light. (*Exodus* 13:21)

The backdrop for Yahweh's covenant with Israel, and Israel's reception of divine law as it was mediated through Moses, was similarly draped by divine fire:

And Mount Sinai was wrapped in smoke, because the Lord descended upon it in fire; and the smoke of it went up like the smoke of a kiln, and the whole mountain quaked greatly. (*Exodus* 19:18)

Before they were written on sheepskin, biblical accounts about the man Moses were filtered through several centuries of oral tradition. They were trickled through creative minds of many generations of storytellers. The present shape of these stories may not have been finalized until seven or eight centuries after the supposed event. Like premium wines, so stories often get better with age and, needless to say, the God of Israel made plenty of time available for Torah stories to ferment and improve.

All the while, it is not the purpose of this book either to establish or to refute textual roots. Our goals are broader and far more humble.

Copyrighted Material

Presenting a few examples that might help illuminate Egyptian aggravations or influences on Levitic, Israelite, and Judaic religion will be a sufficient task for Part Two of this book.

Here and there in this study political history will have to be blended with literary history, to the chagrin of purist historians. The condition of our sources does not always permit a clean line of demarcation. But even though large portions of the landscape may remain shrouded in morning fog by this approach, it is hoped that the general nature and direction of the Hebrew ideological rivulet, which flowed from Egypt through Palestine into the Mediterranean realm, will emerge from this historical sketch clearly enough to be worth our while.

Moses an Egyptian Hebrew

Apart from partial Hebrew scriptures we have no evidence that Moses, the leader of Israel's "Exodus," ever lived. A self-serving cult document is not the best possible source for historical proof. It is necessary, therefore, in much of Part Two of this book, to slide sideways from general history and substitute some history of Hebrew literature. The composition of literary works, in a roundabout manner, is still a historical datum that may be considered for understanding the people who wrote and used them.

The Exodus epic, as recorded in the book of *Exodus*, begins with a brief reference to a time when the "people of Israel" were not yet slaves in Egypt. Perhaps another hand has added the story of how a Levite baby boy was exposed in a reed basket, somewhere along the Nile. He was found and adopted by the pharaoh's daughter, who raised the child in her royal surroundings and, presumably, gave him his Egyptian name, Moses.

Inasmuch as a similar exposure of a baby in a reed basket has been ascribed to the first Mesopotamian imperialist, Sargon of Akkad, the literal historical weight of this Moses story will have to be adjusted downward. Was this story recited to establish the credentials of Moses as a great hero of Sargon's stature? But then, why would later Israelite scribes have wanted to gloss over the Egyptianness of this man before accepting him as a their savior hero? In any case, the story tells about the birth and the early months of Moses' life in Egypt. It leaves a large lacuna concerning the remainder of his life in

Copyrighted Material

that great land. This much is clear, the story explicitly tries to link the man's birth to his later life as a leader who was destined to govern a runaway group of Hebrew slaves.

We are told that at a mature age Moses observed one day how a Hebrew man was being beaten by an Egyptian supervisor. Moses sided with the underdog and killed the Egyptian tormentor. In fear of punishment he then fled to Midian, an oasis in the Sinai desert to the east. A priest named Jethro took the Egyptian fugitive into his home and gave him one of his daughters in marriage. In time she bore Moses two sons.

One day, so the narrative continues, while watching the animals of his father-in-law, Moses saw an apparition: an "angel of fire" burning from the middle of a bush. Miraculously, the fire did not consume its branches. Ever since his flight from Egypt the man Moses must have wondered about his obligations toward the Hebrew slaves who still languished and suffered back in Egypt. His thoughts apparently were fuelled by the nagging memory of his personal violent and "criminal" interference. To justify this deed, it seems, he was predestined eventually to act on this matter. He was challenged to upgrade his status from being a fugitive from Egyptian law to that of a minority representative in exile.

But be that as it may, from the burning bush Moses heard the voice of God. And that voice of God announced the divine decision that the Hebrew slaves were to be delivered from the bondage of Egyptian grand domestication. Then and there God commissioned Moses to approach the elders of these subjugated Hebrews in Egypt with his saving proposition:

You and the elders of Israel shall go to the king of Egypt and say to him, "The Lord, the God of the Hebrews, has met with us; and now, we pray you, let us go a three days journey into the wilderness, that we may sacrifice to the Lord our God." (*Exodus* 3:18)

The reason for which God enlisted here the services of a leader who was familiar with proceedings at the Egyptian royal court is rather transparent. The strategy of Moses was to hoodwink the pharaoh with a ruse of citing religious obligations. Moses and the elders of the Hebrew slaves were to request a furlough, on the pretext

Copyrighted Material

of having to perform religious rites to their God who even by Egyptian reckoning dwelt in the Sinai desert. The motif of a pilgrimage pretext is mentioned again, later in the story, after Moses was actually granted permission for a portion of the people to leave. But Moses rejected a partial exodus and insisted that all Hebrew slaves are required by their God to go on this holy pilgrimage together.

In Hebrew opinion the stated objective of performing religious services in the Sinai desert was amply fulfilled later on, as their Exodus story unfolds. The people's service to their God, who dwells outside Egypt, was intended to last for all time. With the hindsight of tradition it had to be that way, or else Moses could be accused of having paraded before the pharaoh while telling a lie.

Apparently Moses held some initial hope for a diplomatic settlement, to the effect that a measure of religious freedom could be negotiated with an Egyptian pharaoh. And truly, if ever on earth there was a man who could negotiate religious privileges for oppressed slaves in Egypt, it would have been someone like Moses who knew the ways of Egyptian government. Such a spokesman for minority rights would have had to be familiar with Egyptian theology, as well as with political theory, and know that both of these were the same thing. He would have had to be acquainted with the ways of Egyptian as well as of Hebrew religion. And he would have had to be someone who knew how to exploit the differences between these two.

Yahweh as Amun

After we are told by the primary narrator how the Hebrew God has introduced himself as "Yahweh" (*Exodus* 3:7-8), another hand informs those who might still be unfamiliar with the God's manner of referring to himself by means of the word symbol *YHWH* (*Exodus* 3:9-15). We are told that the designation *Yahweh* was ascribed to the God of the Hebrews precisely at the crucial point in Levitic history, in preparation for the Exodus. The question that a thoughtful Israelite might have wished to ask concerning this word symbol is conveniently put in the mouth of Moses, who asks God directly:

> If I come to the people of Israel and say to them, "the God of your fathers has sent me to you," and they ask me, "What is his name?" what shall I say to them?

Copyrighted Material

God said to Moses, "I Am Who I Am." And he said, "Say to the people of Israel, 'I AM has sent me to you.'" (*Exodus* 3:13–14)

Devout readers in later Judaism have avoided reading the letter configuration *YHWH* because to them it signified the unspeakable name of God. It seems as though, somehow, the followers of Moses remembered part of the original lesson of Egyptian theology: that the name of God is not to be pronounced, on penalty of death. According to what else their leader Moses must have known about such holy matters, however, his people need not have worried excessively about this particular theological technicality.

Really! In Chapter Five of this book we have already shown how, in the context of Egyptian Amun theology—which the Egyptian aristocrat Moses must have studied thoroughly—it was impossible to pronounce the real name of the supreme God. Not even the lesser gods, those manifestations of angelic rank who surrounded the hidden essence of Amun, knew their God's real name.

The chances of ordinary humankind ever getting to know and to be able to pronounce the real name of the Hebrew God were equally remote. The word symbol *YHWH*, or *I AM WHO I AM*, is not really a name. If anything, it added up to God gently telling off Moses —letting him know that the Holy Name is not for him to know.

The Exodus story tells about Moses as a leader of Hebrews who was born of Hebrew parents; yet, he lived the early decades of his life as an Egyptian aristocrat in royal surroundings. If the second half of the preceding summary sentence is accepted as a possibility, and I see no reason why it cannot be, it follows that this man Moses also must have been well versed in traditional Egyptian political theory. Throughout Egyptian history the disciplines of political theory and theology belonged together. Moses, the aristocrat, therefore must have known contemporary Amun theology well.

Startled by a spectacular fire and an anonymous divine call, Moses demanded assurance that he would be able to finish the job that, long ago, he had begun with an act of violence. Even though he asked his question on behalf of the Hebrew slave elders who lived in Egypt, he obviously needed additional divine assurance for himself. He needed this assurance to shore up his own confidence.

Our Egyptian-educated potential leader, who still had to be convinced of the feasibility of his assigned (and chosen) task, found himself caught up in an interesting dilemma. Could he who obviously
Copyrighted Material

knew Amun theology very well convince himself to actually obey the
call of a God of Hebrew wanderers? And, if he could obey, could his
faith actually have withstood the challenges and disappointments of
the daring Exodus stratagem he envisioned?

Furthermore, could he have accomplished all these things,
trustingly, if this Hebrew God who commissioned him actually had
told him his name? In Egypt it was the hiddenness of the All-God's
nature, and of his holy name, that rendered Amun the greatest
imaginable power in the cosmos. Could Moses have faced Amun and
the Egyptian pharaoh on behalf of any other God who was defined
less great than Amun? Or, in the Egyptian fashion of doing theology—on behalf of any God who with his magnitude could not
account for all that was known about Amun? Probably not.[1]

But then, *I am* is not a name, as *Amun* in Egypt was not a name
either. To perceive some theological unity between two unnameable
or undefinable configurations of reality is not overly difficult. Both
have their very hiddenness and mystery in common. The Egyptian
root of *Amun* is *imn,* which denotes hiddenness and invisibility.
During the New Kingdom the god Amun also was referred to as "He
who abides in all things" (*Der in allen Dingen bleibt*).[2] How great
is the distance from this theology to that which concerns itself with
an I AM, or with an I AM WHAT I AM, or with an I WILL BE
WHAT I WILL BE, or with a HE CAUSES TO BE?

Hans Bonnet rejects the idea that a close parallelism may exist in
the case of these two theologies. For instance, concerning the
Egyptologist Sethe he remarked that the latter "dares to suspect that
Yahweh was shaped after the model of Amun" (Bonnet pp. 31f).
Obviously, Bonnet's judgment is based on a very spiritualized
interpretation of Yahweh that appears informed more by Hellenic
philosophical dualism than the Moses religion itself. Is pure spiritual
transcendence really the most important aspect of Mosaic mono-

---

[1] This line of reasoning, of Yahweh theology confronting the Egyptian background
of Amun theology, is relevant even in the extreme case of denying the historicity of
Moses and his exodus from Egypt. If the Exodus tradition took shape in Palestine in
confrontation with Philistine-Canaanite traditions along the Egyptian cultural frontier,
then the pressures of the Egyptian imperialistic theology were present just the same.

[2] Sethe, par. 217–230, in Hans Bonnet, *Reallexikon der Ägyptischen Religionsgeschichte* (Berlin, 1952), pp. 31–34.

Copyrighted Material

theism? Is a God who disguises his presence in a burning bush, in a cloud, or in a pillar of fire really "transcendent" in the Hellenic sense of transcendental Platonic "ideas"? This writer has concluded otherwise.

Although an influence of Indo-European dualism on Yahweh theology during the period of the Judges and the early monarchy is being ruled out here, one nevertheless must assume a strong basis of Semitic-Canaanite religiosity for all those Hebrews who dwelled in Palestine. As we shall have occasion to delineate shortly, most of the Israelite tribes may never have been in Egypt—though, in that case all of them have become involved with the Egyptian-Philistine frontier. The actual exposure of the Levites to Egyptian culture and religion, of course, would have depended on the length of their sojourn there. It seems in any case useful to consider in some detail the impact that Egyptian Amun theology, via Moses and the Levites, could have had on the larger Israelite confederation. After all, an Exodus event and a Torah tradition attributed to Moses, in the course of a few centuries, became the central features of Israelite unity. The Egyptian-Hebrew connection is explored here to call attention to a neglected dimension of inquiry.

* * *

And yes, there also were significant differences between Yahweh theology and Amun theology from the outset. After all, the respective cults of these supreme deities engaged in mythological wrangling over the outcome of the Exodus episode. Each sponsored a different unit of people. Amun theology emphasized more the freshness of divine breath and living water, in continuity with Shu's Heliopolitan function and with the fertile blessings of the Nile. This was a function that Yahweh may have assumed only later in Israelite history. It was in the Elijah cycle of stories, *1 Kings* 18, that the Hebrew Yahweh of the desert finally established himself as the bonafide giver of rain for agriculture.

Yahweh theology, at least the Levitic strain that traced its origins to the Sinai area, emphasized much more the fire of God's sternness and wrath. By comparison, this degree of severity was accounted for in Egypt by the lowest Enneadean hypostasis of Seth. In realistic perception of greater-than-human configurations of reality, what else could one have expected? A people who dwell all their lives in the
Copyrighted Material

lush and fertile Nile valley, naturally, will experience more of the
All-God's Shu aspect. And a people who roam in the desert and daily
struggle to survive its fierce heat—such as was the life-style of the
Midianites who harbored Moses—naturally will experience more of
the fiery Seth aspect. Moses surely was aware of this difference, he
is said to have lived at both places long enough to learn about such
things.

A new and far more significant difference between Yahweh and
Amun theology emerges only subsequently, in the story pertaining to
the Exodus struggle itself, especially on the Israelite side. *YHWH*
became the scribal designation of the God of gods at a time when that
deity made a special effort to liberate a chosen group of Hebrew
slaves from bondage in Egypt. For the history and evolution of
religion, this means that a new kind of "God of gods" awareness
thereby was introduced into the world to stay. This new God of gods
theology stood in direct conflict with the very imperial grand
domesticators who originally had defined and traditionally had been
ruling in the name of the God of gods.

The God who revealed himself to Moses, by his very act of revelation, showed himself to be greater than his imperialistic apparitions
that preceded him. He no longer endorsed a human divinized King of
kings in return for his keep or for the maintenance of his state cult.
He was a God who forbade sacred images that, back in Egypt, were
prominently used in the state cult. He forbade these images, apparently, because in the hands of priestly grand domesticators such were
used as levers for political control. In contrast to the Egyptian and
Canaanite deities who blessed artists and sculptor-priests, apparently,
the God of Moses entrusted the management of his cult to a class of
scribes. So it appears, judged by the written legacy these scribes
produced.

The God of Moses was Lord of the entire world and, at the same
time, also savior of a people who previously had fallen victim to
ambitious grand domesticators. During the millennia that followed,
this God, together with the reactionary universal salvation movements
his cult inspired, toppled many a grand domesticator and pretender to
divine authority. He disallowed and reformed many an overdomestication system or "civilization."

Copyrighted Material

Yahweh as Amun-Seth

Before leaving the monotheism of Moses to itself, to watch how its gospel of slave liberation has infected Palestine and lands beyond, it still may be helpful to say a few things about the Egyptian "Seth" element as it pertains to the Yahweh-Amun theology of Moses.

In its Heliopolitan orthodox setting the divine Ennead, which includes Seth, represents a series of hypostases that emanate from a single source, Atum. During the New Kingdom the Amun theology that Moses had learned was still the full heir of the orthodox manner of thinking about theogony, as a process of generation and emanation. Therefore, the theological mind of Moses can be expected to have been aware not only of the essential attributes of the hidden godhead of the New Kingdom, Amun, but also of the God's desert heat emanation—the portion of Seth. As a desert god, Seth was known among Egyptians also as the god of foreigners, of thunder, lightning, and earthquakes. Seth in his cosmic dimension, on a monthly cycle, also was deemed responsible for injuring the poor eye of Horus, the moon.

It has been told that Moses spoke to the pharaoh in the name of the God of the Hebrews (*Exodus* 5:3). To an Egyptian pharaoh that meant in the name of Seth. Of course, the Hebrew narrator happily proceeded to exaggerate the status of Moses another step, at the expense of a supposedly superstitious pharaoh. But then, this is understandable. The story was told to amuse Hebrews, not Egyptians:

... the Lord said to Moses, "See, I make you as God to the Pharaoh; and Aaron your brother shall be your prophet." (*Exodus* 7:1)

It is uncertain how much historical weight may be given to the ten plagues that, with the exception of the last, can be explained in terms of ordinary natural or environmental imbalances. All nine, it must be acknowledged, also proved ineffective for softening the pharaoh's "hardened heart."

The initial ruse of having to make a three-day journey into the Sinai desert, to fulfill religious obligations under the threat of divine punishment, may have been only a cover for a more subtle ruse.

Copyrighted Material

What halfway intelligent pharaoh would not have been able to see through the first one? And yes, the story tells how the pharaoh hardened his heart, as could reasonably be expected of him.

Perhaps the real goal, from the outset, was to nag and intimidate the pharaoh, and wear him down to a point where he no longer would pay attention. Repeated rumors, to the effect that these people were about to leave, could so have been neutralized by the persistent formal diplomatic requests of Moses. Repeated unsubstantiated rumors could have created an impression to the effect that Moses and these slaves would never try to leave without the pharaoh's official consent. Such a subtle strategy could have given the escapees much needed lead time before the ruler would seriously have taken note. Of course, these are mere speculations based on the style of subterfuge by which political problems are being resolved in Near Eastern lands still today.

But then, the tenth and special plague attracts our attention as the pivotal point in the Exodus story plot. All of Egypt's firstborn sons are said to have been slain by an executioner angel of Yahweh. It is high time to rethink this Hebrew story plot from the hypothetical point of view of a twofold Hebrew-Egyptian mind, such as had been the mind of Moses. The God who killed the firstborn sons of the Egyptians would have been Seth to them, the very god of desert dwellers. Furthermore, on the Egyptian side, the color of appearance of Seth, and of all his evil deeds, was red.[3] On the Hebrew side, Mosaic tradition has accented the role of their God with all kinds of red "fire" kratophanies.

Egyptians always have experienced unease in the presence of Seth. Their perception of this lowest Enneadean hypostasis, in Egyptian tradition, clearly has constituted the weakest point in the politico-religious structure within which an Egyptian pharaoh was obliged to operate. Even if critical historiography refuses to accept the tenth Exodus plague as a historical event and even if the rite of Passover is to be understood only as an historicized ancient communal herder sacrifice, both of these motifs together nevertheless may contain a historical kernel of fact. They hint at an actual diplomatic leverage that Moses reasonably could have applied to the Egyptian royal court.

---

[3]See Adolf Erman, *Die Religion der Ägypter*, pp. 37–39.
Copyrighted Material

Traditionally, whenever in Egypt a pharaoh died the god Seth was known to have killed him, reduced him or transformed him into the condition of an Osiris corpse. From the Hebrew perspective, of course, Yahweh upstaged the Egyptian perception of Seth. Instead of waiting to kill an old Egyptian pharaoh, he killed his firstborn son. This means he killed the very person who, on his ceremonial rebirth as Horus during the next enthronement rite, was meant to become the ruling pharaoh.

Egyptian mythology knows the ruling pharaoh as Horus and the avenger of Osiris. The young king supposedly was the one who was to have mutilated Seth during a battle that then ensued.[4] According to Egyptian tradition, however, that victory of Horus over Seth was never a decisive one. Seth was mutilated, and while they struggled the avenger Horus lost his eye. Both divinities had to be healed by Thoth. This meant that after their struggle Seth was again in a position to strike another blow against the next Horus-king of Egypt, whenever he chose to do so. And everyone knew that ruling pharaohs when they suffered death were dispatched by Seth, to be thereby transformed into Osiris. In this manner the god Seth repeatedly defeated a ruling Egyptian Horus. He transformed him back into the mode of his brother Osiris.

To the extent that Moses spoke authoritatively to the pharaoh, in the name of a God who behaved as Amun and Seth combined—or as the Hebrew narrator would have it, to the extent that Moses himself impersonated that kind of a God—he indeed did have a plausible case as to why the Hebrew people should be let go. People who belonged to this dangerous God of the desert, in Egypt, could not be held captive indefinitely with impunity. Moreover, it also was reasonable to think that the people of Seth should want to appease this dangerous God in the desert places where, according to Egyptian perception, he actually lived.

It is quite possible therefore that a diplomatically astute Moses indeed assured the pharaoh that an appeased Yahweh-Amun-Seth would refrain from plaguing Egypt. The presence of a narrative with ten plagues, which now dominates the larger Exodus epic, suggests that at one point some threats of plagues indeed could have been made.

---

[4]See ibid., p. 74.   Copyrighted Material

The clinching plot of the Exodus, which also sequently could have given credence to a series of diplomatic plague threats against Egypt, was Yahweh-Seth's killing of the Egyptian Horus-to-be; that is, the ruling pharaoh's firstborn son. For good measure it is said as well that the Hebrew God has killed all the firstborn sons in all Egyptian houses not marked with Sethian red blood.

The initial diplomatic bait that Moses might have offered to the pharaoh is now coming into better focus. In exchange for letting the Hebrew slaves serve their God in his distant desert, the land of Egypt would be spared the typical calamities that a foreigner's god, like Seth, would be able to inflict. Positively stated, Moses had offered Egypt a conditional blessing.

But that initial diplomatic positivism was overshadowed, in the narrative, when subsequent Hebrew storytellers got carried away celebrating their escape. For good measure they celebrated all the punishments their mighty God could possibly have brought down upon those hated Egyptians.

The death of the pharaoh's firstborn son may be pondered in terms of historical realism still a little further. If Moses actually had approached the Egyptian pharaoh so as to appear to him as a spokesman of a God like Amun-Seth, and if we consider how at some point during these negotiations Moses must have become desperate, then a conditional curse laid by him on the Egyptian crown prince could have been a logical next step. The story has it that the king's firstborn son actually died and that, in a state of grief, the disparaged pharaoh finally ordered the Israelites to get out.

Was this story merely the product of Hebrew wishful thinking? Was it all generated by priestly Levites to anchor an ancient herder ritual in the bedrock of Palestine historical relevance, to commemorate liberation? Possibly, yes. But then, if such thinking was possible by Hebrew minds at all—and the existence of the story testifies to the fact that it was—then it also is conceivable that a desperate Moses could have unloaded on the pharaoh's son some conditional "curse" or "cause" of death. With his Sethian mission, an impatient Moses easily could have cursed the entire sacred Egyptian tradition of royal succession. A strong Amun-Sethian curse laid on the crown prince, possibly even pronounced within hearing range of the lad, conceivably could have contributed to bringing a sensitive young royal heir to his deathbed.

Copyrighted Material

The Hebrew storyteller seems to have remembered that Moses acted like a God! Inasmuch as the curse was conditional, only the pharaoh himself could have removed it by liberating his Hebrew slaves. Thus, in consideration of Egyptian religious beliefs current at the time and in light of experiences that had accrued for Moses, the basic steps of the Exodus appear to have been undertaken in accordance with a well-reasoned strategy.

In all likelihood Yahweh's commissioning of Moses, at the site of the burning bush, was no more than the turning point from theory to practice. While he lived at Midian, Moses had many years to ponder Egyptian weaknesses and Hebrew points of leverage. He probably still knew personally some key Egyptians at the court, and he knew their religio-psychological strengths and weaknesses. He would have been able to exploit these.

Still another question may be asked concerning the Hebrew Exodus, about what exactly might have happened on the Egyptian side. Was a divine curse really sufficient to scare and to kill the crown prince? Was it enough to create confusion, by which Moses and his people could escape? Or, were other death-dealing measures resorted to in the process, perhaps with some inside help at the court? Could Moses have lent a helping hand in the Passover plot by sending a human angel of death into the pharaoh's house? But then again, bodily inflictions may not have been necessary. Curses were taken seriously enough in those days. Could the original Exodus plot indeed have been that simple?

Maybe—and maybe not. The exact historical sequence of events eludes those of us who live over three millennia later. Nevertheless, the religio-political affinity that exists between the Egyptian-educated aristocrat Moses and the man who in Hebrew literature we have come to know as the lawgiver of Yahweh still can be surmised in broad outlines. With help from the history of religions it may be possible to excavate some fresh hypotheses, perhaps with improved historical clarity, beyond what hitherto has been imagined.

Copyrighted Material

Copyrighted Material

7

God and His Created World

Even though the Exodus religion historically and foremostly represents a reaction against Egyptian civilization and its program of overdomestication, its theological tenets nevertheless come into better view when they are seen as having emerged from that same civilization. The form and content of all "antitheses" in this world are determined by "theses" to which they respond. Rarely do religious reforms change everything as thoroughly as, in each instance, the inheritors of those reforms would have liked to believe. For learning more about ancient Israel's theological tenets we must turn to its cosmogony.

According to both Hebrew creation stories in *Genesis*, taken together, God created the world by divine word or command, and then gave life to Adam from his own breath. No essential element in either of these story plots could be classified exclusively as Hebrew or Semitic. The ancient Egyptians had expanded their divine seminal emission metaphor many centuries earlier, perhaps in a first round while educating inexperienced children or semiexperienced juveniles. Already the oldest stratum of Egyptian texts had explained the generative emanational process as Atum's "spitting." It referred to the godhead as blowing forth his breath, or his Shu. Considerably later, but still some centuries before a Hebrew pen gave us *Genesis* 1, Memphite theologians interpreted that same creative emission, or spitting, in terms of spitting forth words or giving creative commands—thus in terms of *logos* theology.[1]

---

[1] The Shabaka Stone of about 800 B.C.E. alleges to be a copy of an earlier text. But, even if its date of copying is postulated, it still precedes the Hebrew source, which generally is dated at 550 B.C.E. or later.

Copyrighted Material

A word of caution, already given in Chapter 5 of this book, must be repeated here. From the late point in time from which we now must view these matters, this *logos* modification may seem like an immense improvement. But examined in a larger historical perspective, it seems as though this improvement or refinement could as well have been very superficial. Already in Memphite theology that same "refinement" added up to a badly balanced theological statement and, therefore, to a mixed blessing. Had the Memphite theology been adopted unilaterally, it would have given to Egyptian kings undue power without sufficient checks and balances. Kings were the ones who issued most of the so-called divine and creative commands that inferior Egyptians had to obey.

For the sake of human rights it therefore was necessary in Egypt to also retain, alongside, the older and more universalistic Heliopolitan Atum mythology, including the phallus and the hand metaphors. Every male and female, high and low, was able to participate to some degree in that dimension of divine creative emanation. A measure of elementary divine status, basic equal rights for all people, could thus be derived much more easily from the older stratum of Heliopolitan Atum mythology. This also means that basic human rights could be hoped for more easily on the basis of the old Heliopolitan theogony than on the advanced *logos* theory of Memphis.

On the other hand, Hebrew scribes, after their liberation from exile in Babylonia, recorded their account of creation in surprising harmony with the Egyptian Memphite mythos of "creation by logos" (approximately 500 B.C.E.). They included a full sequence of divine creative commands, but they did so without having to worry about political checks and balances. The Judaic scribe could afford to do so, because at that time he and his people no longer had a divinized king to establish or a mortal Son of God to keep in check. On that account he and his readers could afford to celebrate the notion of creation of the world by genuine divine command.

All the while, the second Hebrew creation story, the creation of Adam by clay and divine breath, belongs to a much older literary stratum of Egyptian and Hebrew thought. Creation by divine breath is an old notion that certainly antedates the ancient Egyptian idea of creation by Shu. Inasmuch as breath is an essential life function for all higher forms of life, this notion of divine breath could have originated almost anywhere on the globe.

Copyrighted Material

Most of our school books, today, overemphasize the dependency of ancient Israelite religion on Semitic Mesopotamia. We are told that Abraham and his ancestors roamed there, and that the Mesopotamian and the Hebrew flood stories are structurally similar. But these school books generally were written from a post-Exodus bias, that is, from an anti-Egyptian perspective in the shape of which much of the Torah has been cast.

Before this fresh historical assessment evokes unnecessary concerns, I might hurry to add that in light of slavery in Egypt, which preceded Exodus and Torah, this anti-Egyptian sentiment may well have been justified. It probably was justified as much as, earlier, the Egyptian anti-Semitic resentment against Hyksos invaders was justified. Indeed, all these tribalistic and nationalistic sentiments, at one time or other, may have been proper. But should historians of today still permit themselves to be blindfolded by hatreds three millennia old?

Is the polytheistic theological comedy in the Mesopotamian flood story, in the Gilgamesh Epic, really as significant for elucidating its Hebrew counterpart, as it is generally made out to be? Is it very important to know how capricious gods drowned Mesopotamians when we know that the All-God of Egypt inundated the Egyptians every year as well? Flood stories among flood plain civilizations, and in this world of manifest limestone strata and fossils, are numerous and widely spread. And, religiously speaking, most of them are of very little consequence.

Are not creation stories infinitely more important for understanding Near Eastern domesticator cultures and religions? After all, creation stories are what legitimized the ownership of land, of animals and seeds. They represent "primary" scriptures for orderly sedentary living, and they furnish "title" to all kinds of possessions that, first, have been created by an acknowledged divine Creator and that, second, have been given in trust to humankind.

In sharp contrast with the Egyptian "breath" and *logos* cosmogony, the Mesopotamian tradition informs us how the creator god Marduk did his creating in grotesque opposition to *logos*. He drew his sword and cut the goddess Tiamat into two halves. Her upper half became Heaven and her lower half became Earth. Marduk's words of creation that accompany this deed add up to a negative curse. Even the wind he sent represented a negative force against Tiamat. Marduk brandished forces of death, rather than the positive life essence of

Copyrighted Material

Shu. Thereafter human beings were created from the blood of a criminal deity, Kingu, to serve the gods.

All this adds up to a Mesopotamian cosmogony of the Hesiodic hunter-herder-warrior variety. This warrior theology will be discussed in greater detail later, in Chapter 11. Creation by weapon, by sword or knife, is a very ancient theme in theological burlesque. It is a theme cultivated far and wide among the maladapted progeny of male scavengers and hunters. Some groups of that progeny remained part-time hunters; some became headhunters and cannibals; whereas others became herders and aristocratic pioneers of civilizations—their evolutionary maladaptation notwithstanding. And never mind Hesiod who puts into the hand of Cronos a sickle to blackmail farmers.[2] His tale was recited, all the same, by bards who entertained the Greek equivalent of veteran warrior clubs.

"Creation by weapon" was the mythological basis for people who scorned the Egyptian "generation by phallus" cosmogony. And, from the point in history where we now stand, it looks as though those horse-war-and-glory poets, of the Hesiodic variety, have told their epic tales of castration intentionally to mock the unheroic and cowardly priests of the Egyptian variety; namely, those priests who were more disposed toward cultivating "farmer" minds. Hesiod's castration story was clearly intended to be a joke on civilized generative creation theology. A sick joke, yes, but quite "good" as far as the quality of a warrior joke can be ascertained by an audience composed of would-be or nostalgic war heroes.

It must be acknowledged of course that some violence does appear at the lowest Enneadean emanation in Helipolitan theology as well. Seth has killed the Osiris-to-be, and the next Horus avenged his father Osiris. That much violence was admitted by Egyptian priests for a number of reasons: (1) to maintain pharaonic dynasties, (2) to assert the divine ruler's power over life and death, and (3) to explain the king's own dying as divine transformation into Osiris and returning homeward in the direction of union with the godhead.

While the theme of "creation by weapon" is being mentioned in relation to Mesopotamian mythology, one ought to point to a similar blemish in the Hebrew canon. In the second creation story in *Genesis* an embarrassing fragment from a weapon-or-knife version of an

---

[2]See the extensive presentation of this mythology later, in Chapter 11.

Copyrighted Material

origin story has survived. Raw materials obtained by God for the creation of Eve, in the form of one of Adam's ribs, implies some sort of surgical cutting from the first man's body.[3] This bit of Mesopotamian knife mythology has in the history of Hebrew theology been more of an embarrassment than a blessing, it seems.[4]

---

[3] The Sumerian words for "living" and "rib" are homonymous; they are both spelled *ti*. Thus the Babylonian goddess Ninhursag was referred to as *Nin-ti*. Accordingly, the Life-giving Goddess was nicknamed *The Rib Lady*. In *Genesis* 2:21–22 Eve is that Rib Lady, and in *Genesis* 3:20 she is Mother of the Living. See Don C. Benjamin, "The Adam and Eve Story," (1990), and the S. N. Kramer translation of "Enki and Ninhursag: A Paradise Myth" in James P. Pritchard, ed., *Ancient Near Eastern Texts* (Princeton, N.J., 1969), pp. 37–41.

[4] See, for instance, the rabbinic tale that intentionally makes light of this story plot by way of explaining why women must wear perfume: Eve's basic substance was a rib, an organic substance that spoils easily whereas clay, the substance of which Adam was made, keeps indefinitely. See Louis Ginzberg, *Legends of the Jews*, pp. 34ff.

Copyrighted Material

Copyrighted Material

8

Against
Grand Domestication

Civilization, as seen in the long-range context of human evolution and from the perspective of the history of religions, represents a state of cultural achievement wherein the art of domestication has been overdone. From the perspective of the history of religions, as opposed to history of cultures and civilizations, a civilization therefore may be regarded as a kind of grand domestication or overdomestication scheme.

Grand domestication is a human effort, put forth by ambitious folk who thereby progress beyond the mere domestication of plants and animals to also control fellow humans, groups of people, and their gods. Militarism, slavery, exploitation, castration, cannibalism and headhunting, and human sacrifice are examples of excesses and crowning activities that have resulted from purportedly glorious or "grand" domestication schemes. On that account, imperialistic grand domesticators who have become oppressive are more adequately referred to in this discussion as *overdomesticators*.

By contrast, movements of universal salvation are popular reactions to systems of grand domestication that have become abusive—they are normal human reactions against overdomestication. These reactionary movements are universalistic in the sense that their adherents pledge allegiance to more generous types of superior reality configurations. In the ancient Near East this meant allegiance to a deity that was kinder and greater than an emperor's "God of gods" who was worshiped to legitimize the emperor's violence.

Seen within an expanded historical horizon, it was no accident that several movements of universal salvation—including Judaism, Christianity, and Islam—were born between the very fangs of the two oldest civilizations in the Near East, between Mesopotamia and

Egypt. Of course, our expanded historical horizon must allow for the fact that by the time these universalisms were born, Egypt had been dwarfed by Rome and Mesopotamia by Persia. Nevertheless, this changing of the guards among grand domestication systems only drives home the point that, long after the aggressive body of a culture or civilization has been slain and left to decay, its feared ghosts and religious countermeasures may linger some centuries longer. As a case in point the Second Isaiah, eight centuries after the Exodus, still evoked the scarecrow of Egypt to persuade his people to leave Babylon. By the same token, the Hebrew Davidic messiah ideal, and its hope, lingered on a millennium beyond David, and into modern days.

Universalistic reform leaders naturally learned most of their theological methods and logical structures from the grand domestication systems against which they reacted. On that account they reacted against imperial monotheism, invariably, by way of transcending the establishment theology with belief in a God who could embrace more of reality than imperial orthodoxies habitually accounted for. As a rule, a grand domestication system under a God of gods could be challenged only with another kind of God of gods.

Concerning the culture and religion of ancient Israel it may be said that into its cradle were given the hopes and the frustrations of both ancient Near Eastern civilizations. From Mesopotamia the Israelites inherited a passion for the herders' individuality and freedom, whereas from Egypt came its dream of imperial stability and a better-than-human divine kingship. But as it was, in real life all Near Eastern city states were administered by ordinary mortal grand domesticators; and these, in turn, depended for their safety and survival not only on the grace of their own God, but also on the weaknesses of other people's gods. Although greater individual and political freedom was implied by Mesopotamian polytheism—where relationships with various competing gods could be cultivated and balanced to advantage—none of these gods on that account could be respected with unrelenting seriousness.

From among the Hebrew patriarchs Abraham had been in closest contact with Mesopotamia, and from thence his independent herder mind was enabled to listen to God afresh in matters concerning human sacrifice. Tradition has it that he used to roam as a successful domesticator over a wide territory, and that he insisted very much on his nomadic independence. His later domain has been the vicinity of

Copyrighted Material

Hebron. By contrast, Isaac stood in closer contact with the Egyptian frontier in the region presently known as Gaza.

The domain of the patriarch Jacob at the dawn of Israelite history was centered on Bethel; although, much of his life's story has been linked more with Egypt itself. Tradition has it that he and his family took refuge from famine in Egypt. A son of Jacob, named Joseph, is said to have risen there to the rank of a viceroy in the service of some Egyptian pharaoh. Centuries later the aristocrat who was destined to give Israel a more universalistic monotheism was reared in Egypt and trained there in imperial religion and political theory. As has sufficiently been shown in Part One, political theory at the level of the royal house was monotheistic theology.

The stories that narrate the lives of Israelite patriarchs describe conditions that existed a half to a full millennium before the Israelite monarchy was founded. Therefore, in reading these ancient stories, one must take into consideration, with an eye turned to history, the apparent motivations of teachers and scribes who may have recorded them—perhaps as early as the tenth century B.C.E. Some of these scribes undoubtedly were obligated to priestly traditions or were on royal payrolls.

For instance, the brief encounter between Abraham and Melchizedek, narrated in *Genesis* 14, seems to have answered better than anything else a need on the part of King David to justify his ruling of Israelite tribes from the Jebusite or Canaanite city he had taken over. The story also could have been used to justify, on behalf of David and Solomon, the installation of the native Canaanite priestly family, the Zadokites, to henceforth administer the cult of Israel's Yahweh or El (Lord God) in that city.[1] Other episodes in patriarchal story cycles, which pertain to God's covenants with patriarchs and kings, serve similar goals of nationbuilding.

---

[1] It probably is an oversimplification to reconstruct the ancient history of Israel's religion in terms of only two priestly houses, Levites and Zadokites. A more thorough reconstruction would have to consider also Libnites, Hebronites, Mahlites, Mosesites, Korahites, and possibly even the Aaronites as separate priestly lineages. See J. Maxwell Miller and John H. Hayes, *A History of Ancient Israel and Judah* (Philadelphia, 1986), pp. 112f. Among relevant passages concerning Levites and Zadokites may be mentioned in *2 Samuel* 5:8–10; 8:17; 15:24ff; and *1 Kings* 2:35.

Copyrighted Material

The Abolition of Human Sacrifice

One Abraham story, in particular, holds great significance for understanding the meaning of the Hebrew patriarchal contribution in what was to become the religion of ancient Israel (*Genesis* 22). Storytellers remembered their chief patriarch for having accomplished a radical turnabout in Near Eastern religious practice. Abraham considered for a while, then wavered, and by the grace of his God abolished the practice of human sacrifice. He had meant to sacrifice his firstborn son, but as an alternative he took a ram that his God had provided especially for that occasion. He gave it as a substitute payment to the God who had reminded him of this more ancient method of sacrificing animals.

But, of course, the scriptural record is a little more ambiguous than that. In all likelihood it was the original scribe who already made it a point, and subsequent Jewish and Christian commentators vied with him and among themselves, to rationalize Abraham's initial willingness to sacrifice the life of his son. Allegedly the God of Abraham wanted to "test the faith" of his devotee, which means his willingness and his readiness for mindless obedience.[2] In the absence of sufficient historical perspective, still, the Danish philosopher Kierkegaard has magnified this so-called faith of Abraham into a fullfledged nonrational leap of faith.[3]

It is difficult to see how, in historical perspective, any interpretation of the Abraham story could be farther from the mark than that offered by Kierkegaard. Abraham's decision was no leap of faith. He walked every mile of the way rationally and ethically aware, step after step. Overdomesticators everywhere and at all times have understood, rationally well, why they sacrificed humankind. Their motives had to be justified, religiously and with a posture of humble

---

[2]For the original moralized story itself, see *Genesis* 22. The New Testament epistle to the *Hebrews* shows the Christian continuation on that same theme.

[3]Søren Kierkegaard has argued that Abraham was willing to sacrifice Isaac "for God's sake . . . because God required this proof of faith." He rationalized this faith posture of Abraham as the "teleological suspension of the ethical," see "Fear and Trembling: A Dialectical Lyric by Johannes de Silentio" (1843), trans. Walter Lowrie, in Robert Bretall, ed., *A Kierkegaard Anthology* (Princeton, N.J., 1946), pp. 116–134.

Copyrighted Material

obedience, of course. It is a well-known fact that obeying orders, religiously, always has been an alibi of overdomesticators who, for the sake of personal justification, pose intermittently as servants of greater-than-human reality.

In the context of an interreligious dialogue one also ought to keep in mind that, according to Islam, the son who was about to be sacrificed was Ishmael, not Isaac. But, inasmuch as our present discussion focuses on the historical record of human sacrifice as an aspect of general grand domestication, the fact that Abraham avoided sacrificing either of these sons and the fact that he did not become another grand domesticator appears far more important than any other benefits that might have accrued for the estate of either survivor.

The good news here is that both second-generation patriarchs—the one favored by Judaism and the one of Islam—have survived the supposed "faith" of Abraham. The world is a better place for the fact that this old "faith" of Abraham has been abolished more emphatically still by later universalistic prophets and reformers. Thus, the peoples who practice religion in the historical shadow of Abraham are thereby challenged to live—and to let live.

Anyone who stays a while in the vicinity of a potential grand domesticator, soon enough, will see him showing his hand and disclose what is really on his mind. All along a potential grand domesticator will have listened more carefully to such divine revelations that happen to improve his personal destiny and promise fulfillment of his desires. A grand domesticator, even one like Abraham who is only tempted to become one, sooner or later will demand his reward from the God whom he serves so very faithfully. The sacrifice of one's own love toward family and kin—and one's own precious rationality to boot—goes against the drift of life manifest in processes of nature or purposes of divine creation. Presumably life has been created, or has evolved, to be enjoyed and lived in the first place! Therefore both of these types of sacrifice, of rationality as well as of kindred, do call for a special reward from Almighty God himself. At the very least they procure some extraordinary status of righteousness and justification. And behold, Abraham heard the rewarding voice of God even swear an oath:

> ... I will indeed bless you, and I will multiply your descendants as the stars of heaven and as the sand which is on the seashore. And your descendants shall possess the gate of their enemies, and

Copyrighted Material

by your descendants shall all the nations of the earth bless themselves... (*Genesis* 22:17–18)[4]

Indeed, multiplication and paternalistic blessings, as heard by
Abraham or composed by a later Israelite scribe on a grand domesticator's payroll, are only the wrappings of this divine promise.
Possessing the gate of competitive enemies, however, that is the pearl
grand domesticators—and even good folk like Abraham who are
tempted to become grand domesticators—treasure very much.

Yes, there is a temptation hidden in this story after all. But it is
the temptation of overdomestication that ancient Israelite scribes in the
comfort of later monarchic environs, six and more centuries after
Abraham, were no longer able to discern.

But how has this story received its traditional "faith testing"
motive? Any reflective schoolteacher will have had numerous
occasions in the course of work to discover the answer to this simple
question.

First of all, it is unlikely that Israelite scribes, who recorded their
favorite "faith" answer for posterity, actually wanted their pupils
seriously to consider the recurrence of an obediently executed human
sacrifice—living as they did, under their kind of God. But then, with
regard to actual practice in surrounding cultures, "disobedience" is
what the reform of Abraham's religion seems to have been all about.

If confronted with a difficult theological question, as to why God
would have demanded such obedience of Abraham, Hebrew teachers
could not very well have suggested that their story's supreme
patriarch may have misunderstood God or, worse yet, that God
himself is arbitrary. If these scribes really had wanted to dwell on the
horrible notion of human sacrifice, or if in their sheltered scribal
world they still knew much about how it was done formerly, they at
least would have concocted some impressive proto-Levitic description
of such a rite.

As it was, however, old Israelite teachers simply took the shortest
and easiest path to finish off that lesson. And they did so as a people
who knew themselves to be specially chosen by God and redeemed
from grand domestication. They sidestepped the problem of God's

---

[4]Compare here also Jacob's self-interest and bargaining, in *Genesis* 28:20–22, as
a prelude to his subsequent prosperity. Copyrighted Material

right to arbitrariness, because this was too difficult to grasp by the average faithful. Instead, these teachers steered their discussion to schoolroom-level ethics; that is, to the grand domestication portion of theology that could be applied directly to student behavior in a lowly classroom.

Every teacher to a degree is caught up in the exercise of grand domestication. And if an available story happens to teach discipline along with its subject matter, and if it thereby promises to make teaching easier, not many teachers can resist its endorsement and its blessings provided in the form of sweet authority. As all people in a king's entourage had to do, and as most scribes did, so too later generations of students were expected to practice blind obedience.

Therefore, the basic plot of the story remains that Abraham became a different kind of sacrificer, one who did not sacrifice his son. All those who propagated this story about Abraham knew, with all their rational faculties intact, why they wanted to remember precisely the faith of this patriarch and, at the same time, disregard the similar and much stronger faiths of all those who as grand domesticators in the ancient world, in fact, have sacrificed their offspring.

In its historical context the Abraham story carries the full rational weight of a new universalistic theology. The saving message that made this story worth remembering and that made it worth retelling especially among firstborn sons was that Abraham *did not* sacrifice his son, that by his God's own generous waiver a ram was substituted. The implied futuristic theology points therefore to a new God of gods. It points to a new revelation of the God of gods—to the effect that his appetite no longer includes a grand domesticator's hunger for power over human life and flesh.[5] Whether the appetite of the real God actually ever included such craving for human flesh, beyond the possibility of human misunderstanding, is an entirely different faith question. And that question belongs outside the realm of this historical discourse.

---

[5]The theological breakthrough reflected in the Abraham story does not mean that human sacrifice in particular, or overdomestication religion in general, were eliminated as a practice in Israel, or for that matter in Judah. For flagrant exceptions, see *Judges* 11:31ff, 2 *Kings* 16:3, and *Jeremiah* 7:31. Copyrighted Material

Among the civilizations that thrived during Abraham's time it was still deemed possible that such an appetite for human flesh and blood was a genuine divine attribute.[6] But, be that as it may, in the concrete sense of preferring ordinary domesticator food the God of Abraham, in conformity with plain domesticator needs, at once was more archaic and more humane. He was less of a grand domesticator and therefore also less "civilized."

From the perspective of a civilized ruler or a high priest at the time, the theological reform of Abraham meant a step backward. Abraham had recoiled from progressive grand domestication sacrifices and retreated to the simpler primitive animal sacrifices of herder folk. "Retreat behavior" is the primary characteristic of religious movement—retreat behavior in space as well as in time.

Of course, a complete turning away from complex civilization and from overdomesticator religion, and a return to simple domestication, was impossible even for Abraham. No human conscience and no religious repentance from aggressive behavior, not even penitent somersaults and spiritual conversions, will ever completely turn back the clock of history and a people's cultural progress. Hands continue to grasp, teeth continue to bite and chew, and human minds continue to analyze. Time rushes irreversibly along a forward path.

With the help of exciting distractions, such as the Greek Muses were known to provide or religious rites could bestow, the fruits of aggression and progress at times could be deemphasized and checked for a while. And in some societies such fine arts pass then as being "cultured" or "civilized." But gruesome excesses cannot be removed from the actual flow of time. An overdomesticator's practice of sacrificing human victims has become a historical datum, for priestly executioners as well as for prophetic protestants and reformers. Moreover, the reputation of a God on whose tables hapless human victims were once served, by virtue of this God's acceptance of the same to the extent that acceptance has been attested to by scribes, is fixed ontologically in the minds of later devotees. As a God who has

---

[6]Consider, for example, the sacrifice of a young man, excavated in 1979 seven kilometers south of the great palace of Knossos. The proceedings of the sacrificial rite were interrupted by an earthquake and by subsequent fire, some 3,700 years ago. See Yannis Sakellarakis and Efi Sapouna-Sakellarakis, in *National Geographic* (February 1981), pp. 204–222. Copyrighted Material

once shown such an appetite, of course, he can be accepted or resisted. But the historical fact of his cult can never be erased completely from the slate of time.

Consequently, those who retreated with Abraham into a simpler cultic mode of behavior, and who have begun to offer again old-fashioned domesticators' animal sacrifices discovered that their sacrificial animals no longer could be given in accordance with pure and old domesticator logic. Before grand domestication was practiced, firstborn sacrificial animals were given as share sacrifices in payment for domestic herds. This was done to legitimize human ownership under a God who previously had owned them—or who had created and subsequently allotted them to humankind.

The "first offerings" or "share offerings" that hunters gave to their divine tutelaries were amplified by domesticators into ceremonial butchering feasts. Domesticators sacrificed whole firstborn animals to pay for subsequent litters or even for larger herds. And after that these ordinary animal sacrifices of domesticators were magnified still further, by grand domesticators, to pay still mightier divine sponsors with the more valuable currency of human victims—to justify ownership of human herds. This is why in grand domesticator surroundings the stubborn insistence, by Abraham, on simpler animal sacrifices has necessarily acquired new meaning.[7]

In the shadow of Abraham's temptation and in light of his new faith, sacrificial animals, inevitably, have become "substitutional offerings." Animal victims had to be given, henceforth, as substitutes to redeem prospective human victims whom grand domesticator religion had doomed to premature mystic absorption or digestion within a divinity.

On account of this new substitutional dimension it therefore is not warranted anymore to classify Abraham's religiosity, nor the three faiths of Judaism, Christianity, and Islam that descended from it, as nostalgic returns to primitivistic domesticator religion. Rather, it is the case that the spirit of universal salvationism, having gotten quagmired in grand domesticator fascinations and ambitions, was

---

[7]The evolution of sacrificial activities, from the elementary level of religious animal behavior, to hominid hunting, to domesticator and grand domesticator sacrifice, and beyond, will be outlined in greater detail in a forthcoming book on religion in evolution. Copyrighted Material

forced to retreat temporarily to older ritualized primitivisms of animal slaughters and sacrifices. There it had to start anew to regain its momentum for reform.

And of course, all this retreat behavior happened by necessity. Greater-than-human configurations of reality have a way of dampening human ambitions all the time. Reasonable religious responses always are retreat behavior of the balancing kind.

Copyrighted Material

9

Israel's Return to Grand Domestication

Linguistic research and recent archaeological discoveries have taught us to approach the history of Joshua's conquest of Palestine with some serious reservations. The language in *Deuteronomy* and *Joshua* comes from a few centuries later and the supposed pattern of "conquest" does not match the destruction dates of cities in the region.[1] Moreover, the motives in the Joshua epic correspond much better to the grand domestication scheme of a certain king Josiah (622 B.C.E.) who attempted a religio-political reform. Josiah dreamed of a restored and reunited Israel, and it appears that, to advance his ambitions, he and his priestly collaborators embellished Joshua's "conquest of Palestine" that, at the time, lay already six centuries in the past. During the time of Joshua, supposedly, all the Israelite tribes invaded Palestine as a united front and took the land that, perhaps again supposedly, their creator-God had given them.

It now appears that most of the people who belonged to the ancient tribes of Israel were already in the land when Levitic wanderer priests went there to propagate their Exodus tradition. The tribal territories already were claimed, and this might be the reason why the tribe of Levi had no territory allotted to it. Priests ordinarily do not refuse ownership of land, if they can help it. As it was, their Levitic cult of Yahweh was centered on a portable tabernacle tent, and within that tent was kept a chest in which a few sacred mementos

---

[1] See J. Maxwell Miller and John H. Hayes, *A History of Ancient Israel and Judah* (Philadelphia, 1986), pp. 60f and 71f, concerning thirteenth century B.C.E. city destructions. "Conquest cities" like Arad, Heshbon, Jericho, Ai, and Gibeon yielded no archaeological evidence of Late Bronze Age occupation, much less of destruction.

Copyrighted Material

from their escape from Egypt were kept. But more important for the Israelite confederation of tribes became the Levitic annual commemoration of the Exodus experience itself.

Three centuries or longer Levitic tribesmen, as priestly mediators between God and humankind, had been cultivating their tradition of escape from Egyptian rule—under a God of gods who preferred Hebrew slaves over citizens of the mighty Egyptian empire. They roamed as *Hapiru* when they settled at their first place of refuge, at the Midian oasis, on the Sinai peninsula. From there they moved into the hill country of Palestine to interact with Israelite tribes. *Hapiru* was the Egyptian and Mesopotamian designation of foreigners and nomads, rebels, and outlaws; it referred to people who lived or moved about between these two large systems of grand domestication and who, generally, managed to escape the control of both. The label *Hapiru* appears to have given rise, later, to the positive self-designation *Hebrew*. On their part, some Hebrews in Palestine (that is, in the "Philistine" country) referred to themselves as the tribes of *Yisrahel*—a name that seems to have meant fighters, strugglers, or partisans of El (of their Lord God).[2] These tribes later were united into a kingdom as the people of Israel, under David (ca. 1000 B.C.E.) and his son Solomon.

The Levites created and told the narratives of Israel's national epic. They became what might be described as the first "priestly cheerleaders" in the confederation of Israelite rebel tribes. Their Exodus epic and their annual Passover celebration, which remained anchored in memories associated with Sinai as their "Holy Land," have become the foci of their Yahweh religion. Other tribes subscribed to their story and their rituals and, in time, they all learned to commemorate together a joint miraculous escape from Egypt as the always united tribes of Israel. What has been their common experience for this joint ceremonial commemoration?

Up to the time of King David, the Israelite tribes fought separately for survival along the Egyptian frontier, sometimes with and sometimes against the Philistine city states in the Gaza area. And

---

[2]The author gratefully acknowledges this probable etymology as a suggestion of David Wucher. *Copyrighted Material*

sometimes they fought among themselves (*Judges* 12). Only gradually by means of their annual first offerings rite, adopted from the culture stratum of simple herders and historicized in opposition to Egyptian grand domestication, were these rebel tribes ideologically and religiously cemented together into a single nation—at least for a couple generations under David and Solomon.[3]

The historical books in the Bible, *Judges, Samuel,* and *Kings,* in conjunction with recent archaeology in the Gaza area, have given us fresh clues for the early history of Israel. During Israel's formative years, the Philistine kings in that region ruled city-states that had adopted a general pattern of Egyptian culture. Concerning the Israelites, the biblical source tells of a first leader, Saul, who was grudgingly anointed by the priest Samuel for the purpose of leading Israel's defense against the Philistine kings. His kingship was intended only for the duration of an emergency. The general anti-monarchism on the part of Yahweh's priests reflected what all along had been the way of life among tribal herdsmen who led seminomadic lives—a tradition of fierce independence.

Saul's Philistine opponents were well-organized city-states along the northern Egyptian cultural frontier, organized under a well-established aristocracy. During most of Israel's formative centuries these city-states failed to heed the weakened Egyptian pharaohs. Nevertheless, for the Israelite tribes to stand up against the organized might of Philistine city-kings required a more stable military policy than King Saul could deliver on the short leash that Samuel, the priest, was willing to authorize in the name of the antimonarchic Yahweh.

Saul, as a part-time king, succumbed to pressures from Samuel. His dynasty crumbled under the might of the Philistine kings. His rival and successor, David, joined the Philistine opposition for a while, though, in the eyes of the latter he probably was untrustworthy

---

[3]"Historicized" in the sense that the Exodus was made the central guiding theme of the cult, as an acknowledged historical event. The Passover rite, as celebrated by Hebrew-Canaanite refugees from Philistine city states, also may be understood as a ritual of "romantic herder nostalgia." Yisrahel rebels and refugees retreated to simpler living in the hill country and, making virtue of necessity, imitated and idealized the pastoral life-styles of ancient patriarchs.

Copyrighted Material

as an ally. King David's private army consisted of *Habiru* rebels and refugees, many of whom had come directly from those same grand-domesticated city-states, and established *Habiru* tribal bands in the hill country of Palestine. When back in that hill country David at last succeeded in organizing the rival Yisrahel tribes, and when he began deploying their military potential, the Philistine city-kingdoms fell before him.

In stark variance with the conquest narratives included in *Joshua* 1-11 one finds, in *Judges* 1:27-33, a list of seventeen Canaanite cities that the Israelites had been unable to take over. According to *2 Samuel* 8 David finally defeated and subdued the remaining Philistine cities. But even the amount of credit given to King David appears to have been an overstatement in light of *1 Kings* 9:16. There one learns that it had been the pharaoh of Egypt who defeated the Canaanite city of Gezer and gave it as a dowry to his daughter, King Solomon's wife.

During the formative years of the Israelite monarchy the Levitic cult of Yahweh had become a rallying symbol for the young nation. During Israel's formative centuries of rebellion against the Egyptian frontier this revolutionary cult made it possible to orchestrate a semblance of intertribal cooperation.

But what could have been the common experience among the Israelite tribes that made the joint commemoration of Passover and Exodus a meaningful unifying symbol? In light of the freshly established historical context, a reconstruction now can be attempted in a rather straightforward manner. All the tribes held memories in common: about suffering under grand domesticators and resentment toward their Philistine-Egyptian overlords and enemies. They achieved a measure of unity on the basis of their Passover-Exodus cult, which symbolized an underdog's reaction to the presence of Egyptian grand domestication as their common enemy.

Whether someone actually escaped during an "exodus" from the Nile Delta in the company of Levitic leaders, such as Moses and Aaron, or whether someone escaped Philistine-Egyptian city states to join some Israelite rebel tribe in the hills, or whether one participated in the end only in David's victory over these city states, one in any of these situations was liberated from Egyptian bondage in general. The plot of the Exodus epic, that is, Yahweh's victory over Egyptian

Copyrighted Material

taskmasters, has described and given meaning to all subsequent experiences of liberation from overdomestication.[4]

It must be kept in mind that ritualized play acting is a powerful means to routinize human thought and collective behavior, especially among minds caught up religiously in celebrating victory. *Homines sapientes* (men who think) is a misnomer for creatures who, in actual fact, are *homines ludentes* (men who play). And for the coordination of the latter, the staging of civic-religious pageants is of paramount importance. Rituals are more vibrantly alive and effective than all the literary historical footnotes of scribes combined.

Compare, for example, the experience of a typical immigrant to America. Sooner or later he or she gets drawn into celebrating a version of American Thanksgiving—or as a minimum to watch Thanksgiving pageants on television. Like the Jewish Passover, so also this national holiday is celebrated in exchange for divine blessings, for security, and for title to land. Our American epic about pilgrims who arrived on the Mayflower is remembered annually and nationwide with many interdenominational thanksgiving services. The covenant with Manifest Destiny thereby is sealed during a festive communal meal that includes sacrificial turkey as the native American sacrificial "lamb."

This latter-day equivalent to the Jewish Passover is what has redeemed the wanderings of many timid immigrants who came to America. It translated their wanderings into divinely blessed pilgrimages. Rites and celebrations, everywhere, are the real means by which national epics become effective in people's lives. A wanderer who found himself in the company of Levites roaming Palestine, three millennia earlier, could subscribe to Israel's national epic of the Exodus as easily.

Samuel, the priest of Yahweh, resisted monarchy as long as he could. But in the end the first two Israelite kings, Saul and David, as

---

[4]Although arguments over exact motives, means, and ways of Israel's Yawistic revolution still have not been completely settled and the historical synthesis stiil is incomplete, a general consensus appears to have evolved concerning Egypt's over-lordship over the Philistines. For the beginning of this debate. see Norman K. Gottwald, *The Tribes of Yahweh* (Maryknoll, N.Y., 1979), pp. 410ff. It should be kept in mind that, still during the reign of Solomon, it was within the power of the Egyptian pharaoh to take and give the city of Gezer as a dowry.

Copyrighted Material

they competed among themselves, both justified their return to grand domesticator ways with claims of having been anointed king by that same antimonarchic priest (*1 Samuel* 10 and 16). Then David conquered Jebus (Jerusalem) with his private troops and made it his royal city. He also fetched the sacred "ark of the covenant" that used to be in Samuel's shrine at Shiloh, and he brought it home to Jebus (*2 Samuel* 5 and 6). This sacred chest, which was a token of Levitic Yahwism, was placed there under a new tent within the city walls. Using this chest as the relic and legitimate title to the Exodus tradition, the shrewd David then installed the man Zadok as a second high priest to administer the Hebrew cult of Yahweh (*2 Samuel* 8:17 and 15:24). By the time that Solomon became king, Zadok was left as the only high priest; his Levitic competitor was banished from the land (*1 Kings* 1 and 2).[5]

Understandably, the politically and militarily successful David also wanted to build a lasting temple of stone and thereby advance his dream of social fortification and grand domestication an extra step. But the rebel ethos of the Israelite tribes, by the justification of which David had won and organized his kingdom, would not permit him to go that far. The prophet Nathan at one point gave King David permission to build his temple, but quickly he reconsidered and came forth with God's revised order to desist (*2 Samuel* 7). The God of the recently liberated Hebrews would not suffer incarceration in a massive stone structure built by a grand domesticator—at least not yet. He and his appointed priests had to make do for a while longer with a tabernacle tent.

Another one of David's grand domestication schemes concerned the organization of military might. He conducted a census of "valiant men" throughout Israel, that is, a registration for military conscription (*2 Samuel* 24). It is said that David himself was the one who first felt guilty about having ordered this census. Yahweh's verdict, along with the rationalization of an epidemic at hand, was enunciated by David's own court diviner.

---

[5]Zadok was apparently a man of the local Jebusite, that is, Canaanite, family of priests who traced their ancestry back to Melchizedek. A later source, *1 Chronicles* 24:3 and 12:27–28 rationalizes Zadok into having been a Levite. See also *Genesis* 14:18–20 and footnote 1 of Chapter 8.

Copyrighted Material

Religiously inspired roadblocks of this sort were constantly put in the path of Israel's king by antimonarchic men of God who, first ceremonially and later prophetically, continued to live under the spell of their rebel Exodus tradition. Obstacles of this sort clearly defined the perimeters beyond which the divinely sanctioned *Yisrahel* rebel ethos would not permit the king's grand domestication ambitions to progress.

Under Solomon

It remained for Solomon, who rose to the throne with the prophet Nathan's helpful plotting, to build a temple of stone and to bring the Yahweh cult under full royal control (*1 Kings* 6). In his magnificent court temple, the presence of God was meticulously maintained by priests who were on the royal payroll. The structure of the temple itself was built after a Phoenician-Egyptian model; it accommodated a "holy of holies" enclosure inside, the same arrangement as generally could be found in Egyptian Amun temples.[6]

The trouble with all this magnificent temple religiosity was the fact that a God, who accepted the maintenance of his cult from the hand of a king, himself came to depend on the generosity of that king. As a result the divine-human relationship of dependence was reversed. This was the typical outcome whenever the religious behavior of common folk fell under the control of a grand domesticator. Tribes of humankind as a rule became overdomesticated together with their tribal gods.

During the reign of Solomon the Israelite kingdom rivaled in superficial splendor the glories of Egypt and Mesopotamia, and for a while his state even surpassed theirs. His royal scribes collected wisdom literature and recorded it in their king's name, boasting wisdom all the while on behalf of their king. Solomon's wisdom is said to have been greater than the wisdom of all the sages of Egypt (*1 Kings* 5, 10). The fact that his scribes resorted to such boasting in

---

[6]Commentaries ordinarily cite the affinity of Solomon's temple with Phoenician prototypes. But similar floor plans were customary also in Egyptian temples of "Amun," the contemporary name for Egypt's One God. See, for instance, the Middle Kingdom core of the Temple of Amun-Ra, at Karnak. Lionel Casson, *Ancient Egypt* (New York, 1965), pp. 120ff.

Copyrighted Material

competition with Egypt testifies indirectly to the Hebrew religio-cultural indebtedness to that civilization. Along with all that, the Israelite king in fact was married to a daughter of the Egyptian pharaoh (*1 Kings* 3:1).

But Israel's political and religious awareness was sustained, all the while, by its Exodus memory and its religious fervor of partisan-ship—thus by their combined early Mesopotamian and subsequent *Habiru* herder tradition. The Davidic dynasty was not supported by a time-tested and balanced grand domestication organization. Schools of loyal scribes and officials, guilds of artisans, and other groups of citizens on which both Mesopotamian and Egyptian civilizations relied during their centuries of stability and good fortune—all these traditions were in their infancy even during the apex of Solomon's reign. The king seems to have had only his military safely organized. And for a grand domestication system to endure humanely, such a onesided exploitational "law and order" emphasis is never sufficient.

When Solomon died, in 922 B.C.E., the northern tribes of Israel broke away from Judah. They refused to serve Solomon's son, Rehoboam, who stoutly promised to continue the police state tactics of his ambitious father. The northern tribes refused to provide forced labor any longer or pay the king's excessive taxes. They seceded to form their own Israelite kingdom under Jeroboam I (*1 Kings* 12). The two kingdoms, Israel and Judah, existed alongside each other until Sargon II, of Assyria, defeated Samaria in 721 B.C.E.

Josiah's ruthless conquest of the northern Israelite realm, and the "reform" (622 B.C.E) during which he slew all northern priests at their sanctuaries, was duly legitimized with the celebration of a Passover commemoration. A detailed account of this event is narrated in *2 Kings* 23. Under Nebuchadnezzar's sweep, which enforced the Babylonian policy of integrating the Near East, Josiah's dynasty disappeared soon afterward. The southern monarchy of Judah held on a little longer, into the sixth century, when most of its population was deported to Babylonia, in 597 and 587.

Remnants of the southern kingdom, of Benjamin and Judah, eventually returned from exile in Babylon. Another group, which had moved in the direction of Egypt accompanied by Jeremiah, left no written records. But traces of their descendants have been found near the first cataract of the Nile. Throughout their dispersion, the exiles in Babylonia celebrated the freedom from overdomestication that their ancestors had achieved by way of escaping the power of Egypt.

Copyrighted Material

When in 539 Babylonia fell to Cyrus the Great, Palestine came under Persian hegemony as well. With permission from Cyrus, and from later Persian emperors, small remnants of Judaic exiles from Babylonia returned to Jerusalem with a charter to reestablish the semblance of a Judaic state.

Alexander the Great (336–323 B.C.E.) displaced the Persian overlords. He and his successors justified their rule as cultural colonizers. In rebellion against their Greek overlords the small Judaic state for a while became independent under the Maccabees, in 168. But after having become radicalized through revolution against the Greeks, these Hasmonaean priest-kings themselves quickly lapsed into methods of tyranny and overdomestication.

After 63 B.C.E. the period of Roman domination was punctuated repeatedly by brush fires of Judaic rebellion. Their hope for another independent Judaic state was smashed to embers by Roman might during the first century C.E., and the dispersion that followed lasted almost two millennia.

Only during the twentieth century, after persecution and holocaust, have Jews of the Jamnian tradition returned in large numbers to Palestine. Although America and the Western world, under the influence of Christendom, watch these new Jewish pioneers by and large supportively, their present effort at running a modern democratic state, a new Israel, is perceived by most of their Near Eastern neighbors again as a return to grand domestication or overdomestication.

Copyrighted Material

Copyrighted Material

10

Universalistic Monotheism and Messianism

An early trace of universal salvationism that survived from the Israelite past already was noted in the story about Abraham. This patriarch may be credited with having resisted the "temptation of civilization" of sacrificing a human victim—thus implicitly also with having rejected an ancient theology of grand domestication.

Habiru or Hebrew reactionary universalism has become politically significant when, centuries later, under Moses—or with the composition of Exodus stories—the status of the Egyptian "God of gods" was directly challenged and undercut. During that challenge the God of the Hebrew slaves revealed himself, to those freed slaves at least, as the world's mightiest and victorious God of gods. Thus the typical Near Eastern "God of gods" theology, which here and there has legitimized an imperial grand domesticator "King of kings," was replaced by radical Hebrew liberation theology.

Nevertheless, the theology of Moses cannot yet be classified as complete "universalism." The Mosaic reform was only the beginning of an important movement in that direction. The limitations to the universalism of Moses were, as such limitations always are, conditioned by historical circumstances. In their struggle for liberation and survival, the Hebrew slaves acquired fresh ways and means for defending themselves. They needed arms, training, and courage, as well as divine protection when these things proved insufficient. All the while, the God who in his mercy liberated them from slavery continued to support them during the aftermath. It therefore goes without saying that the mundane existential concerns of a fledgling nation, in the end, turned the theological universalism of Moses back onto a return path of defensive exclusiveness. By hindsight it seems

Copyrighted Material

as though such defensive excluding and narrowing scarcely could
have been avoided.

It is a fact in the history of cultures and religions that any God
who has been called upon to serve as a war deity, to lead a people as
their "Lord of hosts," of necessity has ceased to function as universal
Lord of the world. To insist that a Lord of war in his partiality is
nevertheless a universal God, in the past, has led to fanatic warfare.
It has led to the extermination of the enemy side in order to prove the
truth of one's own arrogant theological fixation. Campaigns which are
organized to establish the universality of a war deity can lead either
to calamity for the believers or to imperialistic victory. Thus they
lead to calamity on at least one side of the confrontation. In either
case the universalistic outlook is eclipsed. This predicament constitutes the downside of monotheistic religion wherever such is being
cultivated by advanced humanoid predator minds.

Under David and Solomon

Two or three centuries after Moses, the Hebrew "Lord of hosts"
cult ripened into its next phase. "Yahweh Sabaoth" as foremost deity
of war was invoked to sponsor a new grand domestication system.
During the reigns of David and Solomon such a system came into
bloom and reached its zenith quickly. While living under these two
kings, the heirs of the Israelite rebel tradition gloried for a while in
their united monarchy, as in something that was divinely established.
But then, the abrupt division of the kingdom into northern and
southern portions severely dampened that euphoria.

The Mosaic tradition remained an internal contradiction within
both kingdoms. With an anti-overdomestication religious cult at their
centers, both kingdoms also remained riddles and aggravations unto
themselves. In reading the biblical sources, one should keep in mind
that only the perspective of the southerners has survived in writing.
Thus, at best, our understanding of ancient Israelite history is
onesided; at its worst, and most probably, the cultic depravity of the
northerners has been exaggerated.

To illustrate their confrontationalism, here we need only point to
their most conspicuous bone of contention—the Canaanite cult of the
bovine. Mythologically and symbolically considered, the famous calf
sculpture that the first high priest Aaron set up for worship (*Exodus*

Copyrighted Material

32), and the ones Jeroboam is said to have set up at sanctuaries in Bethel and at Dan (*1 Kings* 12:28), have served similar Canaanite nuances as the twelve calves that supported the bronze basin documented for the Jerusalem temple (*1 Kings* 7:23–26 and *2 Chronicles* 4:2–5). All the complaints about the apostasy of northerners, on the part of southern kings and their prophetic supporters, must be evaluated in light of the fact that, ordinarily in this world, a loss of hegemony breeds resentment and bad blood.

Modern rationalists often dismiss ancient conflicts about cultic behavior as proceeding essentially from irrational thinking, and they include in this judgment all religious behavior to boot. But such evaluations usually fail to see the "rational" or political significance of unified religious behavior. In our introductory chapter we defined religion in general as retreat behavior. Thus, politically and socially, the predictability of religious behavior implies that whosoever bows to, or retreats from, the same greater-than-human configuration of reality as one's own, together with others, such a person can be relied on in emergencies or battles. In posttheistic and secular political ideologies, swearing an oath to a national emblem or a flag, serves a similar function.

Back in the early literature of the Israelite monarchy, one finds the kind of flattery that was customary at grand domesticator courts elsewhere: May the king have a long life! May his dynasty last forever! And in a complete relapse to the Egyptian style of grand domestication, the zealous prophets of Yahweh themselves participated in that idolatrous trend. The prophet Nathan, who personally had been scheming to have Solomon installed as David's successor, is said to have gone so far as to attribute divine sonship to his chosen prince. His words resound as if spoken by God himself:

"I will be his father, and he shall be my son ... I will not take my steadfast love from him ... and your house and kingdom shall be made sure forever before me; your throne shall be established forever." (*2 Samuel* 7:14–16)

The priestly poet who composed the second Psalm has recited this same message even more daringly—as unabashed grand domesticators' breaking and dashing, poetically sublimated of course. This poet, too, has impersonated the voice of God:

Copyrighted Material

"I have set my king on Zion, my holy hill." I will tell of the decree of the Lord: He said to me, "You are my son, today have I begotten you. Ask of me, and I will make the nations your heritage, and the ends of the earth your possession. You shall break them with a rod of iron, and dash them in pieces like a potter's vessel." (*Psalms* 2:6–9)

Born ever so gradually of court flattery and carried on the wings of poetry, a gradual transformation could be observed in Israelite grand domestication etiquette and liturgy. The internal politico-religious contradiction began to stir, stretch, and squirm out from its narrow confines.

A reader of the psalm just quoted, invariably, will be impressed by how a poetic metaphor, an exaggeration, is able to blaze a trail beyond itself and beyond present political realities—"aesthetically," if you like. For contemplating the possibilities of this process of artistic exaggeration, by way of considering still another step in the aesthetic sublimation of this psalm, one need only reexperience it under the wonderful musical umbrella that George Friedrich Händel constructed for it in his inspired oratorio *The Messiah*. There the terrible smashing and the dashing sounds rather wonderful.

Isaiah and Micah

In the poetic prophesies of Isaiah (eighth century B.C.E.), court flattery was elevated unambiguously above the raw desire for dynasty and throne. So, for instance, *Isaiah* 9:2–7 still echoes many polite phrases of Near Eastern court etiquette. Some scholars have suggested that this particular "messianic passage" originally may have been recited while celebrating the accession of King Hezekiah to the throne of Judah:

For unto us a child is born, to us a son is given; and the govern-ment will be upon his shoulder, and his name will be called "Wonderful Counselor, Mighty God, Everlasting Father, Prince of Peace." Of the increase of his government and of peace there will be no end, upon the throne of David, and over his king-dom. . . . The zeal of the Lord of hosts will do this. (*Isaiah* 9:6–7)

Copyrighted Material

Even after making allowances for a generous amount of flattery, this passage in its extant form no longer fits very well the coronation of an ordinary human king. These words of poetry soar high, so as to leave any kind of human Hezekiah far behind in the dust of this world. As a result of having transcended their mortal subject matter, these words actually have ceased to be mere dishonest court flattery. Carried on wings of superlatives and metaphors, such magnificent words were in *homo sapiens* minds miraculously transformed. Resounding as direct echoes from the mouth of God, in the eternal presence of which they were recited, these words suddenly had to be rationalized as honest and serious prophesy—or else risk the human mind getting caught jesting dishonestly in the presence of the holy God.

Isaiah has abandoned the hope of expecting very much from a mortal contemporary king. Prophetically he therefore proceeded to describe an ideal king instead, one whose arrival realistically could be hoped for only in the future. Looking away from the present king who sat on the throne of Judah, the prophet has even permitted his train of thoughts to start afresh with a newly born baby boy who, in a manner of speaking, is at the moment still "out of this world."

If we accept the suggestion of some scholars, that this text represents enthronement liturgy from the days of King Hezekiah, then it is possible that the passage quoted could have been written after disappointment had set in over the king's defeat under Sennacherib of Assyria. In any case, the prophet no longer had an ordinary human king in mind, one who would disappoint again. He anticipated a king who was no less than "Mighty God" himself. Thus, beginning with Isaiah, promonarchic prophets gradually developed their political enthusiasm toward a new kind of antimonarchic transmonarchism.

Micah was a younger contemporary of Isaiah, he too projected the focal point of his hope forward into the future. But he also looked back into the past to the potentiality of a royal childhood. With a fresh start he humbly and ambitiously began to reenvision Davidic history from scratch, beginning at Bethlehem, in the town which had been the birth place of the boy-child that became King David.

But you, O Bethlehem Eph'rathah, who are little to be among the clans of Judah, from you shall come forth for me one who is to be ruler in Israel. (*Micah* 5:2)

Copyrighted Material

Hananiah and Jeremiah

The Israelite experiment with grand domestication began disintegrating after the death of Solomon. It came to an end early during the sixth century B.C.E. when King Zedekiah of Judah put in his lot with an Egyptian coalition against Babylonia's rising King Nebuchadnezzar. Here, at this important turning point in the history of Judah, one finds two prophets speaking opposing revelations on behalf of their God.

Hananiah prophesied in support of joining the Egyptian coalition: "Thus says the Lord of hosts, the God of Israel: I have broken the yoke of the king of Babylon" (*Jeremiah* 28:2). The prophet Jeremiah, who regarded revolt against Babylon to be folly, replied first with ridicule and some time later with a serious counterprophesy: "Thus says the Lord of hosts, the God of Israel: I have put upon the neck of all these nations an iron yoke of servitude to Nebuchadnezzar, king of Babylon." To strengthen his statement further, Jeremiah accused Hananiah of telling a lie and put a curse of death on him.

Such had been, beyond the realm of court flattery, the style of royal advisement in those days. Unfortunately, King Zedekiah heeded the wrong divine promise, or the wrong curse. Nebuchadnezzar destroyed Jerusalem and its temple, wasted the land, and deported most Judeans to Babylonia. There they were given some fifty years to get weaned away from their dream vestiges of the Davidic monarchy.

When Jeremiah's attempt at influencing his king's foreign policy failed, he declared old religious covenants abnegated, including the one that was believed to have existed between God and the dynasty of David. And while contemplating Israel's present situation he hurried back in time to also declare void the covenant that Moses had mediated between God and Israel. Jeremiah saw the old covenants to be replaced by the dawning of a new era of personalized salvation—salvation on a universalistic scope. His new covenant insisted on a complete change of human nature, a new creation, indeed.

> Behold, the days are coming, says the Lord, when I will make a new covenant with the house of Israel and the house of Judah, not like the covenant which I made with their fathers when I took them by the hand to bring them out of the land of Egypt, my

Copyrighted Material

covenant which they broke....But...I will put my law within them, and I will write it upon their hearts; and I will be their God, and they shall be my people. And no longer shall each man teach his neighbor and his brother, saying, "Know the Lord," for they shall all know me, from the least of them to the greatest, says the Lord; for I will forgive their iniquity, and I will remember their sin no more. (*Jeremiah* 31:31–33)[1]

The Second Isaiah

The end of captivity for the Jews in Babylonia came with poetic fanfare. An admirer of the eighth century B.C.E. prophet Isaiah, an anonymous poet now known only as Second Isaiah, tagged an appendix to the old scroll—*Isaiah* 40–56. The fact that he got away with this deed suggests that he was a scribe rather high up in the rabbinic hierarchy. His long poem exploded with fervor about the wonderful saving event that had just occurred and that he himself had been able to decode.

The person who wrote Second Isaiah can be introduced as a poet, that much is quite obvious from his style of writing. But he also must be regarded as a prophet. Poetry spoken in the presence of God, impersonating at times the voice of God or of his angels, is necessarily transformed into poetry that might better be named *prophecy*.

The prophesy of Second Isaiah opens with a song, a song of comfort, which was recited as though it was chanted by the council of heaven itself. It was addressed to the Judaic survivors of the nearly fifty years of exile, sixty years for victims of an earlier deportation. The concrete proof for this freshly announced divine comfort is given at several spots throughout the poem: God has sent his messiah (his anointed one) to conquer Babylon and set his chosen people free. And never mind if that messiah of Yahweh happened to be a Persian conqueror who really did not seem to know much about the God of the Hebrews!

Thus says the Lord, your Redeemer, who formed you from the womb: "I am the Lord, who made all things"...who says of

---

[1]See also *Jeremiah* 32:38–40 and *Ezekiel* 11:19. A similar new relationship between God and people was anticipated in *Hosea* 2:20.

Copyrighted Material

Cyrus, "He is my shepherd, and he shall fulfil all my purpose";
saying of Jerusalem, "She shall be built," and of the temple,
"Your foundation shall be laid." Thus says the Lord to his
anointed, to Cyrus, whose right hand I have grasped to subdue
nations before him and ungird the loins of kings, to open doors
before him. (*Isaiah* 44:24–45:1)

The phrase *whose right hand I have grasped* in *Second Isaiah*
corresponds to a similar phrase on the Cyrus Cylinder, a cuneiform
record inscribed by Babylonian priests of Marduk.[2] It shows the
priests of the Babylonian high god equally enthused, welcoming this
Persian imperialist as their savior. Indeed, it seems as though Cyrus
had saved the Babylonian cult of Marduk as well. Indeed, he had
saved all cults in the land from the hands of a Babylonian revisionist
king, Nabonidus. This invading Persian imperialist, in addition, has
been given credit for having liberated numerous divine statues,
belonging to various city cults in the greater Mesopotamian realm,
also for rebuilding their regional sanctuaries.

All this does not mean that our poet from Judah got his phrase
directly from the priests of Marduk; rather, it means that both priestly
sources probably obtained similar messages from Cyrus' own
generous edicts. All the while, it is obvious that Persian propaganda
in Babylonia was informed and advised by the priests of Marduk
who, unabashedly, collaborated with Cyrus in the government of the
city-state. They probably had collaborated already during Cyrus's
takeover of the city.

Some portions in *Second Isaiah*, for example chapters 44 and 46,
contain explicit ridicule of Mesopotamian polytheism. This hostile
Jewish posture, superficially, has kept many scholars from considering the poet's actual indebtedness to Babylonian religion. However,
a historian who wishes to attain a realistic perspective must assume
that a reasonable Jewish poet, of necessity, would have done some
serious reflecting on Babylonian Marduk religion during his fifty
years of forced exposure to it. A Judaic rabbi could not have helped
but see, and wonder, what the Babylonian Akitu rites (the New Year
rites) were all about. These Akitu rites were as central to Babylonian

---

[2]See James B. Pritchard, ed., *Ancient Near Eastern Texts Relating to the Old
Testament*, 3d ed. (Princeton, N.J., 1969), pp. 315f.

Copyrighted Material

religion and statecraft as Passover had all along been for Israelite and Samaritan traditions. Many Akitu rites were performed in public and therefore could be observed easily.

The disappearance and the return of the Babylonian god Marduk were an integral part in these ceremonial proceedings. Moreover, the behavior of the Babylonian chief deity was closely linked with the fortunes of the king who knew himself to be commissioned by the God. Throughout Mesopotamian history, the king played a key role in this divine-human drama of suffering and redemption. The king was dethroned and deprived of his insignia. He was humiliated to the point where the high priest of Marduk would pull him by the ears, strike his cheeks, and extract a confession to the effect that he had not sinned against the Lord of the countries, had not been negligent in serving the God, and had not destroyed Babylon.[3] Later the face of the king was struck once more, to draw tears from his royal eyes as a good omen for water and fresh growth on the land. All this had to be duly enacted in order to renew the land and the year, thus space and time, for another round of Mesopotamian balance and prosperity.

Jonathan Z. Smith has commented on the negative confession of this Babylonian rite as an incongruity—allegedly for the purpose of stimulating discussion and gaining an entry into this archaic text. He reasoned that, if anyone, it was foreigners who would have destroyed Babylon when given a chance. Disbelievingly he asks, "What native king of Babylonia ever contemplated or was guilty of destroying or overthrowing Babylon, smashing its walls or neglecting/destroying Esagila?"[4]

The Nabonidus Chronicle and the Cyrus Cylinder suggest otherwise.[5] Priests of Marduk and collaborators with Cyrus have accused the last king of the Babylonian dynasty of having attempted just that. In an empire where the central seat of power frequently was moved from one convenient capital city to another, the clause *not*

---

[3]Henri Frankfort, *Kingship and the Gods* (Chicago, 1948), pp. 313ff.

[4]Jonathan Z. Smith. "A Pearl of Great Price and a Cargo of Yams: A Study in Situational Incongruity," *History of Religions*, 16:1 (1976): 1–11.

[5]Pritchard, *Ancient Near Eastern Texts Relating to the Old Testament*, pp. 305ff, 315ff.

Copyrighted Material

destroyed Babylon and Esagila seems to have included the meaning of "neglect" or "abandonment."

In light of a wider religio-historical perspective, the priestly inquest during a Babylonian Akitu rite therefore need not be written off as a "situational incongruity." Any high priest of Marduk, who felt responsible for the God's cult and for the balancing of Babylonian culture and empire, not only would have regarded both ritualized slappings of the king as proper but also reasonable and very necessary. Indeed, often in the past cities and states have been corrupted and ruined from within by follies committed by their own leaders. Human government always represents a two-edged sword: one that cuts inward as well as outward.

One may see in the Babylonian Akitu tradition an archaic system of "checks and balances" that the priestly cult has been able to impose upon the king's secular ambitions, as a means of delimiting a God's generous legitimization of royal ambitions. We all know that royal powers everywhere have tended to become absolute when left unchecked.

Millennia were required to fine tune this blessed "incongruity" and, judging from such religio-political arrangements elsewhere in human history and society, all these balancing measures probably never really worked or endured as well as expected. Every generation of humanists and masters of ceremonies has had to labor and to scheme anew, as *homines ludentes*, to harmonize and safeguard their culture's "cult versus state" balance. Every generation anew has had to invoke greater-than-human reality configurations to safeguard sanctions that prevented leaders from turning privileges into absolute rights. They had to invent rituals that kept benevolent dictators from taking the lead in too many activities.

Citizens of Judea, in 586 B.C.E., went into exile with the Deuteronomic knowledge that their God rewards good behavior and punishes bad behavior. They had been taught how to interpret divine punishments as evidence of guilt and sin. Throughout their exile in Babylonia they were haunted by the very same question Job asked of God: What is my sin? They wondered whether collectively they were guilty of something other than those peoples were who were not exiled. And so, at the end of their sojourn in Babylonia, their Second Isaiah answered these questions by insisting that suffering, although at some point it may have been God's punishment, nevertheless has been a prelude and necessity to redemption.

Copyrighted Material

The poetry of *Isaiah* 53 celebrates the notion of divinely sanctioned and redemptive suffering. The questions that the poet has raised are all typically Judaic, and they have been generated by the Second Isaiah's own experience of deportation and exile. His answers, however, dared to draw heavily from the very core of Babylonian religion itself. During the cultic rites of that religion the God Marduk disappeared temporarily from the land of the living.[6]

The debate still continues about whether in Babylonia the God Marduk actually was thought of as a "dying and rising god," as such deities have been categorized by Sir James Frazer.[7] Indeed, reconstructions of the full Akitu sequence rely on bringing together Mesopotamian documents of several culture strata. But in addition, I suspect, the debate thus far has relied far too heavily on a difference between latter-day Christian and Jewish views. According to the Christian tradition, dying and rising taken together are reasonable divine attributes, whereas historians of Jewish provenance tend to regard such notions as being unnecessary in a context of respectable Semitic religion.

But be that as it may, even if Marduk's temporary disappearance during the New Year's rite is not called *death*, the king's suffering before his national deity by itself demands some kind of theological-imperial parallelism or justification for the priest's assertive actions. The simplest motive of why a high priest should have struck the king appears to have been the imposition of Marduk's authority over that king. Beyond that, for a king to be struck during his annual "re-initiation rite" could best be justified, and can still now be best explained, by referencing such practices directly to the very nature and habits of the sponsoring deity.

But again, be that as it may, we must not allow ourselves to be distracted by the emotive meanings that *death* or *resurrection* carry here or there among scholarly traditions. What in the realm of the gods, or at the level of a God of gods, could *dying* possibly mean? Certainly, it meant not *death* in the finite human sense.

---

[6] See Frankfort, *Kingship and the Gods*, pp. 321ff.

[7] See, for instance, Smith, "A Pearl of Great Price and a Cargo of Yams."

Copyrighted Material

And together with these considerations, the existence of the text of *Second Isaiah* 53 itself is a Judaic-Babylonian datum that needs to be reckoned with. And such historical data definitely do transcend their Christian as well as their Jewish significance.

Thus, the question whether Marduk should be classified as a "dying and rising" deity really is beside the point. The central meaning of the Akitu drama was that divine roles and royal roles were synchronized and harmonized. Then for the duration of a safe ritualized interval of renewal the risk was taken for this arrangement to be interrupted, interrupted only to be reassembled again more solidly. God and king together have "suffered" and have put forth an effort, as it were, for the redemption and the renewal of Babylon. After Marduk had reemerged, the king of Babylon once again could be enthroned.

In full accord with Babylonian soteriology the "Servant Israel" in *Second Isaiah* suffered and was "cut off from the land of the living." The poet considered him dead and proceeded, accordingly, to dwell on what could still be salvaged from this sad situation. Thus, with an application of Babylonian soteriology and logic, the poetry of Second Isaiah progressed from death to reemergence and new life. The poet knows that his gospel may indeed sound incredible to fellow Judaic ears:

> Who has believed what we have heard? And to whom has the arm of the Lord been revealed? For he grew up before him like a young plant, and like a root out of dry ground; he had no form or comeliness that we should look at him, and no beauty that we should desire him. He was despised and rejected by men; a man of sorrows and grief.... Surely he has borne our griefs and carried our sorrows; yet we esteemed him stricken, smitten by God, and afflicted. But he was wounded for our transgressions, he was bruised for our iniquities; upon him was the chastisement that made us whole, and with his stripes we are healed. (*Isaiah* 53:1-5)

It is obvious that Second Isaiah actually believed that to him the purposes of God have been revealed. He proceeded to tell exactly how. God has stepped into Judean history once again. He has led his chosen Persian messiah, Cyrus, by his own hand. On the basis of the "Babylonian Chronicles" students of history can reasonably infer that
Copyrighted Material

Cyrus participated in the Babylonian cult festival: that during the Akitu rites he thus was humiliated, that he suffered and subsequently was reenthroned.[8] As far as the motives of Cyrus himself were concerned, no doubt he suffered all these indignities pragmatically, to legitimize his rule over Babylonia.

But then, the Second Isaiah communicated the will of his God not as it pertained to Persian interests in Babylonia, but as it affected him as one of God's specially chosen people. His immediate goal was to persuade his fellow deportees to return home. He either did not see, or he chose to overlook, the pragmatism that motivated Cyrus in his ritualistic participation, his divine suffering.

As far as Second Isaiah was concerned, this Persian messiah of God invaded Babylonia for the primary purpose of liberating God's special people. As poet he himself experienced this saving event as if it were new light and a first insight sent by God. Then, while he was already at it, he proceeded to decode God's riddle that had been put to Judaism by way of their Deuteronomic theory of suffering.

The identity of the suffering Servant in *Second Isaiah* is dual and triple. One may identify in this text two Servant figures. A first Servant Israel signifies the people of Judea going into exile. This Servant died by the very fact of having been exiled. But then, after the exilic "burial" of this Servant, alongside "the wicked and the rich" of Babylonia, there followed the rebirth of a liberated and freshly prospering Servant Israel. This second Servant was redeemed by the sufferings of the first, of that same designation. The first Servant died at the very moment when freedom was lost to Nebuchadnezzar, and the second was reborn when freedom was decreed by Cyrus.

Thus, the role of Cyrus vis-à-vis Israel corresponded, in Babylonian terms, to the role of Nebu when he liberated Marduk from the confines of his netherworld mountain. All the while, however, from the point of view of Israel's sovereign God, the prophet saw neither

---

[8] The evidence is somewhat indirect and contextual. Upon taking over Babylon, Cyrus slaughtered sacrificial sheep, offered incense, and "constantly prayed to the gods, prostrated on his face" (Verse Account of Nabonidus). The priests of Marduk further wrote concerning their god, that "he scanned and looked through all the countries, searching for a righteous ruler willing to lead him (i.e., Marduk, in the annual procession)." See the Cyrus Cylinder. Both documents are published in Pritchard, *Ancient Near Eastern Texts*, pp. 312–316.

Copyrighted Material

Marduk nor Cyrus emerging from netherworld and captivity; instead, he saw the new Israel. From the point of view of Israel's God, the larger scenario looked like this:

> For a brief moment I forsook you, but with great compassion I will gather you. In overflowing wrath for a moment I hid my face from you, but with everlasting love I will have compassion on you, says the Lord, your Redeemer. (*Isaiah* 54:7–8)

The incorporation of a Persian messiah introduced into the theology of Second Isaiah a third Servant figure, Cyrus, his mission closely fused with the fortunes of the second. This figure was introduced on the strength of Judaic messianism and Babylonian theology, together with the implicit gospel of redemptive suffering. Its introduction into the scriptures of Judaism had far-reaching consequences for the distant future.

The Second Isaiah called for a reenactment of the Exodus, but the immediate result could be counted only in small numbers of people who were willing to return to their Judean homeland. Beyond these meager results Judaism produced later, under Ezra and Nehemiah, much the opposite of what this universalistic Second Isaiah had hoped for. For its survival the new Judea retreated to narrow and defensive provincialism.

The universalistic motives expressed by biblical writers of the postexilic period, such as are reflected in books like *Ruth* and *Jonah*, reveal the posture afforded only by a liberal minority. But the fact that these books, too, were collected and recopied is sufficient proof that some scribes and teachers persisted in laboring for a more universalistic outlook.

It must be said that the universalism of Second Isaiah itself, with all its international openness and awareness, still contained some nationalistic blemishes. Here and there the poet-prophet appears to be still unduly patronizing toward other nations. It seems so at least in these passages:

> For you will spread abroad to the right and to the left, and your descendants will possess the nations and will people the desolate cities (54:3).

Copyrighted Material

Behold, you shall call nations that you know not, and nations that knew you not shall run to you, because of the Lord your God, and of the Holy One of Israel, for he has glorified you. (55:5)

Standing, as it were, suddenly under the protection of Cyrus, a strong messiah of Yahweh who was made to startle nations, miraculously appearing as if from nowhere, the prophet's occasional relapses into nationalistic vainglory do seem understandable. Concerning Israel's special status in relation to fellow humankind he still dreamed the dream of Joseph (compare *Genesis* 37) and he postulated favoritism on the part of his God. Thus, by way of such defensive and nationalistic overstatements the wonderful book of Second Isaiah has to the Judaic tradition not only helped contribute a distorted view of other nations but also reinforced a latent martyr complex. From Judaism that same tendency to sanctimonious martyrdom was passed on to Christianity and hence to some if its secular offshoots.

* * *

Claims to supraegalitarian chosenness, or to divinely sanctioned superiority, among peoples destined to live together in a world also blessed with democratic ideals and awareness of a Golden Rule, in the end always aggravate and invite retributive leveling or persecution. The Christian exploitation of *Second Isaiah*, of preempting the sufferings of the Servant to signify specifically the sufferings of Christ—claiming the promised salvation for followers of Christ alone—has aggravated deadly competition between two "almost" universalistic religious faiths. It has heightened both the irritability and vulnerability of Christian and Jewish egos alike. It has isolated Judaism to persist in its diaspora of sanctified uniqueness, while, at the same time, it has saddled vast stretches of Christendom with an idolatrous scriptural perception of that same divinely ordained uniqueness. A deadly combination, indeed! Democratically considered, the Christian scriptural idol of an ethnic "apple of God's eye," piously garnered from *Zechariah* 2:8, necessarily invites vultures from near and far to peck at that eye.

And so, during the holocaust under German National Socialism, in post-Versaillesian anger, two nationalisms—one seeing itself as

Copyrighted Material

having been "elected by God" and the other, more recently informed about having been "selected by Nature"—in moments of worldwide economic desperation, saw the younger grab the throat of the older. All humanoid cultures thrive on robbing from among the possessions of the gods.

Judaism and Christianity, two ancient universalisms that are more provincial than either side likes to think of itself, persisting in half ignorance about their own histories and full ignorance about each other's, will predispose themselves repeatedly to new opportunities for conflict. Islam meanwhile has entered that same field, and it participates in that same scuffle with similar zeal.

* * *

Still, a historian must try to remain fair. By sixth century B.C.E. Jewish standards, the universalism of Second Isaiah was remarkable and radical. Salvation had come to his people through a God-anointed Persian grand domesticator. And that gospel of salvation, in its Babylonian historical setting, came nicely wrapped in Babylonian logic and soteriology. One wonders what could have happened had this Judaic poet acknowledged the worldly presence of "Persia" as such, or had he spoken a clear word of appreciation to Cyrus's relatives. Some facts of life and relationships are meant to be acknowledged here on earth; they need not be eclipsed, necessarily, by the personal relationships individuals achieve with their gods. But such historical realism apparently was not yet meant to be.

Instead, something else has transpired. The very introduction and presence of such a book as *Second Isaiah* into the thought stream of Judaism was destined, after a period of incubation, eventually to break forth with a new and a different kind of religious rhythm, with a different religious style. A renewed awareness of redemptive divine-human suffering has ushered in a new era in the history of Judaism. And, for the rest of the world, it changed B.C.E. to C.E.

Copyrighted Material

PART THREE:
THE WISDOM OF GREECE

Copyrighted Material

Copyrighted Material

Preface to
the Wisdom of Greece

The information in Part Three of this book, on the Wisdom of Greece, is presented in the reverse order of its discovery. Several years ago I was explaining Heliopolitan theology to a class of students. At one point in our discussion I found myself reaching desperately for an analogy, and I heard myself say: "It is somewhat like...like Neoplatonic ontology." These words came as a complete surprise to me. It had been more than a quarter of a century since I had last looked at the Enneads of Plotinus. And the subsequent confirmation, to the effect that Plotinus and his teacher Ammonius indeed were native Egyptians, led me to reexamine their bequest. The reason for mentioning this incident is to assure my readers that, whatever is being said in this part of this book, it is definitely not the result of trying to prove a preconceived hypothesis; rather, it serves to introduce a new insight.

At a later occasion, after the remainder of this book had been written, I began to wonder how strange my exposition of the *Enneads* must appear to someone who all along has known Plotinus' philosophy to be an elaboration on Plato. And this astonished audience would include practically everyone. In any case, as a "new Plato" the founder of "Neoplatonism" had to be somehow related to the supposed first founder of his own school. I resolved therefore to include a little on Plato in my presentation. But then, inasmuch as Plotinus has quoted sentences not only from Plato but also from other Greek philosophers, the entire history of Greek ontology became a matter of concern.

Another series of surprises followed in quick succession, and each of these demanded that my book be expanded to the size of a multivolume encyclopedia. Not only portions of Plato's dialogues, such as the Timaeus, derived their elementary ontology from ancient Egypt, but so did the writings of most other Greek philosophers before Plato.

Copyrighted Material

The only way to do justice to the prehistory of Plotinus' so-called Neoplatonism, therefore, was to call attention to traces of Egyptian ontology in the bequests of some other philosophers as well. It goes without saying, a broad sketch of this sort can be only preliminary and hypothetical. Future historians of philosophy and historians of religions, together, will have to reexamine the larger picture of Hellenic philosophy in light of the ancient Egyptian connection. In time we surely will end up with a different way of looking at the history of Greek philosophy—and certainly with a revision of the draft presented here as well.

The Hellenic tradition of philosophy has greatly affected the formation of the early Christian church. This happened especially by way of Neoplatonism, which, as we now know, has been Greek philosophy's homecoming to neo-Egyptian ontology. Whereas the history of Greek philosophy does now read like the homecoming of Greek minds to Egypt, Christianity by and large represents a similar return to Egypt by way of mythology, theology, and ritual. Hellenic philosophy, Christianity, Gnosticism—and some of the mystery cults that flourished during the time we call Hellenistic—were ancient Egypt's parting gifts to Mediterranean and Western civilization.

Copyrighted Material

11

From Mythology
to Philosophy

The Philosophical Temper

In one of his famous dialogues the philosopher Plato narrated a playful discussion on mythology, carried on in the shadow of a tree by Socrates and Phaedrus. The latter seemed to remember that it was "somewhere about here that they say Boreas seized Orithyia from the river?" Socrates acknowledged that this indeed was the story. But then comes a surprise. The notorious Athenian gadfly, Socrates, who stood mentally poised to expose the foolishness of any *homo sapiens* he met, refused to demythologize this mythic tale and its divine figures. Instead, he became introspective and mused about his own priorities:

> I can't as yet "know myself," as the inscription at Delphi enjoins, and so long as that ignorance remains it seems to me ridiculous to inquire into extraneous matters. (*Phaedrus* 230a)[1]

The need for introspection and self-knowledge, which Socrates set forth as his immediate goal in his pursuit of philosophy, was put in the *Phaedo* (67c–e) on a more sober common denominator. There, contemplating his own impending death, Socrates saw how his dying has been prefigured dualistically in his lifelong pursuit of philosophy—as a process of "separation of soul from body."

In an earlier instance, speaking from a less ultimate pedestal, Socrates insisted on balancing the Appollonian advice of "know

---

[1]In E. Hamilton and H. Cairns, eds., *Collected Dialogues of Plato* (Princeton, N.J., 1963).

thyself" with the dictum of temperance, "nothing in excess" (*Protagoras* 343a–b). All the same, such religio-philosophical introspective wisdom, on the one hand, and temperance, on the other, were pursued by Socrates and his companions on rather individualistic pretexts. Philosophy generally was pursued in small circles of student associates, under a single tutor. The subject matter of study generally was restricted, therefore, to that teacher's own personal soteriology.

Philosophical quests traditionally have engaged only small numbers of elitist minds, sustained by equally elitist egos. Moreover, those few minds rarely contemplated their subject matter in a time perspective much larger than could be scanned by the two generations that could be represented by a teacher and his students. Knowledge about truth was obtained from moments of intuition, moments that were expected to occur after traversing lengthy paths of formal reasoning. These mental journeys therefore tended to be dedicated to an ahistorical exploration of static eternal relationships and structures. Moreover, such personal quests for intuition, at abstract levels, seldom brought much enlightenment to large numbers of people, to those who struggled for survival in a world that contained many kinds of living beings.

With some glimpses of hindsight, cast on the entire history of Greek philosophy, Apollo's dictum of "know thyself" now beckons us to supplement philosophical with historical introspection. The expanded Apollonian dictum becomes therefore: Know thyself as one knower among many; know thyself as a changing participant in a larger changing tradition of knowing; and know your own tradition as a dribble that trickles alongside and interplays with other traditions of knowing! And not all traditions of human knowledge are philosophical. Our holistic historical introspection therefore must try to embrace, as a minimum, an extended history of Greek philosophy. We must find some evolutionary rootlets in philosophy's prehistory.

The contents and memories of human minds generally are more ancient than their containers can intuit by themselves or under the spell of some momentary fascination. Therefore, even while dwelling still nearer to the fountainhead of their tradition and while pondering ahistorically at ease, Socrates and Plato nevertheless had great difficulty seeing just how much their own methods of reasoning still depended on an ethos that was rooted in mythos. Thinking of themselves as intellectual reformers, Greek philosophers generally disliked

Copyrighted Material

the Greek mythological substratum of more ancient mental habits. At the same time they were unaware of the motherland and mythology that had furnished the ontological substratum for their philosophizing.

Furthermore, Socrates and Plato would have been surprised to recognize how their philosophical analytic methods, as distinguished from their ontological assumptions, were still akin to the habits of destructive herder-bandit-warrior ancestors who, mounted on horses, had pushed out from the Eurasian plains a few centuries earlier. They would not have been any less astonished to learn how their aristocratic talent of analytic reasoning itself had evolved, as a mental substitute, from the predatorial aggressiveness of these early Indo-European intruders.

The analytic physical breakdown of prey and environment, by predators and hunters, gradually over millions of years has been enhanced beyond the basic necessity of biting and digestion. This exaggeration was accomplished most effectively by aggressive male members of the genus *Homo* who, over millions of years, evolved into scavengers and tool-using predators.

An updated Appollonian dictum of "know thyself" obligates individual lovers of wisdom, therefore, to seriously study the entire evolution and history of cultures and religions in light of recent anthropological discoveries. Of course, the more limited philosophical task of personal introspection remains, as it always has been, a good start in this direction.

Intercultural and interreligious understanding can succeed only in continuity with prior introspection into one's own cultural, philosophical, and religious preoccupations. Minds grasp to understand by contrast and comparison. Thus, a student who impatiently rushes toward understanding another culture or its concomitant religion still may lack the wherewithal for making valid comparisons. Without perception of historical depth, without awareness of time and the fact that all things are changing, our own cultural trends, philosophical and religious, will not come adequately into focus for us—nor will those of other peoples. We therefore must begin our introspection afresh, precisely at the point where the proponents of Indo-European glory advised us to begin—at the very beginnings of Indo-European mythology.

Copyrighted Material

Hesiod

Centuries before Greek philosophers and scientists began to reduce divine functions to abstract categories and impersonal principles—nay, even before classical Greek sculptors began to incarnate old divinities in bodies of wood or weigh them down with the inertia of stone—the poet Hesiod penned "Theogony." This powerful mythos was destined to provide ethos for practically everything philosophical and scientific that hitherto has been thought and achieved in Western civilization.

The mythic event, of the divine son Cronos castrating his Father Uranos (Sky-Heaven), at the bidding of Mother Earth, goes a long ways toward explaining how Oedipus complexes thrive in societies afflicted with patrilineality, under gods who themselves rose up against their fathers. It exposes problems inherent in aristocratic succession. And it even provides a few ancient clues about elementary stirrings in women's liberation movements.

But in addition, this myth also exposes the roots of Western philosophy, of Western science and Western culture. It reveals some ancient existential reasons as to why, in spite of the presence of philosophy, certain new religious movements have succeeded. Seen from the angle of Greek history, the dualistic Greek philosophers, Socrates and Plato, and to some extent even Aristotle, added little more than footnotes to this seminal theogonic myth of castration, to this archetype of Western progress. Philosophical advance and scientific progress required for their legitimation this ancient archetype of "progression" from virile theogony to emasculated cosmogony.

It behooves us to refresh our memories concerning this important tale and contemplate afresh its central plot.[2] We are told here, at the dawn of Greek literature, that Earth was primary and Heaven was secondary:

Verily at first Chaos came to be, but next wide-bosomed Earth, the ever-sure foundation of all.... And Earth first bare starry

[2]Hesiod, "Theogony," in *Hesiod, the Homeric Hymns and Homerica*, trans. H. G. Evelyn-White (Cambridge, Mass., 1977), pp. 87, 89.

Heaven, equal to herself, to cover her on every side, and to be an ever-sure abiding-place for the gods.

The mythic narrative, of how Mother Earth subsequently gave birth to hills and nymphs, to Pontus, Oceanus, Coeus, Crius, Hyperion, Iapetus, Theia, and Rhea; to Themis, Mnemosyne, Phoebe, and Thetys; to Cronos, the Cyclopes, and finally Cottus, Briareos, and Gyes, moves on speedily to a divine plot. This mythic incident, as has been hinted already, produced far-reaching results in the mental development of not only ancient Greece, but all of Western civilization.

For of all the children that were born of Earth and Heaven, these were the most terrible, and they were hated by their own father from the first. And he used to hide them all away in a secret place of Earth so soon as each was born, and would not suffer them to come up into the light: and Heaven rejoiced in his evil doing. But vast Earth groaned within, being straitened, and she thought a crafty and an evil vile. Forthwith she made the element of grey flint and shaped a great sickle, and told her plan to her dear sons. And she spoke, cheering them, while she was vexed in her dear heart:

"My children, gotten of a sinful father, if you will obey me, we should punish the vile outrage of your father; for he first thought of doing shameful things."

So she said; but fear seized them all, and none of them uttered a word. But great Cronos the wily took courage and answered his dear mother:

"Mother, I will undertake to do this deed, for I reverence not our father of evil name, for he first thought of doing shameful things."

So he said: and vast Earth rejoiced greatly in spirit, and set and hid him in an ambush, and put in his hands the jagged sickle, and revealed to him the whole plot.

And Heaven came, bringing on night and longing for love, and he lay about Earth spreading himself full upon her. Then the son from his ambush stretched forth his left hand and in his right took

Copyrighted Material

the great long sickle with jagged teeth, and swiftly lopped off his own father's members and cast them away to fall behind him.[3]

Herder Culture

In contrast to the indigenous Egyptian civilization of sedentary farmers, the Greek cultural heritage received its primary impulses from Euro-Asiatic herders. During much of its early history, Egypt had been sheltered from major movements of nomadic peoples. At most, it was obliged to respond to impulses from the Mesopotamian sedentary presence. In later times, especially after the arrival of Eurasian horses in Egypt with the Hyksos and after their expulsion, Egyptian dealings were destined to expand eastward and northward in the general direction from which came the Hyksos kings with their horse-drawn chariots.

For the sake of a broad overview the ancient Near East may be approached, elliptically, by way of its two very diverse ideo-cultural foci. Egyptian culture and religion, together with its reactionary Hebrew offshoot, may be seen as representing one focus. Hellas, a representative of Indo-European intrusions into the Mediterranean realm, may be seen as representing the other.

An approach to the ancient Near East by way of focusing on extreme cultural and religious postures may not do justice to all the ordinary people who, existentially, were living along their spectrum of aggression-retreat possibilities. But then, an understanding of their extreme ideological postures nevertheless may provide a useful shortcut for obtaining an overview on the scope of this book. Nothing during the third and second millennium B.C.E., in the Near East, stood in sharper contrast than the lifeways of sedentary farmers in Egypt, on the one hand, and the ways of nomadic herder folk, on the other. Fanatic devotees to the latter way of life kept pushing from Eurasia into the Fertile Crescent. They arrived with wagons, then with horse-drawn chariots, and finally as skilled warriors on horseback. They traded some of their animals and passed on their new arts of cavalry warfare to the peoples whom they touched—who increasingly needed them for their safety and defense.

---

[3]Ibid., pp. 91, 93.   Copyrighted Material

When Eurasian herders succeeded in domesticating horses, they themselves were electrified by the power and speed of their subjugated animals. When herders perfected the art of riding on horseback, warfare became more fierce and was destined never to be the same again. When these Asiatic horse breeders then brought their animals to sedentary cultures in the Near East, those sedentary civilizations were transformed by cavalry-incited militarism. An equine-inspired cultural dynamic was set in motion that pulsated clear into our twentieth century. World War I was still ignited by it, and World War II erupted among its embers—only to be continued now with variants or "antitheses" of armored, so-called horseless carriages. I personally may have witnessed one of the last cavalry battles in human history, just a few kilometers from my boyhood home.

Nothing in this broad overview conflicts with Colin Renfrew's postulate, of a prior westward expansion of agriculture into Europe by carriers who spoke a proto-Indoeuropean language.[4] In fact, the equine-generated cultural explosion on the steppes of Eurasia might have forced the westward movement of farmers in the first place. After the southern European plains were emptied of farmers by waves of increasingly more spirited horsemen from the steppes, the latter sometimes became acculturated to the remains of the civilization that they failed to destroy.

As adaptive hunters in Asia following remnant herds of grazing animals, they had become herders. As riders on horseback, they became herder-bandit-warriors; and as such they overtook farming communities and civilizations south of the Caucasus. Their kindred by profession caught up with and plundered those planters who had resettled farther west in Europe. They "domesticated" farmers and low-class herders after the manner in which they were accustomed to control herds of grazing animals. They thereby became "grand domesticators" and "overdomesticators," depending on the value judgment applied by objective observers.

In this discussion we are not concerned strictly with the problem of linguistic movements. The mythos and ethos of nomadic herder-warriors, as they vented their "glory and honor" aspirations in their lengthy epics, transcended tribal languages and could easily be retold

---

[4]Colin Renfrew, *Archaeology and Language: The Puzzle of Indo-European Origins* (New York, 1988).   Copyrighted Material

in the media of any lingual configurations; in fact, they most probably have contributed to the formation of new languages. In any case, mythos and ethos rest foremostly on life-style and the justification of livelihood. By contrast, individual languages function only as temporary carriers—and disposable vehicles at that.

Although the appellation *cowboy* in its modern Western sense may not be entirely appropriate for labeling the entire scavenger-hunter-herder-bandit-warrior mentality brought into bloom by Eurasian horsemanship, in this book we nevertheless will use this term occasionally. A "cowboy" may be the closest a modern Western reader will ever have come to the primitive Asiatic horse-oriented megalomania and cultural milieu.

The term *cowboy* enables us to think about much of ancient Egyptian culture and religion by way of a contrast, or as a foil. The ancient land of Egypt represented sedentary farmers who would rather have been left alone by grand domesticators and empire builders to plant their fields and raise domestic animals.

In Hesiod's *Theogony*, earlier, we were told some interesting things about the behavior of traditional Greek "cowboy" gods. And all along we know that the quoted portion was only one conspicuous act of violence among many episodes in Hesiod's theogony. Prior to the significant castration incident, Father Sky tormented his offspring, and afterward Cronos, to whom the cruel deed of castration had been attributed, was defeated and imprisoned by his own son, Zeus.

* * *

What ought a historian make of this grand array of conflict theology? Should one agree with the philosopher Plato when he suggested, in the *Republic*, that story-tellers like Homer and Hesiod should be censured on that account? Plato himself even went as far as to propose an effective method for silencing their literature forever. That literature, according to him, contained only lies.

There is, first of all...the greatest lie about the things of greatest concern...how Uranos did what Hesiod says he did to Cronos, and how Cronos in turn took his revenge, and then there are the doings and sufferings of Cronos at the hands of his son. Even if they were true I should not think that they ought to be thus lightly

Copyrighted Material

told to thoughtless young persons. But the best way would be to bury them in silence.[5]

And here is how Plato envisioned this silent burial. First, the audience should be restricted to a very few. A pledge of strict secrecy should be required. On top of that a large sacrifice should be given—not just "a pig, but some huge and unprocurable victim."

Needless to say, Plato did not want those stories repeated, neither then, nor ever. He was convinced that they were lies and that the gods never waged war or did other cruel deeds. Plato was afraid that people who hear and believe these stories might want to imitate the violent deeds of their gods. And yes, the philosopher was right. Humankind, as a rule, does imitate, usurp, and absorb whatever appears greater than itself. Originally these myths were told to glorify, that is, to "justify," past herder-bandit–type behavior. Castration and killing belonged among their repertoire of skills.

Bards like Homer and Hesiod peddled their warrior theologies among would-be warriors and aristocrats, for entertainment . . . in what would be equivalent to our "veterans clubs." Comparatively speaking, it may be said that these mythic tales were functional equivalents to our blue movies that, in America, first have spread among veterans and warrior clubs as well. But then, because Hesiod's and Homer's epics were so well done, as works of art, they became, as such, regular school-book fare for Greece.

Hesiod by himself should not be blamed for the existence of his craft, nor for the existence of an epic tradition as such. His was a time-honored tradition already among prehistoric Eurasian hordes of horsemen. In fact, this epic tradition was so strong and has been so revered that in Central Asia it remains alive to this very day.[6]

For a better historical perspective on this hero-horse-and-glory religiosity of Homer and Hesiod we do well when we search for an Indo-European tradition that might be even older than theirs. And yes, we do have antecedent Hittite texts, perhaps over a thousand

---

[5]Plato, "Republic" 377e–378a, in *Collected Dialogues*.

[6]This conclusion is based on personal impressions, obtained during repeated travels to Chinese Central Asia in search of oral literature.

Copyrighted Material

years older, that may have been derived from still older Hurrian sources.

The first God of Heaven of the Hittites, Alalus, was killed by Anus. Thus Anus was defeated by Kumarbis. And we are told that Kumarbis bit off the manhood of the vanquished god and swallowed it. Inside his belly the phallus of Anus grew into the Hittite stormgod. After he was born, this stormgod defeated Kumarbis at the instigation of Anus who, understandably, had remained angry and sore about his loss.[7]

Seen from the Hittite angle, Hesiod's version may not necessarily seem an improvement over this older version. The severed members of Anus matured into the Hittite storm god, a counterpart to Zeus. By contrast, those cut away from Uranos according to Hesiodic mythology were neutered some more, by being transformed into their sexual opposite, the female Aphrodite and goddess of love. One may surmise that for Hesiod, personally, the precise outcome of his tale was irrelevant. The transformation of Uranus' manhood into Aphrodite was simply a convenient way of disposing a still powerful masculine "abstraction."

If from the land of the Hittites, about that time, we had traveled far enough north and east we could have come across some Aryan tribesmen who were in the process of descending southward upon the Indus civilization. Aryan poets, perhaps a millennium later in the *Rig Veda*, still ascribed similar cruelty to their chief warrior deity, Indra—such as slugging Dasyu fortifications like pregnant women who, as a result, aborted their black inhabitants.[8] This is the same genre of raw theological burlesque produced by herders who turned warriors. They were men who knew well how to kill and castrate, and who had set out to rob farmers' livelihood. By the systematic pursuit of these activities they became rulers and aristocrats, and they told tales of cosmic scope to ridicule the procreation- and generation-oriented religion of the natives they subjected.

---

[7]See Albrecht Goetze, "Hittite Myths, Epics, and Legends," in Pritchard, *Ancient Near Eastern Texts*, pp. 120ff.

[8]See K. F. Geldner, *Der Rigveda* (Cambridge, Mass., 1951) 1,101,1 and note; 2,20,7; 4,16,13. The Dasyu victims of the Aryan god Indra were worshippers of the cosmic serpent Vrtra. They were also identified as phallus worshippers, as in Rig Veda 10,99,3.

Copyrighted Material

The task of fair historical interpretation always is difficult. Because whenever in history one sees someone score as a great hero, glamorous enough to where that hero can afford to build palaces and other notable monuments or temples and churches for atonement, his most cruel deeds already have been done. As a rule, the scribes and historians arrive at the scene just in time for the whitewash—to be paid royally for their whitewashing labor. For understanding religions we therefore must find additional access to culture-historical data, that is, shortcuts directly to the minds of the people. All the while, we must keep an eye on the larger historical context. Our shortcut to the minds of these horse-and-glory warriors is precisely their shabby mythology of violence, their memorized epics, and marvelous recitations.

Poets as Reformers

The first intent of every genuine religious movement, as religion has been defined in this book, is to save and balance a corresponding culture. Religion constitutes a reorientation by retreat-oriented common sense that limits cultural aggression and thereby establishes, and justifies afresh, a limit of aggression. As has been sufficiently outlined in the introductory chapter, cultures and religions essentially are opposites.

As strange as it may seem, the predecessors of Homer and Hesiod, in their time, actually were spreading some religious sentiments, of a very weak sort. They began the long process of converting actual blood-thirsty bandits and warriors into spoiled aristocrats who, in time, would rather listen to heroism in the form of poetry than do the required cruel deeds on an actual battlefield.

But, of course, the poetic method of reforming cutthroats by means of artistic sublimation does work exceedingly slow. On that account, this method was no longer sufficient, or even decent enough, to be admitted into Plato's ideal state. Belief in God or gods, to the extent that such a belief is maintained religiously, indeed facilitates honest retreat behavior. But to the extent that belief in God or gods has become organized in line with the progressive appetites of culture, it could be used as easily to justify aggression and warmongering. All peoples on earth have had experiences with those types of so-called religious postures.

Copyrighted Material

"As it was in the beginning [in God's behavior], is now, and ever shall be [in human behavior]." This is not only a Christian liturgical formula, it is the logic by which all cultures of *Homines sapientes* evolve, albeit at times only semiconsciously.

Philosophers as Reformers

Where does all of this leave our Greek philosophers in the ancient conflict between herder-dominated cultures and farmer civilizations? In Greek society they functioned approximately as prophets did in ancient Israel and Judah. Of course, Greek philosophers were necessarily different from Jewish prophets. They had no Egyptian imperial God of gods from under whom they needed to escape; they therefore needed no strong theology to upstage or to deny the reality of such a God.

Nevertheless, Greek philosophers were squaring off with their own Hellenic grand domesticator gods just the same. Had they acted like Hebrew prophets, Greek philosophers probably would not have survived very long in their own rough-and-tumble nation, a culture that still gloried in its old youthful "cowboy" ethos, where Homeric cutthroats were still deemed aristocratic and noble.

* * *

It must be acknowledged at the outset that Greek philosophy is not entirely Greek. Its origin was in Miletus in Ionia, Asia Minor, a harbor city that at the time was the primary trading partner of Egypt. This should give us a clue. But trade in material goods is not our primary concern here; and the identity of carrier storytellers no longer can be traced. We therefore have to look for our evidence, concerning Ionia's indebtedness to Egyptian ontology, among the very ontological axioms of Greek philosophy itself. Common sense at that basic axiomatic level can be carried from harbor to harbor by ordinary folk. No exchange of leading thinkers between Egypt and Ionia was necessary for transmitting basic ontology from one place to another, though traveling scholars there surely were.

Regarding Greek philosophy, we must distinguish its method from its content, its analytic habits from its axiomatic ontology. The philosophers' analytical habits by and large have been the indigenous

Copyrighted Material

product of Greek predatorial herder intellect. From an evolutionary perspective, their analysis represents a sublimation of perfected physical butchering skills. There always will be a difference between the knife of analysis and the subject matter to which that knife is being applied. As of late I have permitted myself to become convinced that the ontology to which Greek philosophers have applied their analytical scalpels, all along, has been a residue of Egyptian theology.[9]

No matter how much the Greek philosophers disliked Hesiodic mythology, their own method of inquiry and thinking was still conditioned, all the same, by its very same basic "cowboy" ethos. And that ethos included the very notion of castration, and creation with the help of weapons.

Castration, in its raw physical form, is a condition that domesticators, especially herders, inflict on some of their animals to make them tame. In Hesiod's myth we obtain a glimpse of how such domesticator skills were magnified by Greek poets to the level of overdomestication cosmology and hype. When in the course of human evolution domesticators progressed to the level of grand domestication we find, in the records of history, how divinely mandated despots had their harems guarded by cut eunuchs. When finally this level of overdomestication needed religious justification, the theme of exemplary castration—as the gods themselves did it—provided a reasonable direction of theological and philosophical speculation.

* * *

Up to this point the early prehistory of Hesiod's myth, in herder life, already has been sketched. What follows here as "history of

---

[9]Traces of Egyptian religious influence can be found in a Homeric epic. Garth Alford, in a still unpublished paper titled "Elysion—A Foreign Eschatological Concept in Homer's Oddysey," furnishes convincing linguistic proof that traces the Greek "elysion" to the Egyptian "fields of rushes." In addition, Kjell Aartun, working along the paths of Cyrus Gordon and Rudolf Macuch, recently demonstrated linguistic continuity between ancient Crete and Egypt of four to five thousand years ago. See Lynn Ryne, "The Faistos Disc—Norwegian Researcher Unravels Ancient Mystery," *Norway Now*, no. 6 (1990): 12. All this suggests a flow of "Hellenic culture" from south to north.

Copyrighted Material

Greek philosophy" will be the sequence of Greek rationalizations concocted on behalf of its sublimation.

Soon after Hesiod had postulated Father Heaven's castration, Greek sculptors transfixed the god's divine progeny into concrete and inert bodies of wood and stone. The fact that gods have been entrapped by skilled human hands in static and sometimes compromising humanlike postures proved damaging to their reputation in the longer run. In addition, ingenious playwrights also paraded the old Hellenic gods in some of these compromising postures, like columns of prisoners, to everyone's delight.

At last, when the time was ripe, came the philosophers. These men occasionally quoted the old names of Hellenic gods with an air of feigned piety. But all the same, the Greek divine names they mentioned no longer were related directly to anything basic in their personal world-views. These deities were not seriously expected to contribute anymore to ontology.

Analysis and abstraction are the mental counterparts to physical severance and castration. So, for example, that which survives after philosophical abstraction of, let us say, a Creator deity, remains no longer a personal deity. It is reduced to a static philosophical "principle of creativity."

The realm of Platonic "ideas" has been conceptualized as an eternal but also static dimension of greater-than-human reality. About Aristotle's Prime Mover we are told that, although everything else moves because of him, he himself is an Unmoved Mover (*Physics* 5). The First Mover has no limit or magnitude and is situated at the circumference of the known world (*Physics* 10). Aristotle ruled out the possibility of having a Prime Mover create movement by either pushing or pulling. In his *Metaphysics* he therefore derived motion in the universe from the fact that the Prime Mover still represents "an object of desire" on account of which other entities move.[10] This finally implies that the First Mover is not only unmoved by someone else but in actuality, by himself, also may be impotent and unmoving.

Thus, all these famous Greek philosophical systems, and Western science subsequently, suffer from what one might call the Hesiodic castration syndrome or the Uranian predicament.

---

[10]See W. D. Ross, *Aristotle* (Cleveland, 1959), pp. 95f, 175ff.

Copyrighted Material

Of course, our Greek philosophers were not that negative toward all the gods. It would have been impossible for them to hope to reform their culture from the platform of an all-out atheism. In addition, Greek philosophers have appropriated, perhaps unknowingly, the primary ontology of ancient Egyptian monotheism, at least in its decayed form as monism. What is meant here by *decayed form*? This calls for a brief digression and explanation.

Human rationality proceeds like music, it shifts from one key to another, from a higher octave to a lower one, depending on a composer's inspiration, instrumentation, and cultural context. The language of experiential religion can accordingly be translated into the language of theology, theology into philosophy, philosophy into science, and science into technology.

Thus, genuine religious experiences naturally begin to decay by the yeast of rational theology. And this happens inevitably, because *homo religiosus* is *homo sapiens* as well. Analytic reasoning, an innate activity of the human mind, corresponds to teeth and digestive acids in an animals physical body. Teeth and digestive acids both perform elementary analysis; that is, a kind of breakdown. Systematic theological minds, in a like manner, break down the subject matter of religion—gods or God—by way of distinguishing divine functions, aspects, and attributes.

Then processes, aspects, and attributes of some larger reality configuration subsequently are reduced, by philosophers, to the size of more easily comprehensible and more manageable abstractions. Monotheism thereby becomes monism, and polytheism becomes pluralism. Sped along by the enzyme of analytic reason, the products of analytic theology continue to decay into philosophical abstractions and thinkable principles. It becomes possible to approach what used to be true greater-than-human realities without having to pray to them. Thus, philosophy by very its nature is atheistic.

Philosophies subsequently decay into sciences. Principles are trimmed down to become even more applicable and manageable. For their part, the sciences decay into technologies, into institutions, and into hangovers for Earth and Nature. With fresh theophanies about World and Nature, as truly greater-than-human realities, with divine grace and a little luck, the process of analytic decay may be given a chance to begin anew with a mystic vision. Thus, inherent in Greek philosophy was not only the possibility of decay. There also was the

Copyrighted Material

possibility of redemption and reform, including religious retreats to divinely graced common sense.

Redemption, or religious retreat from analysis, was implied when Ionian philosophers paused long enough to think about substance or *apeiron* as something "divine"—divine in the holistic Egyptian sense. The Enneadean stream of life, or Atum's seminal emission, is what Anaxagoras fell back on when he envisioned Anaximander's *apeiron* as full of "seeds." That same theology of flux and flow, which initially perhaps had been inspired by the living River Nile, still echoed in the philosophy of Heraclitus when he saw reality as alive and flowing. Plato returned to that same Egyptian theology when, in the *Timaeus*, he summed up his description of the cosmogonic process as God generating an "only-begotten universe." And finally, that same theology of redemption was present when Aristotle struggled to overcome Plato's dichotomy—his static "realm of ideas" versus "objects of sense experience." With his graduated theory of "form and matter," the philosopher Aristotle succeeded in constructing a metaphysical halfway house between Platonic dualism and Egyptian holistic emanationalism.

Greek philosophy eventually won its skirmishes against the old imperialistic gods of the weapon-religion type. It left on its battle-ground the ruined reputations of old overdomestication cults. And it also left in its wake, mired in satire and disdain, the old burlesque myths that supported killing, castration, and other grand domestication tricks. The philosophers then arranged for fresh and cautious rapproachment with Egyptian dynamic monism.

Beyond that, perhaps without really knowing or trying, the Greek philosophers redefined the commonsense context and paved the way for a fresh kind of monotheistic vision. The conceptual decay of monotheism into monism was not irreversible. And behold, in the form of the Christian religion, Greek philosophy later found again a new mythological home—new life for its ancient formal skeleton and its abstract brittle bones. Part Four of this book will give important glimpses of that fresh turning point in the history of Greek and Western civilization.

Copyrighted Material

12

Philosophy: From Thales to Anaxagoras

The history of Greek philosophy begins with the sixth century B.C.E. in the seaport city Miletus, in Ionia along the Western coast of Asia Minor. At the time when the first teachers of science and philosophy were noticed in that Greek settlement, the city had become the most prosperous trade center in all of Hellas. A significant portion of the city's trading capacity was developed with the help of Phoenician middle men. The Milesian city-state also maintained its own colonies. Some of these were located along the eastern shore of the Black Sea.

At the same time Miletus also obtained a strong trading foothold in Egypt. The pharaohs of the Twenty-Sixth Dynasty (663–525 B.C.E.), after they regained independence from Assyria, built a strong mercantile fleet. Their primary trading partner during this renaissance was Greece, and Miletus was the seaport most frequented. Inasmuch as Ionia itself came under Lydian and Persian hegemony, the later Persian takeover of Egypt, under Cambyses, did not unduly disturb the Miletus-Nile connection.

It is with a sense of irony and embarrassment that I, a staunch admirer of Greek civilization, have had to acknowledge that Greek philosophy well nigh had its beginning outside of Greece itself. Had it not been for political unrest, and the migration of refugee scholars to the Greek mainland where Athens enjoyed a quick blossoming under Pericles (460–429 B.C.E.), the torch of Greek philosophy as easily could have been scattered abroad among various Greek colonies and farther west. As it was, philosophy flourished but for a few generations in Athens and perhaps already had passed its climax with the death of Socrates.

Greek philosophy's final and most enduring flower, Neoplatonism, grew and blossomed in a situation similar to that in which the Greek quest for *sophia* had first begun—again in a peripheral Greek settlement. Though Platonic by subsequent appellation, Neoplatonism nevertheless was conceived in Egypt, in the afterglow of ancient Egyptian culture and religion. It took form in a more direct and more intimate relationship with Egyptian theology than even the beginnings of philosophy in Ionia had taken. Neoplatonism was taught by two Egyptian wise men in a Greek colony on Egyptian soil, surrounded by Egyptian culture and quiet ancient religion.

The Milesians

Thales

Thales (ca. 624–548 B.C.E.) gained great renown in Miletus for a number of scientific and technological accomplishments. He is remembered especially for having correctly predicted the year of a solar eclipse that happened on May 22, 585 B.C.E. Diogenes took great pains to tell us, secondhand, how most writers have described Thales as a genuine Milesian who belonged to a distinguished family. All the same, we read in Herodotus (1:170) that his ancestors were Phoenicians.[1]

Historical documentation that traces some of Thales' education to other places along the eastern Mediterranean is unavailable; nevertheless, for a family with Phoenician ancestry some such connections safely may be assumed. All the while, it may be surmised that a man of Thales' intellect, living in a foremost Mediterranean port city, scarcely could have remained ignorant of Mesopotamian and Egyptian thinking. Unfortunately, we have only scant direct information about the cosmogony that formed the backdrop for his philosophy. What we do have matches nicely the remnants that have survived of the teachings of his successors, Anaximander and Anaximenes.

Aristotle considered himself distantly related to the philosophical tradition begun by Thales. He credited Thales with having been the

---

[1]See W. K. C. Guthrie, *A History of Greek Philosophy*, Vol. 1 (Cambridge, 1962), pp. 46, 50. *Copyrighted Material*

first thinker who postulated a "material principle" as underlying the nature or substance of all things. For Thales that "principle is water, and for this reason . . . the earth rests on water." (*Metaph.* A, 983,b, 6ff)[2]

We can spare ourselves the remainder of Aristotle's commentary, by which he gave his own oblique rationalizations as to why the wise Thales might have reasoned the way he did. To the delight of a historian of religions, Aristotle showed himself in that treatise not entirely insensitive to mythological and theological modes of reasoning. But surely, Thales would have been amused by his proponent's loose references to Oceanus, Tethys, and Styx—unless, of course, these references permitted also some kind of overlapping among these divinities with an original Egyptian Nun or watery chaos. The larger context is fairly clear, it seems. Aristotle tried to give historical depth to his own discourses, and he invoked the wisdom of Thales as a convenient early Greek historical benchmark.

This is not to suggest that Aristotle was wrong in his overall assessment of Thales' analytic temperament. One may very much suspect, however, that in this particular instance Aristotle appealed to the wrong mythology. The Egyptian myth, of Atum rising from Nun, that is, of an earthen hill rising from watery chaos, matches Thales' world portrait far better than anything gathered from the disjunctive mythology of Greece. The Greek myths of Hesiod and Homer were ill-suited to support a monistic ontology. Indeed, they had very little material to contribute to the reductionistic approaches of the first Ionian philosophers.

Anaximander

Anaximander (ca. 611–546 B.C.E.) is remembered for having elaborated on the cosmogony of Thales. Like his famous teacher, he assumed a singular homogeneous and living substratum of reality, something unlimited:

> it is neither water nor any other one of the things called elements, but the infinite is something of a different nature, from which

---

[2]Ibid., pp. 45, 55f. Copyrighted Material

came all the heavens and the worlds in them.... And from what source things arise, to that they return of necessity when they are destroyed; for they suffer punishment and make reparation to one another for their injustice according to the order of time, as he says in somewhat poetical language. (Simplicius, *Phys.* 6r; 24,26)[3]

Here we have arrived at a crucial point in early Greek philosophy; namely, at Anaximander's vision of the cosmogonic process whereby the ordered world had come into being. This process is a separating out that, in turn, is brought about by an eternal motion in the *apeiron*. All things come from and return to the *apeiron*, the infinite or boundless substratum of the universe.

Of special interest is information on Anaximander, provided by Theophrastus, as originally given by Eusebius:

He says that at the birth of this cosmos a germ of hot and cold was separated off from the eternal substance, and out of this a sphere of flame grew about the vapour surrounding the earth like the bark round a tree. When this was torn away and shut off in certain rings, the sun, moon, and stars came into existence.[4]

Thus, instead of the more concrete "first" in the cosmos, of Nun as the "water" to which Thales had reference, Anaximander has returned to a more vaporlike and less sensate conceptualization of the Egyptian Nun. From within it he derived the world and then the sun, moon, and stars. All these emanated from the center, successively contained within rings of fire. Indeed, in the orthodox Egyptian context these fiery emanational rings provide a rational pattern for visualization. Atum was the central primeval Hill-Sun from whence all lesser realities came. These successive emanations, spewing from the Hill-Sun center, puffed forth as rings of fire, like a playful smoker may blow smoke rings that emanate.

---

[3]In Milton C. Nahm, ed., *Selections from Early Greek Philosophy* (New York, 1962 [1934]), p. 62.

[4]DK,A,10, in Guthrie, *A History of Greek Philosophy*, pp. 89f.
Copyrighted Material

Anaximander thought of these emanations as some kind of a "seed" substance. This metaphor also can be linked with the Heliopolitan prototype of Atum's seminal emission. And this prototype is documented in the earliest stratum of Egyptian texts. There, too, the godhead's emissions are mentioned as fire or as the light of Ra. Thus, the elements of water, earth, air, and fire about which the Milesians reasoned "scientifically," or "philosophically," can be identified still as distinct divine realities that, in Heliopolitan theology, were present as Nun, Atum, Shu, and Ra, respectively. The dynamic link between Atum and Ra (earthy hill and ecstatic-fiery emanation) is in the later generation of Enneadean gods depreciated from Shu to Geb—thus to Father Earth.

Egyptian paintings of the Heliopolitan hypostasis of Geb and Nut sometimes depict stars as decorations along the arching body of the sky goddess. Stars were places in the sky where light bursts shone forth and became manifest. Moreover, Anaximander's allusion to the cyclic return of all things to the original substratum, along a sequence of emanated worlds, personages, or things, nicely matches the full generational and soteriological cycle of the Heliopolitan system.

Anaximander's notion of "injustice" within the cosmological process had been judged and adjusted in Egypt by Mahet about a millennium and a half before Anaximander. Mahet was the same personal determinant who also ordered the remainder of the cosmos. She, who was the ancient goddess Tefnut renamed, represented order in cosmology as well as "justice" and "righteousness" in the sacerdotal monarchy. In ancient Egypt these two overlapped. Thus, terminology taken from jurisprudence in Anaximander's case was not poetic license, as Simplicius suggested in the first Anaximander passage quoted. These concepts were carried to Ionia part and parcel from Egyptian theology and political theory—by thoughtful travelers, it seems. But, be that as it may, the primary point for us is that these Egyptian notions have been found there.

The singular homogeneous and boundless substratum of Anaximander's All-being was deemed still divine. All those ancient philosophers who did not postulate other external causes, such as Mind or Love, assumed the divine nature of the *apeiron*, as Aristotle affirms:

Copyrighted Material

and this they say is the divine, for it is immortal and imperishable, as Anaximander and most of the writers on nature call it. (*Physics*. 203,b,6)[5]

Thinkers who have not distinguished Mind or Love as agents independent from the *apeiron*, assumed that motivational energies resided within. Thus, any way one turns it, Anaximander's primal substratum of reality remains analogous to the Egyptian godhead's emanation. Egyptian theology thereby has lured, and aggravated, Hellenic analytic minds into a new millennium of mindful "civilized" reflection.

Anaximenes

Anaximenes was a younger contemporary of Anaximander who is remembered for having advanced an alternate cosmology. Like his elder dialogue partner, so too he embraced monistic Egyptian ontology. In this case it should be remembered that, in the tailwind of Amun theology, during the New Kingdom, the Egyptian godhead continued to keep his actual name hidden. Accordingly, the elder Anaximander contemplated a nameless *apeiron*.

By contrast, his successor Anaximenes has boldly identified the unbounded primal substance as air or breath:

Anaximenes of Miletus... calls it air, and says that it differs in rarity and density according to the different substances. Rarefied it becomes fire; condensed, it becomes first wind, then cloud, and when condensed still further water, then earth and stones. Everything else is made of these. He too postulated eternal motion, which is indeed the cause of the change. (Simplicius, *Phys*. 24.26,A5)[6]

Appreciative philosophers, such as W. K. C. Guthrie, have done what can be done to preserve Anaximenes' theory of rarefaction and condensation as something philosophically reasonable or even

---

[5]In ibid., pp. 87ff.

[6]In ibid., p. 121.

Copyrighted Material

honorably scientific.[7] After all, a cofounder of Greek philosophy and Western science deserves to be remembered with respect. And it is not the intention of this book to detract from any credit that might have accrued to this ancient thinker along the science trail in history.

However, on behalf of Egyptian predecessors of Ionian philosophy, it is necessary to insist that a millennium and a half earlier some Egyptian minds had concluded that Shu, present as air, was sufficient to account for the entire plethora of Atum's emanations. That tendency is clearly traceable in the Coffin Texts and has been delineated in Part One of this book. It should be remembered that Shu was life-breath and was also understood, more concretely, as representing Atum's seminal emission; he continued the creative "spitting" of Atum.

Ancient priestly minds indeed have envisioned Atum's seminal emissions, or emanations, as radiating outward from an invisible center toward a periphery that had greater visibility and concreteness. Thus, it would not have been at all difficult for them to accommodate Anaximenes by simply referring to that emanational process, in the direction of greater visibility, as *condensation*.

And, inversely, anyone who now reconsiders the theophany of the sun god Ra, or an Egyptian soul's funerary rite for its return journey in the company of the sun god, also will have to grant that these ancient Egyptian thinkers were able to reason homeward; that is, about processes of "refinement" or about the "rarefaction" of visible substances, of air back into fire and light. These considerations point to the conclusion that Anaximenes, as much as Thales and Anaximander before him, still "lived, moved, and had his being" in Egyptian cosmogony and cosmology—as does anyone today, still, who understands this quote from the New Testament a little.

Pythagoras

Pythagoras (ca. 570–? B.C.E.) was a philosopher who came from Samos, an island facing the Ionian coast. We do not know how highly he thought of his three Ionian contemporaries; probably not overly so.

---

[7]Ibid., pp. 119ff.   Copyrighted Material

But we do know that he shied away from their general tendency of materialistically objectifying aspects of the larger divine order. Instead he regarded numbers to be the key to understanding the universe and its contents.

In the course of human evolution, nouns and names have come into use to keep track of individual beings—things, animals, or people, and even gods. The application of numbers has permitted keeping track and taking possessions to a greater degree. A person who applies numbers to the world, selfishly, may claim many things as property without ever having to know their individual names or true characteristics. Numerology was invented as a tool for greater control, and numbers justify the depersonalization and extraction of may things from the greater whole of reality and environment.

In the actual struggle for human survival, numbers have been applied to many things. And once numbers were assigned, they sustained the illusion that all things so numbered are small enough to be manipulated by finite human hands; that is, owned harmlessly as numbers and therewith manipulated by proxy. Thus, the utilization of numbers constitutes the sharpest claw of analysis available to the rational human creature. By means of digital faceless labels, the human mind can snatch away many properties and things from what once was considered the domain of greater-than-human personages. And all the while human "con-science" is kept tranquil and under the euphoria of being mathematically correct, and thereby true and justified.

Nevertheless, extreme analytic or scientific "progress" in its reliance on a measure of rationality sooner or later necessitates its opposite—a religious "retreat" posture for balance and sane survival. Accordingly, the Pythagorean predatorial abstraction of the universe into coordinates and numbers, for its balance, demanded a more holistic faith in cosmic harmony. Into this larger harmony—into the "music of the heavenly spheres" to where numbers also can be traced—the mathematician ego of Pythagoras withdrew for personal refuge, for balance and existential comfort.

Pythagoras and his religious brotherhood repented from their mathematical sins of mental progress by living ascetic lives. It is obvious that some greater-than-mathematics reality—that is, the God of cosmos and numbers—scared these mortals back into more

Copyrighted Material

restricted domains. All the while, their ennobled minds remained preoccupied with the hope of somehow escaping their mortality as immortal souls.

Whereas Milesian thinkers evolved their analytic claws, their brain-tipped teeth, for purposes of breaking down the divine visible cosmos into smaller impersonal units and elements, the Pythagoreans dedicated their minds to perfecting the ultimate mental fishing net of abstract mathematics. To the extent that they became aggressively successful they also became religiously frightened.

As frightened *homines religiosi,* the Pythagoreans were destined to develop for their mathematical "science" a matching religious "conscience." This erupted among them especially in their personal eschatology. Practicing initiation and pursuing purification, they knew their souls caught up in a process of transmigration and reincarnation. This religious posture is what, on a personal basis, has furnished a check and balance, or an atonement, for Pythagorean mathematical ambitions and estrangement.

Comparative historians must remember that in India this was the time when the sons of priests began to doubt the Vedas and the efficacy of the grand domestication cult of sacrifices. This was the time when aristocratic warrior sons expressed their dissent even more adamantly, and when throngs of dropout hippie-monks refused to be fascinated any longer by external spectacles of the cultus. Instead, they opted for inward meditational piety. All their new religious ways, their yoga exercises and their philosophical contemplations, henceforth were defined against the backdrop of samsara; that is, against the cosmic process within which entangled souls must transmigrate after death. The souls of those who died anticipated successive rounds or reincarnation, new opportunities for purification in accordance with the law of karma.

It is quite likely, therefore, that Pythagoras had been touched directly by Hinduism. His doctrine of transmigration and reincarnation definitely points in that direction. It is also possible that, along with these religious tenets, some of his mathematics may have come from India as well. Physical as well as mental "progress," and corresponding religious "retreat" behavior tend to accompany one another for survival balance. On the other hand, some of what is now known as Pythagorean mathematics well may have been inspired by

Copyrighted Material

Egypt.[8] But even at that, Pythagoras with his Hindu religion appears thus far to be the least Egyptianized Greek philosopher.

Heraclitus

Heraclitus (ca. 540–480 B.C.E.) lived in Ephesus, a short distance from Miletus which had become the cradle of Greek philosophy. His ontological inheritance was the same general Ionian-Egyptian monism we detected already among the first Milesian philosophers. Historians of philosophy, thus far, have not been very successful in linking Heraclitus to any known "school." On that account, many of this man's aphorisms have been interpreted thus far on the assumption that he was a haughtily independent obscurant, a fabricator of riddles.

Surprisingly, however, when approached from the direction of the Egyptian ontological heritage, the aphorisms of Heraclitus make sense at least as much, if not more, than any of the fragments that survived from the teachings of his Ionian contemporaries. A good place to begin is the following concise summary of Heraclitus, by Diogenes Laertius:

> fire is the element, all things are exchange for fire and come into being by rarefaction and condensation.... All things come into being by conflict of opposites, and the sum of things flows like a stream. Further, all that is is limited and forms one world. And it is alternately born from fire and again resolved into fire in fixed cycles to all eternity.... Of the opposites that which tends to birth or creation is called war and strife, and that which tends to destruction by fire is called concord and peace.... Change he called a pathway up and down, and this determines the birth of the world. (Book 4, 9, 8-12)[9]

---

[8]A spark of practical trigonometry could easily have reached Protagoras from Egypt, while he contemplated and inquired about the ever so conspicuous triangular surfaces of pyramids.

[9]Heraclitus, "Fragments" in Nahm, *Selections from Early Greek Philosophy*, pp. 89–97. All subsequent quotes from Heraclitus are from this source.

Copyrighted Material

The sequence of emanations that Diogenes attributed to Heraclitus begins, one easily can see, with the radiant fire of Ra. Along the downward path of "condensation," fire transforms into moisture; moisture condenses into water; and water congeals into earth. The return path cuts across the same sequence in reverse. Anyone who has seriously contemplated Figure 10, in Chapter 2, will have no difficulty recognizing here the same basic orthodox Egyptian U-turn pattern.

We are also told by Heraclitus that "the sum of things flows like a stream." He could as well have said that it "flows like the seminal emission of Atum." The "fixed cycles" here, of course, do not refer to sequential disappearances and reappearances of entire divine hypostases or bodies. Rather, they are comparable to sectional swirls or eddies that become visible here and there along the total stream of life and being.

As soon as one considers this broader ancient Egyptian perspective the task of explaining some of Heraclitus' *Fragments* is made much easier. So for instance, what should one make of this?

(The earth) is poured out as sea, and measures the same amount as existed before it became earth. (*Fragments* 23)

This cosmogonic moment pertains to the turnaround point at the lower end of the emanational process. The stream of All-being was made visible to us already when moisture is precipitated into water. It was made more solid after water congealed into earth. And all the while the mass or energy of the divine emanation remains constant. For the broader Egyptian context, one should note how in the more distant mythological past, at the ontological center of All-being, Atum arose as a solid hill from amidst Nun, the latter of which remained watery chaos. All the while the total *ka* essence of Atum remained constant.

Human souls are caught up in the emanational outward currents, as they are in the homeward currents. So the question may rightly be asked: How is it that souls ever appear in material bodies? Any adult who ever has participated intimately in this procreative event of reincarnating a soul, and reflected on it afterward, knows that *Fragments* 72 explains it as well as can be done: "It is a delight to souls to become wet."

Copyrighted Material

Here is how a grandfatherly and patient Heliopolitan priest might have explained this Heraclitean puzzle to us, had we visited him in the heyday of his religion. Consider the experience of prospective parents. First they detect "fire" in each others eyes; then they sense "moisture" welling up inside, and externally they exude sweat as well. Invisible sparks of their ecstatic *ka* souls—reflected as gleams in their eyes—swim onward in the aforementioned fluids to mingle and fuse; and amidst those fluids, in time, evolves and grows a tangible human being, a visible *ba*. How? And Why? Because "it is a delight to (*ka*) souls to become wet."

Of course, in the opinion of a Hellenic lover of wisdom, of the stature of Heraclitus, "a dry soul is wisest and best," or, as viewed from a less personal beam of light that radiates from the greater Atum-Ra and All-being, "a dry beam is the wisest and best soul" (*Fragments* 74f). All this simply means that closer to the divine source of soul, at the hypostasis of rarified light and fire, even an individual soul spark beams brighter. At that refined level of Sun and fire a *ka* soul is less passionate, less visible, less wet, and less messy.

What is the intelligence that steers all things in and through all things? Or, what should the creative godhead be named? Religious Greeks have named him Zeus, whereas contemporary wise men in Egypt, of the Theban persuasion, probably would have refused to ascribe any name at all to Amun, the Hidden One. A similar agnosticism concerning the real name of the godhead speaks from *Fragments* 19: "it is willing and is unwilling to be called by the name Zeus."

When Heraclitus spoke religiously about successive emanations of the godhead, about gods in plural form, he considered some of these emanations to be "gods" only in relation to hypostases still lower than they. Thus, whichever is higher can be thought of as "dying" when its dignity is being compromised; when it is lowered beneath a fellow equal or reduced to the level of an even lesser entity. In turn, an entity at a lower level of existence "dies" when it mystically surrenders to be absorbed by a higher one. And all this happens in full accord with the orthodox U-turn pattern of Egyptian theogony and soteriology. Of course, our wise man from Ephesus, as a diligent student of Egyptian priestly riddles, knew how to say all of this more profoundly and succinctly:

Gods are mortals, men are immortals, each living in the other's death and dying in the others' life. (*Fragments* 67)

Copyrighted Material

Having thus commented on only a few samples near the core of Heraclitean ontology, it may no longer be necessary to puzzle about the famous Fragments 41, 42, or 81 at the usual elementary level: "In the same rivers we step and we do not step; we are and we are not." It means that now we are, and that then we are not. Not only is the river going in and out of existence for us from one moment of perception to the next; we ourselves are becoming other kinds of beings by the time our minds and wills have readjusted to step into a river again. We thus concurrently are in two existential conditions—"we are and we are not"—determined by our own upward and downward movements within the larger two-way stream of life and All-being, which itself is flux.

Parmenides

Parmenides (ca. 515–456 B.C.E.) began his philosophical inquiries among the Pythagorean brotherhood at Elea, in southern Italy. Under the spell of Pythagoras, perhaps, he fell heir to a more shamanic perspective on Egyptian ontology. He became known in the history of philosophy for his alleged insistence on the permanence of all being; *permanence* defined vis-à-vis Heraclitus' fascination for flux and becoming. After reexamining both philosophers from the perspective of a possible common Egyptian ontology, this alleged difference now will have to be reconsidered.

Parmenides' insistence on the permanence of being appears to be no more than a semantic echo from his Pythagorean days when, in mathematical language, he habitually dealt with abstract and fixed principles. These eternal principles, supposedly, govern an equally fixed and impersonal system of numerology.

Our chances for understanding either Heraclitus or Parmenides have been severely impaired by interpretations generated by their latter-day progeny, by generations of materialistic philosophers and scientists. In the course of their respective hermeneutical fates, the integrity of Heraclitus was protected by his own obscurantism and love of Egyptian riddles. All the while, the bequest of Parmenides was severely distorted. If Parmenides had a weakness, it was the fact that he took his opponents too seriously. He invested altogether too heavily in the language of Milesian positivism.

Copyrighted Material

Parmenides' religio-metaphysical poem, "The Way of Truth and the Way of Opinion," was defended and fortified by his well-intentioned student Zeno, before the Athenian tribunal, in the very presence of Socrates himself. It was defended against a wrong set of nonreligious questions and on a battlefield already objectified by others. Its religio-ontological and epistemological message thus was permitted to dissipate in the dry dunes of analysis. Instead of recognizing the conclusions Parmenides had reached religiously—and his existential lesson from the depth of what he called his "mental paralysis"—philosophers exploited incidentals in his poem, to be able to imagine for themselves All-being as something inert, something impersonal or dead. By this distortion of Parmenides' philosophy, the predatorial minds of subsequent budding scientists hoped that All-being might become a fair and easier target for experimental control and devastation.

* * *

There is no essential conflict between the teachings of Heraclitus and Parmenides. They describe the same All-being from different momentary human perspectives. For the sake of an adequate comparison and contrast we must refocus our attention once more on Heraclitus, for the length of a paragraph at least.

As a living and a changing mind Heraclitus had remained conceptually within the All-being. Knowing himself as becoming, he participated in All-being's larger process of change and becoming. Heraclitus was fascinated by the dynamics of finite living, and apparently, he also enjoyed swimming and swirling about among the relative currents and eddies in the larger stream of life and being. All the while, Heraclitus was reconciled to his humble destiny of being a small changing bubble of thought, or hype, in the larger mind of God. Like Socrates later, who appealed to the dictum "know thyself," so Heraclitus with a similar haughty sense of superiority, despised those who seemed unaware of this rational need for introspection and sense of finitude. All Greek philosophers have, as have conspicuous leaders in all cultures and situations, generated a contradiction between the surrenderings of their inward ego and the assertions of their external or public ego. In the case of Greek philosophers one must keep in mind that their love of wisdom was an aristocratic brand

Copyrighted Material

of soteriology, meant to be shared with minds of similar haughty temperament and stature.

By contrast, the mind of Parmenides temporarily had wandered off on a transhuman shamanic journey, estranged and severed even from its own ontology. Temporarily the philosopher Parmenides was able to imagine, and achieve, some sort of visionary focus on objectified All-being. And momentarily this reality appeared to his playful analytic predator mind as a perfect sphere—it appeared to his playful kitten mind like an inviting ball of yarn.

At that point Parmenides had not learned, yet, how the All-being could play possum, feign death, when confronted by an analytic predator mind that had been impressed and numbed by its own activity of objectification. Such objectification implied mental fixation and abstraction—thus castration and killing. Heraclitus objectified All-being; and toward him All-being played possum.

We must ask the central question. How did Parmenides achieve his temporary state of transhuman objectivity, which led to the illusion that nothing moves? And what exactly happened when All-being played possum with him? His poem points to a rational method of usurpation on the philosopher's part. He assumed a posture as if to absorb into himself all imaginable motion and commotion. No wonder therefore when all being, apart from himself, seemed motionless by comparison! We must take, at all cost, the relativity of his own testimonial seriously.

A goddess, who assumedly herself was born from within the divine All-being, somewhat like Isis, took Parmenides for a ride. She took him out on that same kind of glorious ride that, in the concrete material world, easily could have resulted in the destruction of cities and fellow humankind. Parmenides traveled on a war chariot drawn by horses and guided by the sun-ray daughters of Father Helios.[10] Entering thus the Egyptian realm of Ra's splendor, our philosopher tells how he left behind "retributive Justice" (i.e., Mahet), holding her key at the gate between darkness and light. Parmenides traveled onward with his personal guardian goddess as on a shamanic-

---

[10]The entire discussion of Parmenides, from here on, will follow the text given in "The Way of Truth and the Way of Opinion," in Nahm, *Selections from Early Greek Philosophy*, pp. 113–121.

Copyrighted Material

philosophic trance journey. His divine female guide kept for him "horses and chariot straight on the high road."

Amidst this personal visionary motion and commotion, and always in hot pursuit of enduring ontological glimpses, Parmenides was destined to learn his first ontological lesson about All-being. He experienced relative motion between observer and observed. From his fast-moving point of view, in a chariot somewhere out there in nowhere, Parmenides looked back and, objectifyingly, beheld All-being. Thus he distinguished the "abiding essence of persuasive truth" from ordinary "men's opinions in which rests no true belief." And the All-abiding essence of persuasive truth, being mirrored, held, and fixed as abstract concept in the mind of Parmenides, showed no sign of motion. Meanwhile Parmenides completely overlooked the fact that he himself was still contained within that same, now conceptually fixed and abstracted, All-being. And that fact, suddenly, invalidated the entire logic of his motion-packed trance journey. Not knowing that this was so was his tragic mistake.

Such forgetfulness, in the presence of the less forgetful gods, shows off human finitude with unforgiving severity. And it may safely be assumed that Parmenides' sun-maiden escorts, his enlighten-ment mistresses, succeeded by their divinely flirtatious demeanor to dull the otherwise sharp wits of this philosopher. Comparatively speaking, it may be worthwhile to contemplate how even in the ordinary world ordinary sun rays occasionally strike philosophically less gifted human brains with similar paralyzing effects.

The first lesson taught by the goddess seems simple enough. "Whatever is is." All could have been well, amidst the splendor of all that light, had Parmenides not overvalued his own sense of sight and light. Had his mind at the moment been capable of interface with other sense data, such as touch, sound, taste, and smell, he could have heard and smelled that his horses and the chariot containing his own presence, were still part of a sensate swirl within All-being. But, as it was, in his state of supervisionary hype and sensual deprivation, the bubble of Parmenides' thought mistakenly was perceived equal to All-being.

As formerly, during mathematical trance, the realm of numbers became a statically fixed All-being for Pythagoras—and as later for Plato the realm of "ideas" became static—so in this instance the mind of Parmenides has held on to All-being in an objectified state. An objectified mental world no longer is a world, and therefore it no

Copyrighted Material

longer lives and moves. This mental habit of freezing the world portrait, by fixation or objectification, has become commonplace among the many scientific descendants of this philosopher. Objectification serves foremostly as the justification for experimenting with and controlling docile less-than-human things.

But let us not do unto Parmenides as his own friends have done to him—friends for whom his now motionless tongue is sufficient proof that, indeed, he must have taught the immobility of all things. This is no way to treat an ancestor whose legacy of words still speaks as clearly as our own contemporaries. We gladly grant him the ability to consider greater-than-human configurations of reality, among other things:

> Therefore thinking and that by reason of which thought exists are one and the same thing, for you will not find thinking without the *being* from which it receives its name. Nor is there nor will there be anything apart from being; for fate has linked it together, so that it is a whole and immovable.... (p. 117:94–99)

What then about the nature of All-being? Of its existence? Its multiplicity? Its immobility? Its completeness? Its homogeneity and unity? Has Parmenides really intended his words to be useful for a positivistic conquest of God and World, as if both together were an inert corpse? Midway during his statement, just quoted, while he contemplated last movements or twitchings, Parmenides achieved a very sharp focus of introspection on his habit of objectification toward All-being. He perceived the gentle movement of Fate, actively "linking together" into an immovable whole—not "immobility together with All-being" as commentators on Parmenides frequently tell us—but he perceived his own "thinking" as it encountered All-being. There is a tremendous difference between these two readings: a difference of life and death for either Parmenides or All-being.

And behold! Parmenides' individualized thinking and All-being, after being fused together, became instantly immobilized. Instantly, that is, as soon as his objective thought was brought in contact with the living presence of All-being. It was like a kiss of death to him. His analytic thoughts had the efficacy of serpentine venom.

But now we must consider the crucial point. Inasmuch as both sides, the philosopher's thought process and perceived All-being, seemed to have become immobilized together, the poor man had no
Copyrighted Material

way of knowing which of the two had actually fallen victim to the other. Nor, on the basis of his testimony, have we.

In its paralyzed condition, the dazed mind of Parmenides was barely able to finish the remainder of its poem. The man was reduced to where he had to finish his discourse with an admitted play on empty names and words. I shall continue Parmenides' statement, quoted earlier, by repeating its last phrase for the sake of better continuity:

> so that it is a whole and immovable. Wherefore all these things will be but a name, all these things which mortals determined in the belief that they were true.... (p. 117:99–102)

Parmenides' first lesson had stunned his mind. How so? Did this happen because he gazed upon objectified reality? Of course not; rather, his mind was immobilized because it contemplated All-being *as if it were* an objectifiable reality. This kind of self-centered thinking could not help but overload and short out his mental circuits. He noticed himself gazing upon the whole All-being and discovered that he himself was missing in that objectified one and only realm of being.

Gazing on All-being from a constantly changing distance, as from a moving celestial war chariot, happens to be a very dangerous undertaking. The philosopher's sharp mind instantly sensed that it had fallen a victim to itself, into mortal danger; and for a supposedly immortal Greek mind to get into that condition was reason enough to become scared and freeze over. Having caught itself AWOL from All-being, arrested by his own conscience, Parmenides accepted for a moment his mind's own death sentence.

To translate this simple metaphorical assessment into philosophically respectable terminology one might say, summarily, that the very hype of Parmenides' own epistemology, which claimed for itself the status of ontology, is what has done him in. What Parmenides gave us was no longer legitimate existential ontology. Instead, it was epistemological paralysis.

It may be useful to recall how for similar reasons a man named Moses, who had come under the spell of Egyptian wisdom long before Parmenides' time, had learned that "man shall not see God and live" (*Exodus* 33:20). In Parmenides' case this meant that he who saw

Copyrighted Material

All-being, without seeing himself included in it, was doomed by his own logic to collapse into immobility and apparent nonbeing. Or still more precisely, his mind has chosen for itself a content of static notions, thus unverifiable nonbeing. Animal instincts from the long process of evolution still betray the minds of *homines sapientes*. Human predator minds, like most advanced predators on this planet, chase after and can grasp only what previously has been sensed as moving.

Fortunately, the goddess who initially had lured him into estrangement from All-being let Parmenides down gently. "Trustworthy discourse" on All-being went blank in the philosopher's mind. Now, as a confessed and a finite mortal, Parmenides therefore was instructed to learn, instead, more about "these things which mortals determined," thus, about opinions current among mortals. Pure monism was too much to ponder. Parmenides was given dichotomy as second best.

> On the one hand there is the aethereal flame of fire, fine, rarefied, everywhere identical with itself and not identical with its opposite; and on the other hand, opposed to the first, is the second principle, flameless darkness, dense and heavy in character. . . . (p. 118:116–121)

With the extremities of ethereal fire and heavy darkness thus having been placed safely out of reach for human hands and minds, Parmenides proceeded to describe the range of emanational hypostases in between. He was fully aware that between his "one hand" and his "other hand" there extended the divine body of All-being. This body existed, nearer to its center, as circles or wreaths of rarefied fire. Toward the outer periphery it appeared increasingly mixed with darkness. Thus, All-being is surrounded by "the second principle" of solid darkness, according to the forementioned quotation.

In accordance with this basic dualistic conceptualization, some Parmenidean specifics now follow that nicely match the Egyptian emanationalism with which we have become already familiar:

> And the smaller circles are filled with unmixed fire, and those next them with darkness into which their portion of light pene-

Copyrighted Material

trates; in the midst of these is the divinity who directs the course of all. (118:125–130)

This divinity who "in the midst of these" directs the course of all is the godhead of orthodox Egyptian theology. And inasmuch as this divinity still "directs," it certainly is acknowledged here outside the realm of the proverbial Parmenidean inertia. Only the Egyptian gender emphasis is reversed here to accommodate Greek Hesiodic theography, or the primacy of Gaia over Uranos. What else can one expect of someone who does his thinking under the spell of a goddess! Parmenides knew that a "she" devised first love.

Elsewhere, in a more intense confrontation, we are given a hint to the effect that Parmenides might have thought of this central deity as Fate. In our present context this does not really matter, because we know, specifically, what this divinity did by way of continuous activity. She devised love. That same activity also was the first function of Atum's hand, and of Shu and Tefnut subsequently.

Parmenides had returned from his poetic trance journey on the high road, so it seems, reconciled to Egyptian ontology. He was ready to humble himself by learning less important notions about "the wandering deeds of the round-eyed moon" (the eye of Horus). He contemplated "the sky (Nut) surrounding all, whence it arose, and how necessity took it and chained it so as to serve as a limit (Tefnut and Nut) to the courses of the stars." The writers of ancient Egyptian coffin spells definitely were better at describing these sorts of things than Parmenides. But he was a Greek who introduced Egyptian wisdom to his kindred secondhand. He did the best he could.

One interesting comparison remains to be made with the Parmenidean "cosmos devoid of motion." As the hyperactive biblical warrior Joshua is said to have seen the sun stand still (*Joshua* 10:13), so too the mentally hyperactive Parmenides saw All-being motionless during a few visionary trance moments. But then, finite beings who stop short of pari-nirvana must return to paradises of a lesser kind. Parmenides returned smack into orthodox Egyptian ontology. And there, in this cosmos among emanations between light and darkness, between invisibility and visibility, he moved about. From there he lived and died and rose. Or, as an Egyptian wise man might have said, he has had, he has, and he will have his being there. His moments of transient perception are of little consequence.

Copyrighted Material

The Pluralists

For better or for worse, the philosophy of Parmenides and of his defender Zeno have left the impression on analytic minds that All-being is motionless and passive. Whereas such a conclusion would have been in line with Hesiodic castration theology, it would have been unthinkable, if not blasphemous, in the original context of Egyptian monotheism. As much as some later Greek philosophers protested the works of Hesiod and Homer, to the effect that poets have slandered the gods by ascribing scandalous behavior to them, they as philosophers were still children of the same great Mother Earth.

The scandalous behavior of Cronos became the archetypal method for Greek philosophy. It was Cronos who first "immobilized" and "depersonalized" the All-father Uranos; and it was the popularized version of Parmenides' philosophy that applied the analytic sickle to the remainder of All-being as well. Hesiod established the mythological archetype for all subsequent analytic or philosophical treatment of deity and reality, and all philosophers and scientists in pursuit of analysis and experimentation have subscribed to that approach ever since.

Analytic minds are like advanced predators, and advanced predator species, as a rule, shun potential victims that permanently lie still. For the sake of greater excitement, most predators prefer to hunt animals that still are alive and afoot. But then, having once sensed a potential prey as moving about freely, these predators will not rest until their victim is laid low—immobilized, butchered, and abstracted to suit their appetites and fancies.

With the upper half of the Greek cosmos having been neutered by Hesiod, the keen predator minds of the first Ionian philosophers directed their analytic curiosity toward a theology that, at the time, was being carried abroad from Egypt still somewhat alive. Greek analytic thinkers then dealt with the Egyptian All-being with mixed success. Parmenides abstracted from All-being, abstracted even his own moving self in the process. He did so even though his own self afterward was sorely missed in his ontological inventory.

Heirs of Parmenides, by not knowing themselves relatively in motion in celestial chariots, have continued to subtract motion from

Copyrighted Material

All-being all the while. It took several generations of Greek philosophers to be able to explain this conceived absence of motion in All-being, alongside the obstinate apparent presence of motion in the sensual dimension of human existence. The prime years of Greek philosophy were spent on resolving this disparity between permanence and being, on the one hand, and flux and becoming, on the other. Egyptian theologians easily would have diagnosed debates of this sort as the futile life-and-death struggles of mortal humankind with the living God and within his own world emanation. The Egyptian All-God, hidden and unknown, after all, was beyond the reach of Cronos' sickle, and beyond the abstracting scalpels of analytic humanoid predator minds.

Historians of religions, who nowadays concern themselves with the larger evolutionary process, will have no difficulty seeing in the classical philosophical discourses an intellectualized repetition of ancestral hunters' guilt. Pluralistic philosophers, in the Parmenidean tradition, many times have reenacted the moments during which primitive hunters stood, after a stately animal has just been brought down, and contemplated the inflicted stillness of the carcass. Not many novel conflicts happen in the world of predators, nor among all the predator minds together under Helios! Such pursuits, bites, and balancing bites of conscience are of great antiquity.

The experience or the maintenance of life and motion, after Parmenides, needed no longer distract philosophers from "progress," especially not those who came to be classified as pluralists; that is, Empedocles, Anaxagoras, Leucippus, Democritus, Epicurus, and Lucretius. They all invented different ways to analyze, divide, or to cut apart the All-being that the Parmenidean misperception had stunned—stunned sufficiently for a butchering feast—for modern warfare with science and technology, to have begun.

Empedocles

Empedocles (ca. 493–433 B.C.E.), in the paralyzed body of All-being, no longer could perceive any traces of divine life. He no longer could perceive, much less enjoy, those mysterious qualitative mutations from one wonderful hypostasis into a next. Since the onset of Greek philosophy, earlier divine manifestations had been analytically distinguished from their source, as well as from one another.

Copyrighted Material

They had become immutable "roots"; that is, root elements of fire, air, earth, and water. Though these elements had been depersonalized and abstracted, it is not difficult to recognize that the first three of these realities were original manifestations of the Egyptian godhead; that is, Hellenized theoretical "corpses" of three living Egyptian hypostases—Ra (as fire), Shu (as air), and Geb (as earth). By the same method of analysis, an inert liquid had been abstracted from the virile seminal flow of Atum. An impersonal element was postulated. It was water.

The attempt by Empedocles, to dignify his abstracted elements by identifying each again with an old deity of the Hellenic tradition, resulted only in the redefinition of these gods at some points closer to the philosopher's elements—and their implied demise. In the construction of such ontological equations, it always happens that the less understood is absorbed into whatever is better understood. Look at this!

Hear first [of] the four roots of all things: bright Zeus, life-giving Hera (air), and Aidoneus (earth), and Nestis who moistens the springs of men with her tears.

And a second thing I will tell thee: There is no origination of anything that is mortal, nor yet any end in baneful death; but only mixture and separation of what is mixed, but men call this "origination." (*Fragments* 33–34)[11]

This half-hearted attempt by Empedocles to revitalize his basic categories, or root elements, by linking them to Greek polytheism seems almost pitiful. Monotheism for analytic minds defaults into monism (i.e., monism describes God from whom life has been abstracted), and polytheism defaults into pluralism. All modes of depersonalization in this universe, and all modes of human progress, are accomplished at the expense of the living gods, or of a living God.

What, in Empedocles' fourfold world, accounts for life and motion? What or who does the mixing and the separating of elemental roots? As efficient causes for this process he named Love and Strife.

---

[11]Empedocles, "Fragments" in Nahm, *Selections from Early Greek Philosophy*, pp. 128–144.

Copyrighted Material

But what were Love and Strife apart from personal beings who now were mere aggregates mixed together? Set in an almost Buddhist context of "origination," Love and Strife as analytically ascertained efficient causes were no more than the inert extracts of what used to be the living souls of Aphrodite and Mars. They had become abstractions who depended for their mobility on a new set of godlike beings—on philosophers who, alone among the world's intellectual beings, were left to ascribe efficacy or withhold it from the configurations of reality for which they had become managers and definers.

Anaxagoras

Anaxagoras (ca.500–428 B.C.E.) was an older contemporary of Empedocles, and to him he responded. He, too, denied the ontological status of "coming into being" and "perishing." The general pattern he saw in the universe resembled the one Empedocles already had postulated. But a selection of only four elements, mixing and separating, seemed overly simple and crude to him. He therefore postulated a creative Mind that issued forth an infinite number—and watch this!—of first principles or "seeds."

Over against the Egyptian heritage we can recognize instantly the "novelty" of this idea of Anaxagoras. Procedurally, he disagreed with Empedocles' dissolution of four hypostases of the godhead into four separate elements. But then, as a first aid remedy to this depersonalization of reality he attempted to return to basic orthodox Egyptian process theology. The stream of All-being still could be explained best by him as an infinite number of "seeds" flowing, joining, and separating—as if still within an unnameable Egyptian godhead's seminal flow.

From such a postulate, which is traceable to the land of the Nile, Anaxagoras deduced his ontology of "seeds." But his aim was not to establish an Egyptian cult. On the contrary, he contributed to Greek philosophy and made his intellectual progeny ever more curious about what kinds of distinct small seeds actually do exist within All-being—seeds awaiting analysis by human minds and manipulation by hands.

The remaining pluralists, the atomists Leucippus, Democritus and Epicurus need not be discussed to provide additional perspective for

Copyrighted Material

this book. Their contributions lead off in the opposite direction. Once the principles of division and subtraction had been applied in philosophical methodology, predator teeth and appetites could finish off what was left.

Philosophical debates, thereafter, needed to concern themselves only with analytic "scientific" questions, about how much smaller first principles, atoms, or seeds should be imagined for easier manipulation and experimentation. If they were imagined large enough to be still somehow visible, reasoning could proceed quantitatively. Whenever they were too small to be seen, philosophical discussion continued, just the same, on the basis of distinguishing qualities inherent in things. But then, qualities in turn could be quantified, abstractly, along numbered and arbitrary scales.

For down-to-earth industry and applied sciences, pluralistic thought was a blessing. It provided many more pieces and fragments that could be gathered, owned, and brought under control. Thus, the numerology of those religiously timid Pythagoreans has served philosophers and scientists well—as it had served ambitious domesticators and grand domesticators earlier.

Copyrighted Material

Copyrighted Material

13

Philosophy:
Socrates, Plato, Aristotle

For the purpose of merely showing the dependency of Greek philosophy on ancient Egyptian ontology, one could stop at this point in the history of philosophy and sketch nothing further. Continuity of subject matter between the Egyptian parent ontology and her offspring among the founders of Greek philosophy has been displayed sufficiently. Anyone who wishes to reconfirm that overview need only read Part One of this book comparatively, together with what already has been written here in Part Three.

But then, Greek philosophy not only has had its past, it also has contributed to the future. Socrates, Plato, and Aristotle have become the most famous philosophers of classical Greece. And then, beginning with the first century C.E., students of philosophy in the Graeco-Roman world were destined to interact increasingly with another glow of Egypt-inspired spirituality, which as a spark had escaped from "Hebrew Fire." It was the Christian gospel.

Athenian analytic rationality, especially that of Plato and Aristotle, and their successors, squeezed the life juices from many a remaining grand domestication religion within range of the Hellenistic influence. The cultural landscapes were left dry and ready for fresh religious brush fires, and new life, to start up after the conflagrations. Many new religious syncretisms and universalistic cults flourished and were tolerated within the intellectual climate of the philosophy-illuminated Graeco-Roman civilization. Then the brush fire of Christian "kingdom of heaven" soteriology, a Hebrew-Egyptian spark of spirituality, swept the Graeco-Roman lands and grew into a large conflagration. It illuminated and reshaped the life rhythms of Western civilization from within, beginning at urban centers and spreading to the countryside. Neoplatonic philosophy and soteriology, spreading

Copyrighted Material

from Alexandria during the third century C.E., played a significant role during the institutionalization phase of early Christendom.

Socrates

Socrates (ca. 469–399 B.C.E.), the principal founder of Greek philosophy in Athens, need be mentioned here only in passing. The fact that this discussion will pay less attention to Socrates than to some of his Ionian predecessors may indeed seem unfair. However, the motive for this abridgement is not to deprive Socrates of his rightful place in the annals of intellectual history. Nor has it been our aim to write here a full historical sketch of Greek philosophy or revise the biographical sketches of those who are considered to be philosophers. All these tasks have been done more thoroughly by other historians. Our aim here is to show enough of ontology, cosmogony, and cosmology to expose the ideological continuity between ancient Egyptian theology and what, in Ionia and Athens, became "philosophy."

In his younger years the man Socrates, like most progressive minds of his time, was attracted to the study of natural science. This implies that he seriously concerned himself with the Egyptian-Ionian ontological tradition already sketched in the preceding chapter. But by the time Socrates finally became acquainted with the younger Plato, his social conscience already had matured to a point where he preferred to dwell on questions of ethics and socio-political reform.

Socrates placed his hope on the honest confrontation of *logos;* thus, on the direct rational struggle for truth. Of course, this is not to say that he failed to appreciate playfulness in his discussions. But, in comparison to the Confucian way, his was a more boisterous aristocratic puppy play.

The philosophical method of Socrates was designed to educate leaders for a still youthful and confident Hellenic civilization, one that was not yet very far removed from the parent hunter-herder-bandit cultures that earlier on the prairies of Eurasia had developed a taste for horsemanship, adventure, heroism, and epic poetry. Sparks from the eyes of these ancestral horsemen, from their horse-and-glory ethos of heroism, still glowed in the eyes of Socrates and his contemporaries. His own confidence in the positive power of intellect, and in its

Copyrighted Material

direct applicability to the ordering of human society, still drew from the well-spring of that same positive fighting spirit.

The confidence Socrates placed on the ability of human reason knew few bounds. It remained unshaken to his death. To steer the Hellenic virgin intellect in the direction of a rational and humane political order, Socrates baited young aspirants with puzzles and enduring existential questions. He lured them into membership in his intellectual aristocracy. Admission into that circle of philosopher friends had to be earned by rational discourse, by a kind of mental dueling.

People from lower social classes, whose menial labors and struggles had numbed and humbled their spirits, generally had little appreciation for the Athenian philosopher and the progeny of wise guys who sought out his company. Yes, his methods of interrogation inspired some bright young men of leisure to intellectual competition, to self-confidence and the perfection of mental skills. But these same methods quite easily alienated ordinary folk. The haughtiness of philosophers inflicted intellectual defeat on ordinary slow-witted folk. Their embarrassments festered and frequently aggravated into hate. Enough Athenian people disliked Socrates in 399 when the death sentence was proposed at his trial, and the motion passed.

Plato

The primary aspect of the philosophy of Plato (427–347 B.C.E.) that needs to be summarized here is his famous theory of "ideas." We offer some statements from the *Timaeus* to suggest a few clues concerning his cosmological orientation.

Indeed, the theory of "ideas" is central to Plato's system. With its help he achieved a position of compromise between Parmenides' supposed insistence on permanence and Heraclites' emphasis on life as flux. Accordingly, Platonic "ideas" *are*, whereas things in the sensible realm are merely caught up in a process of *becoming*. The data obtained concerning objects of sense experience are known to fluctuate and change. These data only "share" or "participate" temporarily in the intelligible world, in the realm of "ideas."

While contemplating the Socratic-Platonic theory of "ideas" from the point of view of a more nominalistic and process-conscious

Copyrighted Material

epistemology, a critical perspective is called for. All inclusive plurals or universal ideas, as these are abstracted from their concrete and specific associations in the visible world—that is, once they have been committed to memory and fixed as word symbols or as Platonic "ideas"—will be envisioned necessarily and self-servingly by finite minds as worthwhile and eternally valid. Finite minds will grasp anything that promises eternity.

In contrast to "ideas," which in memory reappear as permanent and fixed, the sense-experiential world naturally appears transient, changing, and therefore less dependable. To mortal eyes and hands, who would like to grasp and possess eternity, the dimension of finite experiences will never satisfy completely nor lastingly.

Plato intuited his universal "ideas" as realities that transcend sense data. He regarded them as real beings that, themselves, participate in still greater units of permanence. Of course, Plato presumed that universal "ideas" were more than just inert (i.e., memorized) symbology. He postulated the notion that his ideas participate in the most permanent kind of reality. As all sense objects that come into human awareness "participate" in "ideas" at some lower level, thinkable by human minds, so all these same lower-level ideas themselves may be regarded as participating in more inclusive and greater, but equally permanent, ideas. And so this hierarchy of ideas extends to where it culminates on high in the still more-inclusive ideas of Goodness, Truth, and Beauty.

Within the domain of human recollection, these more-inclusive "ideas" can be traced further, metaphorically speaking, to ever larger accumulations of inert generality where, formally and logically, they may be envisioned as "sharing" or as "participating" in still-greater reality. The most inclusive and supreme, the most lastingly fixed sum of all goodness, truth, and beauty is the *summum bonum*, is the *GOOD* itself.

Looking back at Plato through the eyes of his younger contemporary, the philosopher Aristotle, the eternal Platonic "ideas" represent an ontology by which life and motion could not be adequately explained. In response to this deficiency, Aristotle introduced his own doctrine of no less than four distinct causes: material, formal, efficient or motive, and final causes. Could one, five, or a hundred distinct causes, perceived through analysis, have gotten Aristotle's universe better into motion under the auspices of his

Copyrighted Material

unmoved and unmoving Prime Mover? Cosmogonically speaking, that seems doubtful.

Every historian of philosophy sooner or later will be confronted with the fact that the world of every Greek philosopher in the footsteps of Hesiod has tended to come apart at some seam: along some fine line of demarcation between heaven and earth, between being and becoming, between a conceptually fixed reality and the changing apparitions of still throbbing life.

In the *Timaeus*

The most elaborate textual source for Plato's cosmology is a dialogue named after its primary speaker, Timaeus. It generally is agreed that this character, who in the dialogue converses with Socrates, speaks as a proponent of Plato and so expresses the writer's own ideas. The dialogue format therefore was the philosopher-playwright's convenient way of raising a number of weak cosmological hypotheses without risking his personal reputation. Religious theogonies and scientific cosmologies from different ages, and of variable credulity, have so been given a voice in this treatise.

Whether Plato's speculations in the *Timaeus* actually are believable anymore, or whether they should now be discarded, is of no great concern for this historical task. For the time being we are interested in exploring the presence of Egyptian traces in Plato's ontology.

Posterity has made use of the *Timaeus* in a great variety of ways. The so-called Middle Platonists and Neoplatonists in Alexandria favored the *Timaeus* for what many modern philosophers have come to regard as its weakness—for its voracious variety. This loosely structured treatise enabled Neoplatonists to remain within the sphere of Greek philosophy and, at the same time, dip heavily into their long-lost substratum of Egyptian wisdom, to their hearts' content.

Christian theologians naturally preferred the *Timaeus* to other Platonic works. In the dialogue's underlayment of Egyptian ontology they discovered a natural affinity with their own christology and theology. After all, Christendom was born from, and overtaken by, the same Alexandrian-Hellenistic undercurrent of Egyptian theological notions that entrapped a Porphyry and a Saint Augustine. Both men embraced the Egyptian process theology under the guise of religiously

Copyrighted Material

neutral philosophy. Each did so for different reasons, of course. With its amazing openness toward the ancient Egyptian ontological core, which has puzzled students of Plato ever since, the *Timaeus* eventually provided materials for building a bridge, a rational bridge of rapproachment between Christian theology and Platonic philosophy.

Egypt Romanticized.—The major dialogue portion of the *Timaeus* is introduced by a quaint secondhand tale; and that tale is traced to an old priest who served the goddess Neith, in Sais, Egypt. The significance is not in what Plato makes Timaeus communicate about Egypt. In light of the fact that the Egyptian priest shared only historicized Athenian conceit, that amount of communication seems almost negligible. The tale contains fantasies about the fabled glory of ancient Athens, nine thousand years earlier, and a thousand years before the city of Sais itself had been founded.

Such a tale, obviously, amounts to no more than a round of self-congratulation on the part of members of the Athenian philosophers' club. Moreover, the goddess Neith was deemed significant only to the extent that she could be identified with Athena. By the same token, Plato's knowledge about the Nile being Egypt's never-failing savior and about the fact that Egyptians know stories about many floods is of the superficial type, like the gossip of Greek tourists or traders.

Nevertheless, the intellectual dependence of Greece on ancient Egyptian tradition is implicit throughout this introductory tale. The assertion made by the very old Egyptian priest, to the effect that in comparison with Egyptian sages "Hellenes are never anything but children" and that "in mind [they] are all young" (*Timaeus*. 22b), is not contested by Socrates in the course of the dialogue, nor by anyone else. So, although specific evidence of Plato's familiarity with Egyptian culture and religion is lacking, the reader nevertheless is left with the distinct impression that, in Plato's own estimate, Egyptian wisdom preceded Greek *sophia*. And this fabled Egyptian prehistory, in all likelihood, was meant to vouch for what the character Timaeus was about to teach at the behest of Plato.

The Cosmogony.—Even though he was introduced as an astronomer, Timaeus quickly comes around to one of Plato's own central concerns: the distinction between Parmenidean *being* and Heraclitean *becoming*, or, eternal "ideas" vis-à-vis "objects" of sense experience:

Copyrighted Material

First then, in my judgement, we must make a distinction and ask, What is that which always is and has no becoming, and what is that which is always becoming and never is? That which is apprehended by intelligence and reason is always in the same state, but that which is conceived by opinion with the help of sensation and without reason is always in a process of becoming and perishing and never really is. (*Timaeus* 27d–28a)[1]

The method by which the universe was created is explained at the very outset. It assumes a generative process that, although mentioned repeatedly, never is questioned throughout the dialogue: "The creator made this world of generation" (*Timaeus* 29d). And, when the creator framed the universe, "he put intelligence in soul, and soul in body...the world came into being—a living creature truly endowed with soul and intelligence by the providence of God" (30b). The original universe is and was invisible; it "contains in itself all intelligible beings, just as this world comprehends us and all other visible creatures" (30c–d). Timaeus calls the realm that includes all intelligible creatures the "one only-begotten and created heaven" (31b), and thereby he specified this divine process of generation as essentially having been one of procreation.

True to the pre-Socratic tradition of Greek philosophy, Plato gives precedence to the "biological nature" of this living and only-begotten universe, over and above the need for clarifying astronomical structures. Ontological concerns predominate here over bare cosmological questions. Plato's relational density scale, applied to the four elements of his "bio-physics" so to speak, is the traditional Ionian one.

"As fire is to air so is air to water, and as air is to water so is water to earth" (*Timaeus* 32b). The universe is a "creature" spherical in shape, soul diffuses from its center throughout its body and represents "a circle moving in a circle." As far as soul is concerned, "in origin and excellence" it or she "is prior to and older than the body" (*Timaeus* 34a–c). The creator has "formed within her the corporeal universe" (36d). And "when the father and creator saw the

---

[1] *Collected Dialogues of Plato*, ed. Edith Hamilton and Huntington Cairns, (Princeton, N.J., 1963), pp. 1151–1211. All translations from the "Timaeus," herein, are quoted by permission of Princeton University Press.
Copyrighted Material

creature which he had made moving and living, the created image of the eternal gods, he rejoiced" (37c).

The actual arrangement of sun, moon, and planets in orbits around the earth was made by God for the establishment of time: "The sun and moon and five other stars, which are called the planets, were created by him in order to distinguish and preserve the numbers of time... he placed them in orbits... in seven orbits seven stars." The moon was placed in the nearest orbit circling earth, next the sun, then the morning star and the star sacred to Hermes (*Timaeus* 38c–d). Over against these moving stars, for contrast, "the fixed stars were created, to be divine and eternal animals, ever abiding and revolving after the same manner and on the same spot" (40b).

Interlude.—Two very interesting paragraphs follow here (*Timaeus* 40d–41a). Timaeus pleaded agnosia with regard to knowing something about "the other divinities." As a mature individual he goes along with the folk wisdom to the effect that one "must accept the traditions of the men of old time who affirm themselves to be the offspring of the gods—that is what they say—and they must surely have known their own ancestors." Subtle irony here is transposed, rhetorically and without wasting an extra word, into mild satire: "How can we doubt the word of the children of the gods?"

It appears as though the Greek gods, mentioned next, were added only for good measure. Oceanus and Thethys as children of Earth and Heaven, along with Phorcys, Cronos, and Rhea; Zeus and Hera. Together they seem almost as foreign to the cosmology of the *Timaeus* as the arbitrary insertion of an American Indian "Earth Diver" origin myth would have been. These paragraphs represent no more than a courteous bow in the direction of Greek mythology and religion. They were intended to excuse the writer from having to relate seriously to his Hellenic religious heritage. Plato hurried to return to what, earlier, we already identified as orthodox Egyptian ontology.

Toward a Hellenic Tefnut.—Earth herself is first introduced as "our nurse" (*Timaeus* 40b). It appears as though Plato is careful here, so as not to present her as a potential equal partner of God the father. Earth is definitely situated at the opposite end along Plato's invisibility-visibility continuum. This reading is supported by the fact that

Copyrighted Material

later (49b) the "receptacle" or "nurse of all generation," or "mother" (50c–d), embraces the entire creation, not only earth.

On that larger cosmic scale the receiving principle is mother, whereas the source and well-spring of all being is father. The entire creation is the creator's generation or offspring. If there were no castration plot in Hesiod's theogony it would be conceivable, up to this point, that this portion of Plato's vision of the universe could be traced to some Greek Father Heaven and Mother Earth mythology. But as the case happens to be, Plato's statements rest solidly on an Egyptian basis. We may suspect that he had an inkling about this. Why else, with all his Athenian pride, would he have Egyptianized this dialogue from the outset with an exotic tall tale about Athens and Sais?

The road back to Hesiodic theogony, or to general Indo-European religion, was efficiently blocked by Plato himself. The first mother he had in mind resembles far more the invisible and receptive Tefnut than Hesiod's concrete Mother Earth:

> the mother and receptacle of all created and visible and in any way sensible things is not to be termed earth or air or fire or water, or any of their compounds, or any of the elements from which these are derived, but is an invisible and formless being which receives all things and in some mysterious way partakes of the intelligible, and is most incomprehensible (*Timaeus* 51a–b).

This Platonic statement almost certainly earlier, at Heliopolis, would have passed as an adequate description of Tefnut and her matching polarity in relation to Shu. The amazing thing is that Plato does not even stop at this point of rapproachment to Egyptian orthodoxy. He does not let this postulated invisible mother dangle, so to speak, from his Platonic heaven of eternal "ideas." Instead, Plato assures us that fire inflames her from time to time, that water moistens her, and that her motherly substance becomes earth and air (*Timaeus* 51b). She indeed is the full Tefnut, Atum's receptacle "hand," and the All-Mother of the Heliopolitan universe.

Pythagorean Numerology.—Traces of Pythagorean number mysticism and geometric structuralism are frequent in Plato's *Timaeus*, especially in sections 43–44 and 53c–57d. In all likelihood, Plato had his theory of "ideas" already in place by the time he exposed his

Copyrighted Material

mind to Pythagoreans in southern Italy. Moreover, their numerological key to the cosmos could be accommodated easily into his much broader "theory of ideas." For Plato the invisible world of Pythagorean numerical abstractions became simply another dimension, another register or level, within the greater realm of eternal "ideas."

The pragmatic continuity between numbers and words already was alluded to in the preceding chapter, in the section on Pythagoras and his place in the history of Greek philosophy. Ciphers or numbers correspond in their function to words or names; but they differ from words and names in that they have been subjugated more severely to the human mind and will. To be specific, numbers are faceless "names or words," deprived of personal or individual characteristics, reduced and thereby grasped more easily, possessed and manipulated for manipulation's sake.

Number "ideas" do match Platonic word "ideas" quite nicely. But they furnish greater confidence and greater justification of human assertiveness vis-à-vis the cosmos—much more control than name "ideas" can provide. Inasmuch as numbers can help us reduce greater reality configurations to smaller manageables, they also can contribute significantly to shore up our otherwise finite philosophers' and scientists' egos.

In the same manner in which "numbers" in Plato's mind have become fused with "ideas," so both of these were deemed to fuse in the mind of God. Therefore, "when the world began to get into order . . . God now fashioned them by form and number . . . as far as possible the fairest and best, out of things which [initially] were not fair and good" (*Timaeus* 53b).

Souls and Salvation.—The creator has delegated the task of creating mortal animate beings on earth to his first generation of offspring, the immortal gods. But before assigning this task to the firstborn gods, the creator himself made a great number of immortal souls, equal in number to the stars (*Timaeus* 41a–e). Lesser gods then created mortal bodies, and into these they incorporated the immortal souls that God himself had made. Not being the creation of a single Father throughout, the unions of immortal souls and mortal bodies are temporary arrangements. Moreover, the immortal principle of reason thereby is assigned the task of transforming or sublimating the mortal portion, or as Plato writes, "to draw in its train the turbulent mob of

Copyrighted Material

later accretions made up of fire and air and water and earth" (42c).[2] The immortal soul, guided by reason, thus is given the task of achieving some kind of victory over the sensate and irrational dimension of a human being. For its reward the soul is returned to its better and original divine state.

But then, Hindu notions about samsara and karma, introduced into the *Timaeus* perhaps together with a heavy presence of Pythagorean number mysticism and fueled by philosophers' intellectual elitism, left Plato with a rather twisted notion concerning soteriology for a total humankind:

> He who lived well during his appointed time was to return and dwell in his native star, and there he would have a blessed and congenial existence. But if he failed in attaining this, at the second birth he would pass into a woman, and if, when in that state of being, he did not desist from evil, he would continually be changed into some brute who resembled him in the evil nature which he had acquired. (*Timaeus* 42b-c)

The Summary. —A quick glance at Plato's concluding sentences in the *Timaeus* will help place his larger conceptual framework into the broader Egyptian-Hellenic perspective postulated by this book:

> We may now say that our discourse about the nature of the universe has an end. The world has received animals, mortal and immortal, and is fulfilled with them, and has become the visible animal containing the visible—the sensible God who is the image of the intellectual, the greatest, best, fairest, most perfect—the one only-begotten heaven. (*Timaeus* 92c)

If contemplated for its ontology and structure, from the greater to the smaller, this summary statement recognizes an Intellect-God who is the greatest, best, fairest, and most perfect. No doubt, Plato associ-

---

[2]The soteriology described here may be understood as a reversal of direction, a reversal of the creative descent of the soul, as described by Wordsworth in "trailing clouds of glory we have come from God, who is our home." However, Plato's return journey here seems more like "trailing billows of fury and weight."

Copyrighted Material

ates with this Intellect-God his entire realm of "ideas"; that is, associates them at some point prior to where distinctions are made among strata or levels of these "ideas." So far so good. But are the sensible and the intellectual manifestations of God, together, called *the one only-begotten heaven?* Separately as well as jointly, either of these implies a more supreme begetter who exists beyond the static and sterile realm of Platonic "ideas."

I doubt whether Plato knew very much directly about ancient Egyptian theology. But he inferred enough from the implied "living" or "divine cosmos" that had been presupposed by most of his Greek predecessors in philosophy. When the inertness of his abstract "ideas" disappointed him, Plato, like everyone else, was forced to think of the remaining cosmos as being somehow alive. In this manner the philosopher ended by assuming a godhead who could "beget" intelligent as well as living offspring.

Of course such a conclusion, obtained while reasoning from the God's offspring, is ontologically inverted. Nevertheless, in the context of concrete existential living, the philosopher Plato, like everyone else, comfortably inferred the greater from the presence of the lesser; and then, he told his tale of deduction forward from the greater cause to the lesser effect.

The visible universe that Plato contemplated was a God; that is, one that was begotten by the higher invisible Intellect-God and creator of souls. In turn, that visible universe "conceived"[3] its animals with all the implied philosophical-zoological ambiguity: "Of the divine, he himself was the creator, but the creation of the mortal he committed to his offspring" (*Timaeus* 69c).

Gnostic prophets and teachers, especially those inclined toward Iranian dualism, made much of Plato's ever so slight Hesiodic separation between God and his mixed and mortal offspring. Plato's profane metaphor portrays God as mixing immortal souls with lesser elements, as in an ordinary "bowl—as if taking souls and lesser elements from separate realms." The unity that existed in Heliopolitan

---

[3]Conception somewhere between the Intelligible and Sensible realms can be read in the philosophical sense as "conceiving" an idea. At the next lower or sense-object level it can be taken to mean the conception of bodies. Both belong to the same process of divine procreation and begetting. The presence of this dual meaning of *conception* in our English language still may be appreciated as a trace of our Egyptian-Platonic heritage.

Copyrighted Material

emanationalism, between the godhead and humanity, thereby conceptually is severed. In spite of Plato's earlier protestations to the contrary, the rightness of Cronos' deed thereby was underwritten by the philosopher himself, after all, in the *Timaeus*.

Aristotle

A half generation later the philosopher Aristotle (384–322 B.C.E.) has attempted, somewhat half-heartedly, to heal the Hesiodic wound in his own learned way. This former student of Plato was dissatisfied with the gash his mentor seemed to have cut, as a line of separation, across his entire ontology between the static reality of "ideas" (the sterilized Father Heaven) and the realm of transient sense experience (the fruitful Mother Earth).[4]

Between Earth and Heaven

With the healing hand of a physician, Aristotle arranged Plato's "ideas" along the vertical continuum of a hierarchy. He arranged them as convertible "forms" that, individually, could be seen as imposed on inversely convertible stratified "matter." That is to say, a higher "form" (formerly a Platonic "idea") contains a lower form as its "matter." For example, an entity such as a "chair" constitutes matter (i.e., content) in relation to the larger form "furniture," whereas "chair" at the same time also provides shape or form to the "wood" it contains. Thus, in this next context of a lower order, "chair" is form whereas "wood" is matter. Furniture, chair, and wood are so interrelated hierarchically, participating as entities in some next higher form and embracing a next lower as matter. They may be so distinguished from one another as belonging to different levels of reality—to different degrees of potentiality or actuality—but as form and matter they are interrelated.

---

[4]In presenting Plato's ontology, we for obvious reasons relied heavily on his most Egyptianized dialogue, the *Timaeus*. In other Platonic dialogues the dichotomy of "ideas" and "objects of sense experience" is more explicit. Aristotle's response therefore must be appreciated in the larger context of Plato's writings.

Copyrighted Material

Levels of reality are so knitted together in a hierarchy from the highest to the lowest. Pure matter, the lowest, is pure potentiality, whereas pure form, the highest, is actuality. In Aristotle's astronomy these designations are applied to a single geo-centric universe—to a single cosmic hierarchy of beings that range from matter and earth here below all the way up to pure actuality, the Prime Mover.

By this stairway of forms and matter Aristotle attempted to subdivide the primary line of ontological separation—the line which divides Plato's realm of ideas from his realm of sense experience, or, the old slash by which Cronos cut apart Heaven and Earth—into many smaller and therefore less gruesome incisions. His conceptual stairway, paralleled with the attributes of potentiality (for matter) and actuality (for form), extends so from earth to the outer perimeter of the universe, to the Prime Mover.

However, the famous student of Plato was unable to heal the Uranos wound by this method. Even the best analytic mind, with many smaller analytic cuttings, cannot subdivide a large cut back to its former state of uncut wholeness. A human mind can imagine only how to divide or to "cut up" the larger wound, hypothetically, into smaller ones. In real life, a wound treated in this manner invariably is enlarged, at least for the duration that predator minds continue to gnaw at it analytically.

By way of his questionable science of astronomy, not by way of his surgical metaphysics, the philosopher Aristotle most showed his Hesiodic hand. His model of a perfectly circular universe had earth at its center, with earth representing the low level of matter and potentiality at the same time. This earth is encircled by spheres that, like her, all contemplate in succession some higher moving celestial body, some higher epicycle, or some higher orbit of motion. Inasmuch as Greek philosophers disliked infinite regresses, it seemed reasonable that there should be a farthest circling star or sphere that has no concrete and moving celestial entity left to contemplate. Beyond that outer sphere, surrounding and extending beyond, is the Prime Mover.

Though everything else moves beneath him and on account of him, Aristotle assures us that the divine Prime Mover is himself an Unmoved Mover (*Physics* 5). This first mover has no limit or magnitude and is situated at the circumference of the Eudoxian-Aristotelian world (10). Aristotle ruled out the possibility of having the Prime Mover create movement by either pushing or pulling. Thus,

Copyrighted Material

in his *Metaphysics* he derived motion in the universe from the fact that the Prime Mover still represents "an object of desire" on account of which other entities move.[5] This finally implies that this God not only is unmoved by someone else, but he himself also may be unmoving.

As a mental First Cause who himself is thought of, here, as contemplating after the fashion of an armchair philosopher and who exists beyond the planets, this First Mover demonstrates no physical motion. Being "pure form" and mind he only can contemplate motion. He thinks about motion unencumbered by the uncertainties being displayed at the lowest matter-laden earth or by her physical rhythms of commotion and productivity.

The Legacy of Hesiod

Centuries before philosophers pondered these matters abstractly, the Greek heavenly Father, "mythologically" if you like, lost his ability and his desire to be an active participant in creation. This celestial inaction of Aristotle's First Cause of the universe resembles, remarkably well, the condition of Hesiod's once forcibly retired Father Heaven. At least since the days of Hesiod the Greek Father-god of Heaven no longer was able to actively affect the productivity and the life of Mother Earth, or life on her. All contemplation of celestial motion that leads to responsive motion on Earth, in Hesiod's as well as in Aristotle's system, happens from desires awakened in lower regions.

All the while, a dynamic Earth still moves and continually renews her landscapes and generates fresh life. She produces mortal nourishment for her mortal offspring to thrive on. In contrast, the anciently castrated Greek Father of Heaven is left by Aristotle to contemplate the motion to which his paternal energies no longer can contribute actively. He seems to have barely enough energy left to contemplate what motion might be, apart from himself.

The epistemological fact of the matter is that, in a self-centered philosophical perspective, the human activity of thinking conveniently presents itself as the cause of all motion. Modeled after the contents of a human mind, Aristotle's farthest celestial reality thereby is

---

[5]See W. D. Ross, *Aristotle*, (Cleveland, 1959), pp. 95f, 175ff.

Copyrighted Material

dedicated to the comprehension of ideas. Motion, after all its associations with matter have been subtracted, is motion at its purest, pure form and actuality. Indeed, only a divine mind, and just possibly yet a philosopher's mind, can comprehend that kind of "motion."

Eudoxus of Knidos

Of course, there is more to Aristotle's story than a Platonic education and Hesiodic mythology. Aristotle also has learned a few things from the astronomer and mathematician Eudoxus of Knidos (ca. 400–350 B.C.E.), a teacher who once went to Egypt and shaved his head. He lived with Egyptian priests for sixteen months in order to learn from them.[6] It can be assumed that a man of the caliber of Eudoxus, while undergoing such inconveniences, sought out Egypt's most prominent thinkers to make his efforts worth his while.

Unfortunately, we can trace the teachings of Eudoxus only indirectly by way of the imprint they have left on Aristotle. So, whatever value still can be attributed to the geocentric astronomy of Eudoxus and Aristotle, two and a half millennia later, it will necessarily have been reduced to what their doctrines appear to have added to Western intellectual history.

Based on what already is known about Egyptian theology, it no longer should be difficult to envision how something like the geocentric astronomy of Eudoxus could have been concocted in Egypt —by a Greek materialist dabbling in Egyptian theology. All one needed for a start was Heliopolitan orthodox theology. When astronomical observations are added to the emanational Atum theology, the Eudoxian astronomy comes nicely into focus. It comes into focus together with Aristotle's metaphysics of "forms and matter" that was based on, or at least harmonized with, that same hybrid of emanational astronomy.

Over against the Egyptian theological background, surprisingly, even Aristotle's astronomy begins to make some sense. Heavenly bodies move as they can be observed, and creative thought-power still somehow can be traced back through its levels of emanation to a

---

[6]Diogenes Laertius, VIII 86–89; in Martin Bernal, *Black Athena* (New Brunswick, N.J., 1987), pp. 103, 108, 514. Copyrighted Material

distant Atum-like source. A semblance of harmony between Egyptian theology and Greek scientific observation thereby has been achieved.

But obviously, there is also a problem associated with Eudoxian geocentric astronomy when it is contemplated in relation to its orthodox Egyptian setting. Egyptian ontology with its Atum-Ra or "Hill-Sun" synthesis was geocentric as well as heliocentric. By contrast, the cosmology of Aristotle and Eudoxus was only geocentric. Eudoxian astronomy lacked the creative motion of the Egyptian model according to which motion, as well as intelligence, emanated together from the same source and direction. Motion in Heliopolitan theogony was accounted for as the central godhead's seminal emission, in his shining, his radiation, his spitting, and later in Memphite theology in his speaking of commands.

The Greek mythico-philosophical background, however, which had inherited Hesiod's castrated or immobilized Father Sky and which assumed that motion originates from Earth and her son Cronos and from her remaining progeny, blocked the full Egyptian two-way path of reasoning for Aristotle. It distorted Egypt's larger mythology of emanation for him. This much is certain, that without some concrete mythological underpinnings the abstract foam of any analytic philosophy, or science, dissolves into nothing—deprived of ontological foundation as well as of ethos.

Egyptian Metaphysics

Let us for a moment nevertheless consider the positive side of Aristotle's thought. What made him want to heal the Hesiodic wound? We may never know the full answer to this question. Long before Pascal's ditty was being recited—to the effect that the heart has reasons of which reason does not know—the "heart" of an Egyptian thinker had reasons of which Greek "reason" understood relatively little. But Greek minds nevertheless were attracted to Egyptian thoughtful "hearts" (compare the Memphite theology in Chapter 5).

We therefore must restate our question: Was Aristotle's metaphysics of "form and matter" perchance also a philosophy born from an Egyptianized heart? If Aristotle's starting point is seen as a confrontation with Plato's implied ontological dualism, then we can truly say that in response he set out on a path of reasoning toward orthodox Egyptian monistic process theology. The challenge to reconcile his

Copyrighted Material

philosophy with Eudoxian-Egyptian astronomy could have stimulated him to think along the line of this implicit rapproachment. Even though Aristotle ended up building a metaphysical stairway of forms and matter—with many steps to match the progression of genus and differentia in his scheme of classifications—he nevertheless also managed to restore therewith some sort of continuity that resembled the Egyptian emanationalism.

Inasmuch as Aristotle characterized Earth and "matter" together as "potentiality," and the Prime Mover and "pure form" together as "actuality," he insisted implicitly on some ontological cohesion from heaven on high all the way down to the dark earth. Thus the only important difference that remained, between Aristotelian and Egyptian cosmology, was the assumption that the first cause of motion in the universe was not at the center of the universe. For Aristotle this first cause was diffused along the outskirts of his known world. He obviously was led to this conclusion in an attempt to still conform to the whereabouts of the Hesiodic impotent Uranos.

But then, if no real life energy was emanating from Aristotle's Prime Mover, at least thoughts of motion were being inspired beneath him by his sheer benign presence. Somehow this retired sky deity has remained an object of desire, in conformity to the Egyptian godhead. Somehow the universe still moved, if no longer by divine desire from above, then at least by creaturely desires from below.

It seems as though Aristotle struggled, even yet at this point, to repair his inverted structure of Egyptian ontology and cosmology with a genuine glimpse of Egyptian soteriology. The nostalgia expressed by lower entities toward the distant Prime Mover, as toward pure actuality and an object of their desire, still reminds us of the homeward yearning of Heliopolitan *ka* souls toward Atum. Only—the celestial bodies in Aristotle's universe do not return home to the Prime Mover, as Egyptian *ka* essences did. This demonstrates the fact that cosmology, by itself, does not make a complete soteriology make.

The final victory of overcoming the spell of Hesiodic separation, in the history of Greek philosophy, was left to two other men who were not only Greek philosophers but also Egyptians: Ammonius Saccas and Plotinus.

Copyrighted Material

14

The Neo-Egyptian Philosophy of Plotinus

Plotinus conceptualized Supreme Divinity as a trinity that manifests itself in three hypostases: as One, as Mind, and as Soul. The prototypes of these hypostases still can be traced in the history of Egyptian thought to the first three divinities who make up the basis of the Heliopolitan Ennead: Atum-Ra, Tefnut-Mahet, and Shu. These correspond in the philosophy of Plotinus to the One, Mind, and Soul. To designate each of his three hypostases Plotinus had recourse to a number of synonyms. Inasmuch as some of these designations will occur frequently throughout this chapter, they must be introduced here.[1]

Plotinus in Brief

The One

The Greek term *to proton* is translated most simply as the *One*. It also is called the *First*, the *Good*, the *Simple*, the *Absolute*, the *Transcendent*, the *Infinite*, the *Unconditioned*, and sometimes even the *Father*, and the *God*. The One is unknowable, beyond evaluation, and transcends our concepts of ordinary being. What can be predicated

---

[1]For this summary I have availed myself especially of the translator's "Extracts from the Explanatory Matter in the First Translation," in *Plotinus: The Enneads,* trans. Stephen MacKenna (New York, 1962) pp. xxi–xxxiv.

Copyrighted Material

about its existence is only that "nonexistence" would be a wrong ascription. The One also is beyond thought, because thought implies analytic distinctions; and analytic distinctions, in turn, imply the presence of parts and therefore also the possibility of deficiencies and imperfections.

The Mind

MacKenna translates *nous* most often as Intellectual Principle. It is also given as Divine Thought and Universal Intelligence; or, as the first something of which existence can be predicated. It is the act, the offspring, as well as the unseen "image" of the One; it is a mediation with the unknowable One. Its function is to know. *Nous* or Mind is the highest something knowable or approachable by human minds. In that sense it also may be named *Spirit* or *Supreme Soul*.

Together with the Divine Mind, with Divine Intellection, or with the Divine-Intellectual-Principle, so too plurality alongside complexity and multiplicity have their beginning. Mind is the Intelligible Universe or the totality of Divine Thoughts. The content of the Divine Mind is the "ideas" of Platonic philosophy.

Like the One from which they emanate, so too the Platonic "ideas" are real beings, eternal originals, archetypes, and intellectual forms of whatever exists in the lower spheres. The Intelligible Universe extends to, or encompasses, all particular minds and intelligences that—metaphorically speaking and still unseen—are the images, representations, phantasms, or reflections of the invisible Universal or Divine Mind. All the progressively degenerate beings, which emanate from the One on down in the direction of lowly matter, which happens to be the faintest presence of Real Being, nevertheless are more realistically present, concurrently, as archetypes or Platonic "ideas" within reach of the hypostasis of Divine Thought.

Divine Intellection operates two-directionally. Downwardly or outwardly it generates creative power that, in turn, displays Thought with increasing degrees of visibility; whereas upwardly it contemplates its still more invisible source, the One. The visibility or concreteness of the Mind hypostasis increases thus along the path of emanation or descent. At the same time, Mind generates such Real Being as can be found, still, in conditions that prevail within the reaches of the next hypostasis.

Copyrighted Material

The Soul

The lowest hypostasis of the Plotinian trinity is *psyche* or Soul, the All Soul, Universal Soul, or Soul of the All. After the manner in which Mind is an emanation of the One, so Soul is an emanation of the One and Mind together.

In the same manner of a two-directional orientation as the aforementioned hypostasis, of outward and return flow within the range of Mind, so too the Soul has its dual tendencies. Its high-soul aspect contemplates the Intellectual Principle or Mind, whereas its low-soul aspect may be identified as the effective Logos or Creative Word of the Universe.[2] At the level where humankind exists, the low-soul aspect generates body as a temporary home; but following its embodiment, that concretely situated human soul experiences a desire to return homeward. Nostalgically the soul contemplates or retraces its way, homeward, first toward the Intellectual Principle all the while longing for closeness with the One, and then returning beyond, merging into the One.

The All Soul, which is downward oriented, creatively with involvements along its low-soul dimension, becomes involved along its high-soul dimension in upward contemplation. In the downward or outward dimension, soul is the cause of all visible movements and forms. It is the cause of the visible cosmos and world, of everything that can be experienced by the human five senses. The All Soul comprises all emanating sparks of high and low soul together.[3]

* * *

Thus, the Plotinian trinity is an entirety that is manifest in three hypostases. Within these hypostases a singular stream of generative

---

[2]It is truly amazing how the continuity of meaning between Atum's seminal emission, attested in the Pyramid and Coffin Texts and the creative words of Ptah, has been maintained by this late neo-Egyptian philosopher-theologian. *High soul* corresponds to *ka*, and *low soul* corresponds to *ba*—as in the Heliopolitan and Memphite theologies in Part One of this book.

[3]Or, in orthodox Egyptian language, all sparks of *ka* as well as all lower apparitions of *ba*.

Copyrighted Material

creativity or vitality flows outward from the One, all the way toward *meon* or matter, which shows off the outer edge of Real Being in general and Soul in particular. Along this outer edge the souls, elements of the All Soul and Real Being, turn inward upon themselves to initiate a counter current that flows homeward again into the One.

For conceptualization, using the metaphor of light, it may be helpful to visualize the outward flow of "generation" and the homeward flow of "contemplation" together along a luminous and shiny spectrum ranging from light to darkness. The One is represented in that spectrum as the source of all light—of light so bright that the human eye is unable to distinguish content. Psychologically speaking, the One can be said to transcend all human faculties of perception and knowledge. At the opposite or darkened end of the spectrum, Soul as Real Being fades out into sluggish materiality by way of becoming visible and creating body. Soul, at its lowest or outermost extremity, stops itself just short of non-Being.

What, in the larger context corresponds then to the hypostasis of Mind? It is represented by the intermediate portion on the total spectrum, between the unknowable One and the visible Soul. The contents of Mind are invisible but knowable.

If radiation of light, as it affects whole mortal persons, is to be chosen as the metaphor for our discourse, then intellectual en*lighten*ment at the level of mind transcends, but corresponds analogically to the enjoyment of visible *light* rays in the lower realm where soul has become visible through involvement with matter. At the outer reaches of this radiation, souls become visible and involved in sensate bodies. In that lower realm, the experience of light is brought within the range of vision by the "shadows" of nonbeing. Souls, at that level, therefore are enabled to sense the purer light rays of luminous bodies in contrast with the shadows of nonbeing in which they themselves have become existentially involved.

Thus, whereas for Plotinus there are three hypostases, there is only one source, one essence, and one movement that along its outer reaches coils in unto itself, defensively. There is only one reality, one godhead, one process. All of being, or, All Being, which makes up this process, is considered good. Only the absence of detectable being, the happenstance of void or nonbeing, from a transient human perspective can be experienced or described as apparent evil. In this context the category of "evil" therefore indicates merely directionality for the soul. If the soul were able to continue further in the direction

Copyrighted Material

of matter and nonbeing, presumably it would vanish forever. But that will never happen. Soul is a manifestation of All Being. As such it will adhere to Being and keep returning.

Samples from the Sixth Ennead

The extant writings of Plotinus are fifty-four essays or treatises that have been gathered by Porphyry into six Enneads—six volumes containing nine essays each. It is clear that these essays initially had not been written to make sense in their present sequence as *Enneads*. Any one Ennead, and even certain portions within an Ennead, may be approached as an independent unit. Individually and taken together, all of them attempt to explain a single reality. They represent variations on a single theme, on the All Being and its emanation.

This book has limited aims and therefore provides commentary on only two Enneads. The Sixth Ennead will be utilized here as a wide-angle lens, to assist our focus on the larger ontology and total process. The Fifth Ennead will be consulted for a more specific view on Plotinian trinitarianism.

To begin our readings somewhere in the Sixth Ennead, we shall take a hint from Emile Brehier who, in a lecture on "The Orientalism of Plotinus," in 1921–1922, suggested that "the fourth and fifth treatises of the sixth Ennead...can be easily read without any reference to Greek philosophy."[4] Similar observations can be made regarding other Enneads. In any case, we begin with a quick preview of the climax endings of the treatises that Brehier has singled out.

An Egyptian Clue in VI,4

A discussion of the omnipresence of Soul, in the fourth treatise of the Sixth Ennead, concludes with statements that easily could pass for meditations on ancient Egyptian funerary liturgy:

---

[4]Emile Brehier, *The Philosophy of Plotinus*, trans. Joseph Thomas (Chicago, 1958), p. 111.   Copyrighted Material

As for the entry into the World of the Shades, if this means into the unseen, that is its [the soul's] release; if into some lower place, there is nothing strange in that, since even here the soul is taken to be where the body is, in place with the body... (*Enneads* VI,4,16)[5]

This afterlife anticipation offers comfort for the time when funerary rites must be performed for deceased mortals. What follows after these words of assurance reintroduces a dualism of souls that is not foreign to Egyptologists; namely, the distinction of authentic soul (the *ka*) and image soul (the *ba*). Elsewhere Plotinus has identified these as *high soul* and *low soul*.

But on the dissolution of the body?

So long as the image-soul has not been discarded, clearly the higher will be where that is; if, on the contrary, the higher has been completely emancipated by philosophic discipline, the image-soul may well go alone to that lower place, the authentic passing uncontaminated into the Intellectual, separated from that image but none the less the soul entire.

Let the image—offspring of the individuality—fare as it may, the true soul when it turns its light upon itself, chooses the higher and by that choice blends into the All, neither acting now nor extinct. (*Enneads* VI,4,16)

The *ka* ascends, and as it does it returns to blend with the All, all the while approaching and seeking its future in the direction of the One. The high soul's former association with a soul, the soul-generated body, the body's condition as corpse, and even all ghostly or "prehuman flux" *ba* apparitions following death remain behind to disappear eventually in the shadow play of nonbeing, of which they are temporary instances. Body and corpse were never more than images. After light is withdrawn no reality is left in what used to be

---

[5]For this sketch of Plotinian philosophy the new Armstrong translation has been consulted, but quotations nevertheless have been chosen from the freer MacKenna translation for easier access by nonspecialist readers. See *The Enneads* by Plotinus, trans. Stephen MacKenna, (New York, 1962). Quoted by permission of Faber and Faber Ltd. *Copyrighted Material*

a shadow. The authentic *ka* energy therefore reunites and blends with divinity, the *ka* of the All.

An Egyptian Clue in VI,5

Looking for a moment to the culminating sentences of the fifth treatise of the Sixth Ennead that Brehier has mentioned as reflecting an extra-Greek origin, we find the same theory of soul. Only nonbeing, we are told, is abandoned as the authentic high soul travels, purified and whole, toward the hypostasis of Mind and homeward beyond.

> you become an All. No doubt you were always that, but there has been an addition and by that addition you are [were] diminished; for the addition was . . . from non-Being. It is not by some admixture of non-Being that one becomes an entire, but by putting non-Being away.

Visibility and apparitions result from turning away from All-being, and from looking toward its opposite, nonbeing. Plotinus then moved on to illustrations concerning general folk religiosity. It must be kept in mind that he does not rationalize here the existence of lesser gods, as if he were pursuing philosophical apologetics. On the contrary! The philosophy of Plotinus becomes more relevant, here, by its capacity to make its basic tenets agree with those of popular religion. Apparitions of lesser popular gods happen, as Plotinus concedes, under well-known circumstances.

> the gods who "in many guises seek our cities"; but there is That Other whom the cities seek, and all the earth and heaven—Him who is everywhere self-abiding and from whom derives Being and the Real Beings [i.e., Ideas] down to Soul and Life, all bound to Him and so moving to that unity which by its very lack of extension is infinite. (*Enneads* VI,5,12)

One cannot help but be impressed by the summary statement of the seventh treatise. The emanational process of the All is explained, there, as a sequence of dependent hypostases:

Copyrighted Material

Soul dependent upon Intellectual-Principle and Intellectual Principle upon the Good, all is linked to the Supreme by intermediaries, some close, some nearing those of the closer attachment, while the order of sense stands remotest, dependent upon soul. (*Enneads* VI,7,42)

Inasmuch as no attribute pertaining to the Supreme Good is thinkable—inasmuch as it extends beyond ideas and attributions—all relationships and dependencies must be explained from the perspective of the lower hypostases. Sense experience happens in the domain of soul. Then Soul is dependent on Intellectual Principle or Mind; whereas Intellectual Principle is dependent on the Good or Supreme One. Envisioned objectively, the continuum, which from the One extends down and outward to some lowly sensate soul, in the Enneads repeatedly has been characterized as emanation, radiation, or flow. The beginnings of this conceptualization of the total dynamic process can be traced, convincingly, to ancient Heliopolitan mythology.

Does not the aforementioned passage also make reference to Plato's supreme Idea of the Good? Indeed it seems so. But does this mean that Plotinus borrowed his total ontological vision from Plato's Dialogues? The more one contemplates the words of Plotinus in their Egyptian context, the more obvious it becomes that *Good* was used here to communicate the orthodox Egyptian notion of the godhead—of Atum, Ptah, or Amun—to Greek minds. The writings of Greek philosophers, together with their specialized philosophical vocabulary, for Plotinus foremostly were a tool for dialogue. With their help he was able to communicate with the intelligentsia of Graeco-Roman colonial culture. Although he so shared his basic Egyptian ontological orientation, Greek philosophies were of only limited use to Plotinus.

Samples from the Fifth Ennead

Greek ontology is built largely on nouns. Platonic ontology, in particular, has contributed to this idolatry of nouns by its habit of elevating many nouns to the status of eternal "ideas." Plotinus' ontology, we now can see, has not been shaped so much by contemplating the static nouns or "ideas" that Platonic philosophy left inertly on a bier; rather, it has been affected by the way an inherited

Copyrighted Material

Egyptian theology could be paraphrased in the idiom of Greek philosophy. Inasmuch as the godhead of Egyptian orthodoxy always has been beyond the reach of human conceptualization, and descriptive names or nouns always have been viewed with playful suspicion by Egyptian theologians, the process verbs have become more significant.

At the same time, verbs that describe the divine process of emanation ordinarily have escaped notice among Plotinus' critics who, all along, had been predisposed toward "Hesiodic" Hellenism. This is not to say that Plotinus taught theology underhandedly. As far as his religious openness is concerned, he was not even afraid of pointing to the godhead as an "All Father." In addition, Plotinus never hesitated to describe this All Father's creative activity as a virile process of engendering.

No further discussion of this basic feature is necessary, at this point, except to say that some emphases in italics will be added to the quotes from the Enneads which follow. Our purpose is to highlight some significant verbs or verbalizations that specifically characterize the emanational activity of the godhead as a process of engendering and bringing home.

Ennead V,1,1

Porphyry placed the treatise "On the Three Principal Hypostases" at the beginning of the Fifth or "theological" Ennead. This treatise is perhaps the most important among those that have paved Neoplatonism's inroads on Christendom. Eusebius of Caesarea, Basil, Augustine, Cyril, and Theodoret all quoted from it.[6] Plotinus began his discussion at the human level of existence; that is, with the fact of divine creation or our soul's estrangement from God. Throughout Part One of this book the reader will have found that this was a favorite theme in the ancient Egyptian funerary cult as well.

> What can it be that has brought the souls to *forget* the father, God, and, though members of the Divine and entirely of that world, to *ignore* at once themselves and it?

---

[6] See Paul Henry, "The Place of Plotinus in the History of Thought," in *Plotinus: The Enneads*, trans. Stephen MacKenna (New York, 1962), p. xliv and note 6.

Copyrighted Material

The evil that has overtaken them has its source in self-will...
(i.e.) *desire for self-ownership ... drifting* further and further they
came to lose even the thought of their origin in the Divine.
(V,1,1)

The epistemology implied by these sentences describes, accordingly, the existential upward and homeward yearning of Plotinus' own
estranged soul. His epistemology and ontology are the road map for
his return journey to God. His philosophical doctrines, in fact, are
soteriology.

Ennead V,1,2

After the existential position of his soul has been determined and
plotted, soteriologically and epistemologically, Plotinus focused on his
position in life as the starting point for his ontology.

Let every soul *recall*, then, at the outset the truth that *soul is the
author* of all living things, that it has *breathed the life* into them
all, whatever is nourished by earth and sea, all the creatures of
the air, the divine stars in the sky; it *is the maker* of the sun;
itself *formed* and *ordered* this vast heaven and *conducts* all that
rhythmic motion... (all these living things) gather or dissolve as
soul brings them life or abandons them, but soul, since it never
can abandon itself, is of eternal being.

Continuing with this postulate of the soul's eternal and divine
nature, the discussion that follows moves from the smaller human
souls to the presence of still greater souls, to such who have not
succumbed to the downward lure that bewitched and estranged the
souls of ordinary humankind. Without soul, in Plotinus's words, there
would be only "stark body—clay and water—or, rather, the blankness
of matter, the absence of Being, and, as an author says, 'the excretion
of the Gods.'" In search of that greater Soul and to better understand
its nature and power, Plotinus contemplated the heavenly system in
the upward direction:

By the power of the Soul the manifold and diverse heavenly
system is a unit: through soul this universe is a God: and *the sun*

Copyrighted Material

is a God because it is ensouled; so too the stars; and whatsoever we ourselves may be, it is all in virtue of soul; for "dead is viler than dung."

This, by which the gods are divine, must be the oldest God of them all: and our own soul is of that same Ideal nature... (it is) honourable above all that is bodily. For what is body but earth.?

Plotinus still points here from the human condition to higher divinities, such as the universe, the sun, and the stars. These are divinities to the extent that Soul empowers them. Of course, the statement also implies that these cosmic divinities, to the extent that they have become visible, still are somewhat tainted by matter. Plotinus does not hesitate to inject here momentarily, for contrast, a scatological metaphor that classifies human corpses as being somewhat lower than dung. In the same impressive manner of basic speech, matter in general and when devoid of soul is likened to "excretion of the Gods." The metaphor of divine "procreation" thereby temporarily is replaced with an even more vulnerable metaphor, divine "alimentation." One is reminded of the Heliopolitans who shifted from "masturbation" to "spitting."

The presence of ultraearthy metaphors in lofty philosophical discourse provides a reliable clue to the wider range of dynamic experiential data with which Plotinus felt comfortable. Only a mind that has been nurtured in a rich mythological background can achieve such a wide scope of ease with concrete imagery. In the evolution of human thought, one must not forget, mythological events and figures preceded philosophical principles. Mythological beings preceded philosophical generalities and abstractions. Mythological reasoning always has been, and remains, the earthly parent of philosophical reasoning.

Occasionally some of Plotinus' mythological background shows through his thinly woven, and sometimes worn, fabric of Hellenic philosophical discourse. Ancient deities appear then only slightly veiled under the masks of abstract "hypostases." One may wonder why Plotinus ever classified the godhead simply as another hypostasis.

"Hypostases" have been introduced pragmatically by Plotinus, for the sake of communication. They are the philosophical abstractions, the single picture frames or abstract veils, projected unto the three

Copyrighted Material

"personae" of Plotinus' supreme Egyptian trinity. Without these "abstractions"—or shall we call them *intentional acts of memory fixation*?—the mental subtraction of personhood and virility from mighty divinities would have been unthinkable. Without these hypostases Plotinus could not have held discourse with fellow philosophers who dealt in Greek analysis and abstraction.

Nevertheless, during moments of greater inwardness and honesty, Plotinus placed himself mystically inside the All that he described. This is what happened very early in the Fifth Ennead when, seeing himself situated at the lower end of the hypostasis of Soul, he introduced—as he often did—his epistemological perspective as personal soteriology.[7]

Ennead V,1,3

The recognition of one's own soul, by faith and mind, implies upward contemplation and the approachment of God by finite minds. Above Soul is a more divine and more prior source—another hypostasis to be recognized.

Soul, for all the worth we have shown to belong to it, is yet a secondary, and image of the Intellectual-Principle: reason uttered is an image of the reason stored within the soul, and in the same way Soul *is an utterance* of the Intellectual-Principle: it is even the total of its activity, the *entire stream of life sent forth* by that Principle for the *production* of further being: it is the *forthgoing* heat of a fire which has also heat essentially inherent. . . . *Sprung*, in other words, from the Intellectual-Principle, soul is intellective, but with an intellection operating by the method of reasonings: for its perfection it *must look to that Divine Mind*.

The interrelationship of source and image, of Intellectual Principle and reasoning that enlivens Soul, Plotinus has explained with an Aristotelian type of "form-and-matter" progression. If Plotinus had chosen to apply his scatological metaphor this high up on his scale, he as well could have referred to Soul as "excrement" that issues

---

[7]He will be speaking from this inside perspective also at the completion of his mental journey, in Section VI. Copyrighted Material

from the Intellectual Principle. But, of course, Plotinus reserved his scatological process metaphor to explain the lowest transition in the larger emanational process; namely, the downward drifting of Soul toward visible matter and nothingness.

Ennead V,1,4

The Divine Mind, or Intellect, also can be approached by contemplating the world with its myriads of sense experiences, indirectly of course, by contemplating the archetypes of all creatures. Above all particulars presides unsoiled Intelligence and unapproachable divine wisdom.

Thus, another paragraph of Plotinus represents a proverbial "bone thrown" to Greek philosopher minds who, long ago, lost touch with their own Hellenic mythological tradition. For the rhetorical purpose at hand, Plotinus' allusion to a non-Egyptian mythology, and to linguistic analysis, needed not be very precise. Judge for yourself:

> That archetypal world is the true Golden Age, age of Kronos, whose very name suggests (in Greek) Abundance and Intellect. For here *is contained all that is immortal*: nothing here but its divine Mind; all is God; this is the place of every soul.

The sermonette on mystic bliss in the true Golden Age of Cronos nevertheless sobers up to a description of the process of intellect infusion into the hypostasis of Soul:

> Soul *deals with* thing after thing—now Socrates; now a horse: always some one entity from among beings—but the Intellectual Principle is all and therefore its *entire content is simultaneously present* in that identity: this *is pure being* in eternal actuality; nowhere is there any future, for every then is a now; nor is there any past...and the total of all is Intellectual Principle entire and Being entire.

Ennead V,1,5

The divine Intellectual Principle exists above the Soul. However, both Mind and Soul together constitute a single continuum. Even at

Copyrighted Material

the lower end, all souls stand fused as members with the higher divinity—unless estranged by deliberate apostasy. From this basis, established earlier, the upward contemplation proceeds from the Dyad of Soul and Divine Mind, toward immersion in the One.[8] Inasmuch as Plotinus is here contemplating, onward and upward against the creative current that overflows from the One, he tightens his conceptual net. The number of permissible attributions to deity become more scarce. Thus, rather than letting the complicated text speak for itself in this instance, it may be useful to exegete and paraphrase small steps and sentences:

1. The Intellectual Principle exists above the Soul.

2. Contemplating upward, the Soul brings itself closer to divine Intellect.

3. The Soul unites with the Intellect, as a Dyad, and the Egyptian question is asked: What Being has "engendered" this twofold God?

4. The Soul contemplating divine Intellect is a number quantity, or member, of this divine Dyad.

5. This Dyad of Number (i.e., Soul) and Intellectual Principle is undetermined; it represents, so to speak, the underlayment or "matter" for the Mind.

6. The Dyad is shaped in two ways: by Ideas rising within it, and by the presence of the One.

7. The Dyad in this homeward intellection is subject; the One from whom Mind emanates is object.

8. Within this current of creativity and countercurrent of nostalgic intellection, the subject and its object become identical.

Thus, the reunion of Soul with Intellect is attained by the wholesome homeward yearning of individual souls. The subsequent reunion of the Dyad (of Intellect and Soul already reunited) with the One is a process of a more advanced mode of intellectual homeward contemplation. In a diluted mode, at a lower level, this same kind of philosophical contemplation has only begun with the incitement of souls to yearn homeward.

---

[8]The conceptualization, of Mind and Soul together as a Dyad, follows time-honored orthodox Egyptian conventions. See in Part One the references to Ruti, the lion pair; i.e., Shu and Tefnut. Copyrighted Material

Ennead V,1,6

With this section Plotinus completes the sketch of his contemplative homeward journey; he anchors himself again in cosmogony and theogony. Wrapped into the receptive Dyad, as a soul that penetrates the Intellectual Principle or Divine Mind, Plotinus as a sharp-witted mystic contemplates the question of his relatedness to the Divine Mind:

> But how and what does the Intellectual Principle see and, especially, how *has it sprung* from that which is to become the object of its vision?

> The *mind demands the existence* of these Beings, but it is still in trouble over the problem endlessly debated by the most ancient philosophers: from such a unity as we have declared The One to be, how does anything at all come into substantial existence, any multiplicity, dyad, or number? Why has the Primal not remained self-gathered... ?

The contemplative journey of the soul of Plotinus reaches its happy goal. He lays aside philosophical objective description and then humbly, as a soul knowing itself already enveloped in the Dyad, prays as religiously and humbly as very few philosophers who followed in his steps have dared to do:

> In venturing an answer, we first invoke God Himself, not in loud word but in that way of prayer which is always within our power, *leaning in soul towards Him by aspiration*, alone towards the alone. But if we seek the vision of that great Being within the Inner Sanctuary—self-gathered, tranquilly remote above all else—we begin by considering the *images stationed at the outer precincts*, or more exactly to the moment, the first image that appears. How the Divine Mind comes into being must be explained.

A few additional statements generated by this prayer complete the sketch. Everything moving needs an object toward which it advances—motion is relative—therefore, motion cannot be ascribed without such a goal. Movement is an attribute of the second hypostasis. But

Copyrighted Material

then again, how does multiplicity result from the Supreme unmovable One? Plotinus answers that it must be happening through *"circum-radiation."* The creative emanation from the static and unaltering Supreme "may be compared to the *brilliant light* encircling the sun (as it is) *ceaselessly generated* from that unchanging substance."

With the static process of the One's creativity thus defined as circumradiation, Plotinus would have been set to narrate the story of his journey in the outward and downward direction, traveling on or trailing the rays of creative radiation. He could have dwelt on the Mind reaching out to become radiantly manifest as Soul, and thence he could have flirted with matter and the shadow play of nonbeing. But, true to orthodox Egyptian theology, having invoked the narrow Atonistic metaphor of solar circumradiation, Plotinus in honor of the total Atum-Ra quickly returned to the larger metaphor of creation by begetting:

> all that is fully achieved engenders: therefore the eternally achieved *engenders eternally* and eternal being. The offspring is always minor...the Divine Mind. The *offspring must seek and love the begetter*; and especially so when begetter and begotten are alone in their sphere; when, in addition, *the begetter is the highest Good, the offspring is attached* by a bond of sheer necessity, separated only by being distinct.

The philosophy of Plotinus is soteriology, not fatalistic resigna-tion. Theoretical philosophy for him was the handmaiden for redeemed living; it was never an end in itself. It therefore seems safe to say that what has held Ammonius and Plotinus together, for eleven intimate years, was their mutual concern for traditional Egyptian soteriology.

Ennead V,1,7

Plotinus began Section Seven with an exhortation to himself and to his readers: "We must be more explicit." It seems significant that although he described his soul's entire journey homeward to the One he referred to Hellenic mythology only once—that is, the Golden Age of Cronos (V,1,4)—and very imprecisely at that. Now that he promised to be more explicit he added nothing more than ordinary

Copyrighted Material

commentary. He simply undertook to rationalize the sketch of his homeward journey in greater detail, which for Greeks meant to have recourse to philosophical jargon.

If Greek philosophy had been Plotinus' actual starting point, why would he not have begun with Greek philosophy and ended his treatise with some kind of a concluding synthesis? The answer to this question is simple, indeed. Plotinus has given us Egyptian religion, theology in the linguistic garb of Hellenic philosophy. His philosophical and Greek linguistic cover and his scarce links with Platonic philosophy sufficed to hold the attention of a few Greek students of philosophy. From his personal "Sitz im Leben" Plotinus wrote orthodox Egyptian theology and apologetics, first and foremost.

Copyrighted Material

Copyrighted Material

15

Neoplatonism:
Ammonius and Plotinus

Neoplatonic Scholarship

Neoplatonism, as the name implies, traditionally has been studied as a natural offspring of Platonic philosophy, taking into account a reasonable amount of stimulation from other Hellenic philosophical schools. The first suggestion, that "oriental" influences might be present in the philosophy of Plotinus was by Franz Brentano in 1876. Thirty-eight years later H. F. Mueller refuted Brentano's assertions. More recently, in an essay prepared for an international conference on Neoplatonism and Indian Thought, which was held at Brock University in Ontario, Albert M. Wolters surveyed this "orientalism" controversy up to 1976.[1] He traced the primary stimulus for the Ontario conference question to the well-known Plotinus scholar Emile Brehier.

During the winter of 1921-1922 Emile Brehier gave a series of formal lectures at the Sorbonne, which were published six years later. In his seventh chapter he discussed the orientalism of Plotinus, whereby he observed that the fourth and fifth treatises of the Sixth Ennead easily can be read without reference to Greek philosophy. He concluded, cautiously enough it seems, that the non-Hellenic place of origin for these "oriental" ideas could have been India. Unfortunately he omitted, in this lecture, to name any specific literary or historical points of contact. Wolters observed in his survey that Brehier's thesis has found almost no support among other Plotinus scholars.

---

[1]Albert M. Wolters, "Survey of Modern Scholarly Opinion," in R. Baine Harris, ed., *Neo-Platonism and Indian Thought* (Norfolk, Va., 1982), pp. 293–308.

Copyrighted Material

Also indicative of this mood were the presentations made at the 1976 Ontario conference itself. As a rule, the papers remained non-committal about specific Indian influences on Plotinus, and most of them also roamed within the safe realm of topical and ahistorical comparison.

For the English translation of his lectures, Brehier wrote a new Introduction.[2] He concluded that statement with an evasive apologia:

And we have deemed it legitimate and even necessary to advance a hypothesis of the relations of Plotinus to India which others who are more competent will perhaps want to investigate and verify.

An additional curiosity emerges from Brehier's new Introduction. In preparation for his defensive finale he appealed to a bit of historical common sense:

After Alexander the Greeks, without doubt, did "Hellenize" the Orient; but, inversely, Egypt, "the land were gods are invented" [Brehier quoted here Asclepius], stamped its powerful imprint not only upon the customs but upon the ideas of the Greeks, in spite of the efforts of the rulers of Egypt to keep the Egyptians in a subordinate state. But we have come to believe, as will be seen, that it is necessary to look beyond Egypt in order to render the thought of Plotinus intelligible.

Brehier has not told us whether, before voicing his conclusion, he ever searched among Egyptian sources for precedents. Nor are we told why he abandoned searching in Egypt so quickly to hurry on toward India—to come up emptyhanded there as well. But then, what else could be done? His lectures by that time were several decades old, and he had to introduce what was at hand and what was about to be released in English. Moreover, Brehier shared with many Neoplatonism scholars the peculiar lumped notion of "Orient." Presumably several centuries of Hellenistic expansion, of Greeks reaching Egypt and India, have obliterated most essential cultural differences in the lands traversed by Alexander's armies.

---

[2]Emile Brehier, *The Philosophy of Plotinus* (Chicago, 1958), pp. 1–12.
Copyrighted Material

In the case of real historical situations, and on considering the conservative nature of human cultures everywhere, such thorough obliteration of local traditions is well-nigh unthinkable. On the other hand, had Brehier wanted to pursue this issue a little further, his momentary one-sentence hunch about an Egyptian cultural backlash against the Hellenizers would have been realistic and on target.

Ammonius and Plotinus

Ammonius Saccas (ca. 175–242 C.E.), or Ammonius the Porter, is acknowledged as being now the most shadowy figure in the chronicles of Hellenic philosophy. He left no written work, and most of what we can still infer about his philosophy must be gleaned from the teachings of his students, Plotinus and Origen the Christian. Actually, we depend for information about Plotinus on the later writings of Porphyry, and concerning Origen on Eusebius and Hierocles.[3]

Posterity has remembered Ammonius as a *theodidaktos*; that is, as one who was taught by God. So, apparently he had never studied formally under a recognized Greek teacher of philosophy.[4] Whenever he commented on the writings of earlier Greek philosophers he seemed to have followed the biddings of his own mind.

We know from Porphyry that his teacher Plotinus (205–270 C.E.) had been Ammonius' most devoted and famous student and had developed a similar habit of commenting on philosophical works.[5] As a result of knowing this, all references in the *Enneads* to the writings of earlier Greek philosophers can be read in conflicting ways. Those who presuppose that Plotinus was foremostly a Platonist, generally see his primary dependence on Greek philosophy. On the other hand,

---

[3]For a treatment of this question see E. R. Dodds, "Numenius and Ammonius" and subsequent conference discussions in E. R. Dodds et al., *Les Sources de Plotin*, in *Entretiens sur L'Antiquite Classique*, Book 5 (Geneva, 1966), pp. 3–61.

[4]Dean Inge, in Grace H. Turnbull, *The Essence of Plotinus* (Westport, Conn., 1934), p. 2.

[5]Porphyry, "Life of Plotinus," par. 14, in *Plotinus*, vol. 1, trans. A. H. Armstrong (Cambridge, Mass., 1978).

Copyrighted Material

those who approach him without this presupposition will discover that, even if all references to Greek philosophers were removed from Plotinus' fifty-four treatises, they would still teach the same ontology.

Ammonius probably would have been amused about the credit given to him by Hierocles, in a text by Photius, to the effect that "Ammonius reconciled the doctrines of Plato and Aristotle."[6] Indeed while approaching this teacher of Plotinus, as we shall attempt, from his home background of Egyptian theology, we easily can see how Ammonius could have generated all his commentaries without himself becoming overly indebted to the ontologies of either Plato or Aristotle. "Ammonius bypassed the doctrines of Plato and Aristotle" probably would have been more correct.

The fact is, no one knows exactly how much he actually learned from these Greek masters. It could have been little, or it could have been a little more. In light of the dependence of Platonic and Aristotelian philosophy on ancient Egyptian ontology, demonstrated earlier, it no longer matters as much as it did at the outset of this study.

The "reconciling doctrine" which Ammonius taught was older than the teachings of Plato and Aristotle, even older than those of Thales and Anaximander. It was Egyptian orthodox emanationalism, ancient enough to have nourished Greek philosophy in its infancy, with almost two millennia to spare. Why, then, should anyone who has seriously reviewed Greek philosophies still be surprised to find how nicely an Egyptian intellect could harmonize them with his native Egyptian common sense!

Ammonius remained true to the long-established tradition of Egyptian priests: he left no writings. Beyond that, his students were obligated to him by some vow of secrecy not to publish their mentor's lectures. Porphyry of Tyre (233–304 C.E.), who for a time became Plotinus' editor and biographer, accused Erennius and Origen of having broken that agreement. Supposedly these men published Ammonius' teachings under two titles: "On the Spirits" (Origen) and "That the King is the Only Maker."[7]

---

[6]See Inge, in Turnbull, *The Essence of Plotinus.*

[7]Plotinus, trans. Armstrong, p. 10.

Copyrighted Material

Although most commentators nowadays doubt the Ammonian authorship of such titles, the fact remains that both titles can be reconciled easily with a background in ancient Egyptian theology. The first could have been a general theological treatise on gods in relation to the All-God, whereas the second could have been a takeoff on the enduring Egyptian question about a monarch's identity with the creative godhead, the Heliopolitan Ennead. This possibility makes unnecessary Armstrong's severe judgment—to the effect that the second of these titles amounts to a "fulsome piece of court flattery." An identification of divine Creator and King was clearly developed in Memphite theology, as it was also explicit in Akhenaton's haughty exclusivism. Unfortunately, the Ammonian works themselves are lost, and a discussion of them beyond this paragraph therefore would be a waste of time.

In an essay, "Ammonius der Lehrer des Origenes," Willy Theiler followed Fritz Heinemann (in *Hermes* 61 [1926]: 1ff) in believing that much of Ammonius' philosophy is still extant in written form.[8] He postulated a line of succession that began with Ammonius Saccas and led through Origen to Plutarch, and thence to Hierocles. We then are advised to look for the lost teachings of the founder of Neoplatonism among the legacy of Hierocles, of two centuries later (pp. 2ff). Theiler thus proceeded to reconstruct for us an Ammonius Saccas who conveniently matches the profile of a typical Greek Platonist.

But then, unfortunately, this reconstruction of Ammonius, based on quotes from the two century younger Hierocles, left the better-known founder of Neoplatonism, Plotinus, stranded "like an island in the stream of Platonic tradition," as Theiler himself observed (p. 42).

Such speculative tracing of Ammonian texts, over several generations of students and teachers and across a major religious fault line, indeed seems farfetched, too farfetched for comfort. I personally remain convinced that a historical refocusing on Ammonius Saccas, in the absence of the philosopher's own writings, will fare better by first having a closer look at the bequest of Plotinus.

One may object that Plotinus himself published nothing and that his editor, Porphyry, is a generation removed from Ammonius. In that regard we may note that the relationship between Plotinus and his editor seems fairly well documented. And as far as Plotinus himself

---

[8]Willy Theiler, *Forschungen zum Neuplatonismus* (Berlin, 1966).
Copyrighted Material

is concerned, he remained a student of Ammonius over twice the time that Origen spent in his vicinity, assuming for the moment that we can be sure as to which Origin that student of Ammonius actually was. Beyond that, Plotinus began his studies a year after Origen had left, about 232, and he therefore benefitted from Ammonius' more mature years.

We are told by Porphyry that, on coming to Alexandria, Plotinus listened in on the lectures of all prominent philosophers who could be found in that city at the time. He was summarily disappointed by all. Only after listening to Ammonius the "Porter," somewhere along the periphery of the Alexandrian establishment, was Plotinus' enthusiasm for philosophical learning rekindled. When Plotinus, an Egyptian, finally found this teacher, a fellow Egyptian by all indications, he remained his faithful student for eleven years. Such a long span of time suggests that the student was determined to learn nothing short of the teacher's total ontology.

The *Enneads* of Plotinus therefore still appear to be the best window through which one may see a reflection of the mind of Ammonius. And, in turn, the philosophies of both men are still best understood as mirrors that, in the twilight of antiquity, reflected the ancient theology of their homeland civilization. It now appears as though the Greek philosophical tradition, in itself, for both men has been never more than a convenient modus operandi for intellectual and intercultural discourse.

It is significant that Porphyry of Tyre was unable to elicit from his Egyptian master, Plotinus, any information "about his race or his parents or his native country." And it is indeed remarkable how Porphyry, the man who thought of himself as one of Plotinus' closest friends, was kept completely in the dark about his teacher's family and religio-ethnic background. Yet, in spite of Plotinus' silence about these matters, the profile of his relationship with Porphyry emerges surprisingly clear.

Porphyry was the industrious student who succeeded in prodding his master into doing more systematic writing. In turn, Plotinus responded by letting Porphyry take the lead as his personal editor. Their friendship therefore primarily was a pragmatic one. Porphyry had a superior command of the Greek language and Plotinus, whose native language and thought structure were Egyptian, depended on someone like him. That pragmatic friendship endured to the end, even

Copyrighted Material

after the master had politely persuaded his student to take a permanent vacation.

The fact that Plotinus never entrusted information about his cultural, religious, and family background to his student Porphyry need not seem surprising, after all. As an Egyptian who sought the company of colonial Greek philosophers in Alexandria, from somewhere along the sidelines, Plotinus was dedicated to his mission as a bridge builder between the two cultures. He accepted the challenge to communicate more effectively nearer to the apex of Greek high society. To that effect his Greek students needed to be assured about his Hellenic authenticity and compatibility. On that account he also was obliged to quote occasionally from prestigious Greek philosophers. He knew quite well that haughty Hellenic minds easily would lose interest in him had they seen through, all the way down, to his deep Egyptian religio-ethnic roots.

In other words, Plotinus, whose status as a teacher rested on the pretence of Hellenic authenticity and competence, had nothing to gain, and much to lose, by chatting about his Egyptian background. On the other hand, given what else we know about the kind and saintly nature of Plotinus, it is almost impossible to imagine that he himself was emotionally cut off from his Egyptian family. Rather, we may assume safely that, aside from protecting his intercultural role, Plotinus also regarded it as his duty to protect his Egyptian kin from his own Greek friends. They needed to be protected from the local stigma that would have resulted from the presence of gawking foreign tourists, of tourists from the outer empire. In addition, it even is conceivable that a proud Egyptian family had severed its ties with their son when the latter began to associate with the Greek intruders at Alexandria.

Nevertheless, secrets about ethnicity, home, and family are not as impenetrable as studious men of the type of Porphyry have reckoned them to be. Such family secrets are standard material for gossip among common folk everywhere. Accordingly, a certain Eunapius told someone that the birthplace of Plotinus was Lyco or Lycopolis. Two towns at the time were known by that name, one in Upper Egypt and another in the Delta.

Perhaps more than any commentary thus far published on Ammonius and Plotinus, this discussion focuses on the manner in which both men have appeared and operated along the periphery of Alexandria's academic community. An analogy from Western
Copyrighted Material

civilization may help illuminate this situation. For instance, the dual bridge builder roles played by Ammonius and Plotinus are being replicated, in our days, many times by American Indian intellectuals who interact and communicate with the dominant Anglo-American civilization. Very few among them are equally conversant in the dominant civilization and in their home culture, and all must apply relational double standards.

A rather obvious clue about the background of Ammonius Saccas has been consistently overlooked by earlier commentators—his name. *Ammonius* was a common Egyptian name at the time, and this fact testifies to the persistence of New Kingdom Amun religion. The man Ammonius had been dedicated, as a child, to the Egyptian hidden godhead Ammon. This means that the boy grew up under parents who, at least, explained to the curious boy the meaning of his name or who, at most, were able to explain to him portions of orthodox Egyptian theology as well.

Thus, after taking into account the strong rational-mystic impulse Ammonius was able to impart to Plotinus, it appears on average that this shadowy founder of Neoplatonism somehow had been reared in accordance with devout Egyptian patterns of piety. It remains doubtful that these patterns were Christian, even though Eusebius has quoted Porphyry to that effect.[9]

In any case, Plotinus, an Egyptian boy of the next generation, became disillusioned with the leading Greek philosophers at Alexandria. In the native pietism of Ammonius the searching mind of Plotinus discovered a comprehensive view of the world that preserved his Egyptian cultural identity. And over against the background of his own daring impiety toward Greek scholasticism he worked out a replica of that world-view for himself. A consistent theological emanationalism, and nothing short of that, was the home ideology Ammonius imparted to this student. And in response Plotinus devoted eleven years of his life to studying Egyptian wisdom under Ammonius, as well as its rationalization in relation to Greek colonial philosophy.

The affection that Plotinus, an Egyptian, had for the philosophical wisdom of Ammonius, a fellow Egyptian, seems to have been rooted

---

[9]See footnote in *Plotinus*, trans. Armstrong, pp. 10f.

in simpler folk mythos and ethos. The life story of Plotinus has all the marks of an Egyptian student finding his Egyptian roots, his ontological home, in the teachings of Ammonius. And his searching and finding happened in dialogue with the dominant Hellenistic civilization. Ammonius succeeded in rationalizing for himself, and for Plotinus, the Egyptian theological emanationalism and expressing it in the language of the Eastern Roman Empire, in Greek, and in the medium of respectable Hellenic philosophical jargon.

Two Egyptian men thus have intruded from along the periphery of Hellenism, from along its Egyptian flank, and infused Greek philosophy with an apparently "brand new" monistic ontology that, at the time, was several thousand years old. Traditional dualistic Greek philosophy could not withstand that impact and that affinity for very long. After all, the basic Ionian ontological presuppositions from which Hellenic philosophy was conceived, by which it was secretly nourished for its primal mythos and soul, had been dependent on monotheistic Egyptian process theology all along.

Ancient Egyptian gods who operated in Alexandria must have delighted in the business of creating ironies. To that effect the foreigner Porphyry felt moved to group Plotinus' bequest of fifty-four treatises into six groups of "enneads," hence the title of the book. All the while the editor, Porphyry, was in all likelihood unaware of Saccas' and of Plotinus' distant divine "Enneadean" source. And so, it appears that the ancient gods have here personally intervened, have lent a helping hand, to Porphyry in his choice of numerology! Plotinus' *Enneads* do contain, indeed, elaborations on the Heliopolitan godhead in his threefold as well as in his ninefold emanation.

On the Originality of Plotinus

As the founder of a new Graeco-Egyptian philosophical school called *Neoplatonism*, Plotinus consistently has been studied with regard to what he might have owed to Plato and Socrates. The presence of quotations from Plato's Dialogues, in his writings, has been weighed in, often, as primary evidence. So, for example, we are told that the most frequently cited Platonic sources were the Timaeus, Republic, Phaedo, Phaedrus, Symposium, Theaetetus, Philebus,

Copyrighted Material

Sophist, and the Parmenides.[10] Comparisons of Plotinus with Plato thus have identified specific fragments of doctrines from both sides. And in this simplistic manner, similarities have been chalked up as indebtedness; differences have been credited as original contributions.

But such a narrow comparative approach works only until new similarities are discovered elsewhere, in ancient sources that hitherto were deemed outside the family tree of the Greek philosophical school. When such sources turn out to be in a favorable geographical position, and are precedents as well, then the possibility of other historical indebtedness no longer can be ignored. Early friends of Plotinus, grudgingly, had to acknowledge his debt to certain predecessors. Porphyry, his principal biographer, is invoked as first witness for the prosecution:

> In writing he (Plotinus) is concise and full of thought. He puts things shortly and abounds more in ideas than in words; he generally expresses himself in a tone of rapt inspiration, and states what he himself really feels about the matter and not what has been handed down by tradition. His writings, however, are full of concealed Stoic and Peripatetic doctrines. Aristotle's *Metaphysics*, in particular, is concentrated in them. . . . In the meetings of the school he used to have the commentaries read, perhaps of Severus, perhaps of Cronius or Numenius or Gaius or Atticus, and among the Peripatetics of Aspasius, Alexander, Adrastus, and others that were available. But he did not just speak straight out of these books but took a distinctive personal line in his consideration, and brought the mind of Ammonius to bear on the investigations in hand.[11]

Not so much the indebtedness of Plotinus to his antecedents, but more so the independence of his mind, is highlighted in this eulogy by Porphyry. This begs a number of crucial questions: (1) What has been the cultural and intellectual context for his "rapt inspirations?" (2) Could a common source of doctrine be postulated—beyond the

---

[10]So for instance Paul Henry, "The Place of Plotinus in the History of Thought," in *Plotinus: The Enneads*, trans. Stephen MacKenna (New York, 1962) pp. xxxv–lxx.

[11]Porphyry, "Life of Plotinus," par. 14, in *Plotinus*, trans. Armstrong, vol. 1.

Copyrighted Material

Stoic, Peripatetic, and the other ones of which Porphyry was aware? (3) During conferences, what motivated his momentary requests for books of Platonists and Peripatetics? Was it to learn and borrow, or was it to prove his own point? (4) Was his utilization of Plato's Dialogues in any way different from his treatment of other sources? (5) And finally, was Ammonius' original contribution to Plotinus really a method?

Tentatively, and in a simple preliminary fashion, these questions may be answered as follows: (1) Inspirations and revelations come from the direction toward which a receptive mind is oriented. I suspect that the realm from which inspirations mostly came to Ammonius, and to Plotinus, was ancient Egyptian theology in a variety of current native Egyptian derivative forms. (2) Anyone in the Near East who considered emanational theology or ontology, after they had been taught throughout millennia at Heliopolis, could not avoid being caught up in the tailwind of this ancient heritage. (3) Porphyry leaves no doubt that Plotinus followed his own agenda. Momentary calls for books indicate that these sources were exploited to help establish Plotinus' own perspective. (4) Upon reflecting on his use of Plato, in the *Enneads*, it appears that he mined the Dialogues in the same manner as other authorities and for the same purpose.

And then (5) it is quite understandable how Porphyry, a Greek student of philosophy, initially in hope of perfecting his Socratic skills, would have approached the philosophy of Plotinus in search of a "method." Unable to point to Socrates, Plato, or Aristotle, Plotinus simply deferred to the lesser-known Ammonius as the source of his "method"—inasmuch as he was expected to somehow identify a method. But clearly, method to Plotinus was secondary to content and ontology as, surely, method already had been secondary to Socrates, Plato, and Aristotle. All the same, in the marketplace of subsequent philosophers' academies, methodology always has been in high demand. Methodology is sought by beginners as a substitute for vision. Ontology begs "methodological proof" and commentary.

Copyrighted Material

Copyrighted Material

PART FOUR:
THE BIRTH
OF CHRISTENDOM

Copyrighted Material

Copyrighted Material

16

The Kingdom of Heaven at Hand

Premonitions in Jewish Mythology

Christian theology and soteriology, their indebtedness to ancient Egypt, are the primary focus in Part Four of this book. At the same time, our exposition aims not in the least at diminishing the significance of the life and teachings of Jesus, Christianity's founder. And most certainly, his personal religious impulses and contributions have come to us by way of Judaism.

Nevertheless, to understand the formative years of Christendom, as a world religion, it is necessary to distinguish between Hebrew and Egyptian contributions. The primary Hebrew seed element, imparted to the Christian movement by Jesus, has been his personal dedication to the "kingdom of heaven" or the "kingdom of God." Popular angelology at the time of Jesus, information about God's heavenly entourage, may be considered a good indicator of how the nature of God's kingdom was understood by Jesus and his Jewish contemporaries.

Other Jewish contributions also must be mentioned in this connection, in passing. The memory meal, which the apostles and the Christian Church have continued to celebrate after their Lord's departure, was modeled formally after the Jewish rite of Passover—even though the food mysticism of bread and wine, as such, goes beyond Judaism. But, as it began, by virtue of this revised Passover ritual and by accepting the Hebrew Bible as "old testament," the Christian Church was able to appropriate much of the ancient Abrahamic reform tradition. That reform tradition began early on to delimit the types of sacrifice that supposedly God Almighty still expected of humankind.

Copyrighted Material

The heavenly Father of Jesus Christ reformed sacrificial rites beyond Jewish expectations, at least beyond what was expected by Sadducees. Even though the early Jewish Christians still went to worship at the temple (as in *Acts* 2:42ff), the consensus gradually prevailed that Christ not only came to endorse Abraham's abolishment of human sacrifices, but to disregard animal sacrifices and circumcision as well. In the sacred meal celebrated by Christians, the plant substances of bread and wine came to substitute for the meat of lambs. Moreover, to underwrite the new Christian gospel and the new world order, the execution of Jesus came to be viewed as the last efficacious and redemptive human sacrifice necessary under God's heaven. Christ's death was understood as the supreme sacrifice intended by God to end all human sacrifices. His death was understood as culmination of the Abrahamic tradition of sacrificial reforms.

The "kingdom of heaven" idea continued to change after the death and resurrection of Christ Jesus, to accommodate the fact that churches had evolved instead. There is nothing unusual about this change, inasmuch as the "kingdom of heaven" concept had been fluid all along. It had begun to change in Jewish consciousness in the direction of Christian radicalism already in the thought of Hebrew prophets. The larger process by which kingdom of heaven awareness was effectively transformed, in the teachings of John the Baptizer as well as in those of Jesus, also can be perceived in light of what before their time had happened to the Jewish belief in angels. Angels in Judaism staffed and populated God's kingdom of heaven.

* * *

Ancient Hebrew narrators, plain domesticators, who told stories about the patriarchal age, were still unspoiled by worldly and otherworldly royal glories. As far as these ancients were concerned, the messenger angels of God Almighty appeared regularly in the guise of ordinary human travelers.

Nevertheless, during the formative period of Israel's monarchy, during her grand domestication phase, God increasingly was acclaimed as a "Lord of hosts." Inasmuch as the godhead was then honored as a deity of war, his angelic hosts were understood, accordingly, to be of the warrior type as well. As a result, the distinction between angelic warriors and Israelite human warriors became blurred. So for example, it is said that when the warrior

Copyrighted Material

David faced the Philistine giant, Goliath, he spoke confident words like these:

You come to me with a sword and a spear, and with a javelin; but I come to you in the name of the Lord of hosts, the God of the armies of Israel. (*1 Samuel* 17:45)

The prophet Isaiah, who still lived in the bright afterglow of the Davidic monarchy, envisioned Almighty God as sitting on a high cosmic throne. The earth was God's footstool and the entire universe was his monarchy. The prophet saw and heard God's messenger angels shout toward one another. Their shouts of praise and glory, in those moments, modified their original military posture:

Holy, holy, holy is the Lord of hosts; the whole earth is full of his glory! (*Isaiah* 6:3)

In postcanonical Jewish literature, angelology reached new and sometimes amazingly beautiful heights. The philosopher Philo, having come under the spell of Egyptian emanationalism in Alexandria, has arranged Yahweh's angels in a hierarchy of created beings. Generous readers could easily have reconciled Philo's angelology with so-called Heliopolitan polytheism. In the Egyptian perspective, their religion has been monotheism with polymanifestations all along. It may in the final analysis not matter whether, historically considered, certain divine beings are being called *gods* or *angels*. For religions that belong to the family of Egyptian tradition, only the function of these beings in the larger divine emanational hierarchy matters.

The primary differences between ancient Egyptian theology and the later intertestamental Jewish version of angelology concerned, foremostly, the mode of divine creation and the style of divine government. The Egyptian godhead first generated divine offspring and then, remaining still actively and "organically" involved within his offspring, generated the visible world through the latter. By contrast, in Jewish perspective the divine creator simply commanded, inorganically and somewhat despotically, that there should be creatures. By that same voice method he also decreed that there be angels to serve him as his messengers.

The distinction therefore turns on only the small question as to what came first in God's world. Was it the presence of his servants
Copyrighted Material

in the divine hierarchy? Or was it the Lord's autocratic commandeering that brought them into being, first, to serve?

In contrast to Egyptian emanational theology, Jewish apocalyptic literature presented the angels of God with a tinge of Zoroastrian confrontationalism. This situation can be accounted for easily by considering Persian-Jewish relations during the postexilic period. Inasmuch as all commands, including the divine commands of the Creator, could be disobeyed by strong minds it became necessary for Jews to define what in Egypt used to be distant emanations of God—to define them as more or less estranged and disobedient creatures. Not only humankind, but also some angels, henceforth had to be counted among God's disobedient or fallen creatures. God's obedient angels were those who continued to dwell in his realm of light, whereas the disobedient Satan and his angelic accomplices existed in darkness. Both types of angels were interacting in constant strife.

Theogonically explained, and still somewhat in accord with Egyptian emanational "poly-theistic" logic, the dark and evil angels were those who had descended from the presence of God to defile themselves in union with human maidens (*Genesis* 6:1–4).

In the Egyptian context this would have meant only that for the time being these angels went too far out in the emanational process, in the direction of nonbeing. However, according to the Jewish perspective their behavior was more tragic. It meant that the offspring of such estranged angels became monsters, and that these monsters were responsible for introducing warfare among humankind.[1] Altogether, this amounts to a wonderful Hebrew diatribe on aristocratic warriors anywhere; namely, on heroes and cutthroats who were in the habit of claiming descent from the gods. All the while, when seen under a beam of Zoroastrian light, sideways, with stark contrasts and shadows, some of these far-estranged angels appeared to be devils.

The book of *Jubilees* (2:2), a late second century B.C.E. source, identifies a number of angels as *spirits* (life principles or souls) embodied in natural phenomena; that is, embodied in fire, winds, clouds, darkness, snow, hail, hoar frost, voices, thunder, lightning,

---

[1]James H. Charlesworth, ed., *The Old Testament Pseudepigrapha*, Vol. 1 (Garden City, N.Y., 1983), pp. 6ff, 13ff.

Copyrighted Material

cold, heat, winter, spring, autumn, and summer.[2] The acknowledgment of the presence of an "angel of fire" echoes the Torah story of Moses and the burning bush. But then, in a wider historical perspective, this Jewish angelology represents already a translation of the so-called Egyptian polytheism, along with Jewish angelology as its twin, into the idiom of Hellenistic "naturalism." Angels here correspond to natural phenomena and forces of nature.

The changing perception of angelic beings has thoroughly redefined the idea of God's kingdom of heaven. This much is suggested in *Second Enoch*.[3] It is said that during his visionary journey through ten heavens, Enoch traversed space in the upward direction and explored the entire heavenly hierarchy. At the level of the third heaven he found three hundred angels worshipping the Lord with "never-ceasing voice and pleasant singing" (8:8). In the fourth heaven, whenever the Lord commanded, phoenix and khalkedra birds burst forth into song (15:1).

Angelic hosts might still be seen carrying Bronze Age weapons, but the basic importance of arms increasingly has been upstaged by the prominence of musical instruments. Accordingly, Enoch saw in the "middle" of the heavens:

armed troops, worshiping the Lord with tympani and pipes and unceasing voices, and pleasant... and various songs, which it is impossible to describe. And every mind would be quite astonished, so marvelous and wonderful is the singing of these angels. (17:1)

From the sixth heaven, seven bands of archangels gave orders on how to maintain order in the world. They were informed by "the goings of the stars, and the alteration of the moon, by the revolution of the sun, and the good government of the world." Apparently,

[2]James H. Charlesworth, ed., *The Apogrypha and Pseudepigrapha of the Old Testament*, ed. R. H. Charles, Vol. 2 (Oxford, 1913), pp. 13f.

[3]Charlesworth, *The Old Testament Pseudepigrapha*, Vol. 1, pp. 130ff. The contents of all extant "Enoch" traditions cannot be dated with certainty. Nevertheless, their presence in Jewish libraries, centuries later, does indicate the general direction in which angelology has been evolving.

Copyrighted Material

ancient Babylonian wisdom supplied the writer of *Second Enoch* with rudimentary information about astrology in the first place. But be that as it may, it is important to note that order in this heavenly world was maintained musically.

And they (the angels) make all celestial life peaceful; and they preserve the commandments and the instructions, and sweet voices and singing, every kind of praise and glory. (19:3)

Angelic men then lifted Enoch up and onward to the seventh heaven, the very stairway to the Lord's own dwelling:

And all the heavenly armies came and stood on the ten steps, corresponding to their ranks, and they did obeisance to the Lord. And then they went to their places in joy and merriment and in immeasurable light, singing songs with soft and gentle voices, while presenting the liturgy to him gloriously. (20:3–4)

Enoch's vision in the tenth heaven is expressed in terms of humble insufficiency. Incomprehensibility is explained no further than to a point of "indescribability":

And who am I to give an account of the incomprehensible being of the Lord, and of his face, so extremely strange and indescribable? And how many are his commands, and his multiple voice, and the Lord's throne, supremely great and not made by hands, and the choir stalls all around him, the cherubim and the seraphim armies, and their never-silent singing. (22:2)

Thus, along heaven's entire hierarchy, from the very face of God all the way down to the third heaven, the visionary Enoch is said to have heard God's kingdom break forth with singing and musical joy.

* * *

All this constitutes marvelous background information for understanding the Jewish context from which the Christian gospel of the kingdom of heaven sprouted forth and whence it was first introduced. Even though the intertestamental Jewish notion of the kingdom of heaven still contained armed soldiers—an assumption that

Copyrighted Material

also still has been ascribed to Jesus in *Matthew* 26:53—the divine monarchy was no longer thought of as essentially a military regime. All the same, to the extent that the writer of *Second Enoch* has shared his secrets with mortal humankind, his "kingdom of heaven" idea had to be communicated to a world where some kind of soldiers were still necessary for defense and for a people's collective survival.

The important progression in kingdom of heaven symbolism, during the intertestamental period, called for angels breaking forth into the world of human awareness with singing. Eventually, in the gospel story told by Christians, angels could be heard bursting forth, singing, even downward and earthward from the lower levels of heaven, all the way down to earth where their messages and songs reached the ears of lowly humankind.

The Christian story about the birth of Christ Jesus, of course, originally was a Jewish story, and it took off precisely at this point in the evolution of Jewish angelology. According to *Luke*, the new "kingdom of heaven" music had been heard, no longer audible only to scribes who composed pseudonymous stories about the trance journeys of ancient holy men, but heard instead by unsophisticated shepherd folk (2:13f). Luke's introduction to the Christian gospel, by way of his story about the birth of Jesus, thus made the new "heavenly kingdom" idea accessible at the level of common folk. At the same time, Luke added nothing that is essentially different from the angelology implied elsewhere among the sayings of Jesus.

The announcement of God's messenger angel was heard during the night, on earth—therefore in darkness. And a multitude of heavenly hosts appeared from on high, radiating the glory of God that was about to tingle some of the lowliest among human ears. Momentarily the kingdom of heaven erupted with gentle music—explicitly not with the commotion or violence of a heavenly army. The reign of God was made manifest as an otherworldly kinder regime that intruded from beyond. A gentler kind of kingdom broke into our world with the birth of a helpless baby boy. The story of that humble event, which came to introduce the new Christian universalism, has God's own great messenger angel appear and announce the new world order at the level of lowly herder folk. The simple story speaks for itself:

And the angel said to them: "Be not afraid; for behold, I bring you good news of a great joy which will come to all the people" ... And suddenly there was with the angel a multitude of the

Copyrighted Material

heavenly host praising God and saying, "Glory to God in the highest, and on earth peace among men with whom he is pleased!" (*Luke* 2:10–14)

Jesus and the Kingdom of Heaven

The Christian universalism spread into the Greco-Roman world with time-conscious proclamations, such as the one quoted next from a letter written by the apostle Paul to Christians in Galatia, Asia Minor:

But when the time had fully come, God sent forth his Son, born of a woman, born under the law so that we might receive adoption as sons. And because you are sons, God sent the spirit of his son into our hearts, crying, "Abba! Father!" So through God you are no longer a slave but a son, and if a son then an heir. (*Galatians* 4:4–7)

An awareness of time and history all along has been an integral dimension in the rational structure of the Hebrew-Christian tradition. Hebrew Torah mythology begins with the creation of the world and moves on from there, along a linear time line, to visions of divine election that, in due time, resulted in a people's liberation from Egyptian grand domestication. God's interference in human history set up a group of Hebrew slaves as his divinely chosen people. Other Hebrew writings report on the establishment and demise of their monarchy. They also describe exile in Babylonia and the return of a remnant people to their homeland of Judea.

Similarly, the Christian good news story broke forth from Judaism during the first century C.E. with the confidence of a cosmo-political event. It happened "when the time had fully come" and when conditions were ripe. Of course it may be said that, with hindsight, all significant events in human history, as well as in human awareness, happen in *kairos* or when the time is ripe.

A man named Jesus in his early thirties, from Nazareth in Galilee, appeared among the followers of John the Baptizer somewhere along the Jordan River. John led an ascetic life; he also led a popular "kingdom of heaven" movement that his followers joined by way of an initiation rite. The simple ritual required immersion in

Copyrighted Material

water, and those who participated in this procedure expressed repentance thereby. Ritualized bathing in water came to symbolize some kind of preparation in anticipation of the kingdom of heaven. In light of the general Egyptian background to Jewish piety, delineated in Part One of this book, we have now come to suspect that the Jordan River flowed for John the Baptizer somewhat like an extension of Atum's primordial Nile.

The Jordan waters probably represented God's creative "water of life," after the manner in which such waters were recognized in *Genesis* (2:10ff) and in the gospel of *John* (4:10 and 7:38). It is significant that the "fourth gospel," *John*, happens also to be the most Egyptian tinted among the canonical gospels. All in all, the baptism of John appears to have signified an initiation into the kingdom of heaven, a dimension of "transformation" into divine life, rather than mere cleansing or purification from old sin. By contrast, the notion of baptism as "purification," as such, may constitute a later dualistic Indo-European interpretation.

For a less Egyptianized and more Hebrew account we may turn to *Matthew*. John the Baptizer's mission is there summarized as follows:

In those days came John the Baptist, preaching in the wilderness of Judea, "Repent, for the kingdom of heaven is at hand." (*Matthew* 3:1-2)

Then we obtain our first historical glimpse of the man Jesus as he appeared among the followers of John. Like numerous others, so too Jesus participated in the conspicuous hippie preacher's rite of immersion. And perhaps in accordance with his prior expectations this experience became extraordinarily meaningful to him:

he went up immediately from the water, and behold, the heavens were opened and he saw the Spirit of God descending like a dove, and alighting on him; and lo, a voice from heaven, saying, "This is my beloved Son, with whom I am well pleased." (*Matthew* 3:16-17)

Matthew was a disciple of Jesus and, notwithstanding the possibility of subsequent editorial adjustments in the gospel text attributed to him, it is likely that either he or a fellow disciple

Copyrighted Material

obtained this tidbit of information directly from his beloved rabbi. This means that the original experience of Jesus presupposes a divine auditory revelation that originally had been cast in the second- and first-person singular: "You are my beloved Son, I like you!" The narrative continues to tell us precisely what effect these very personal words, heard by Jesus as spoken by God, have had on him:

> Then Jesus was led up by the Spirit into the wilderness to be tempted by the devil. And he fasted forty days and forty nights, and afterward he was hungry. (*Matthew* 4:1-2)

The three temptations that Jesus in the wilderness was said to have resisted concerned (1) the avoidance of hunger and suffering, (2) stuntmanship and heroism, and finally (3) grand domesticator ambitions on an imperialistic scale. According to this story, the tempter's allurements progressed from the satisfaction of physical hunger to craving for public notoriety, and thence to the added glamour of ruling the world with absolute power.

Jesus emerged from his wilderness ordeal with a resolution; that is, with a renewed commitment to John the Baptizer's cause. This development is attested a few sentences later:

> From that time Jesus began to preach, saying, "Repent, for the kingdom of heaven is at hand." (4:17)

Even a small amount of thoughtful reading in the canonical gospels will render it obvious that the retreat of Jesus to the desert, and his temptations there, were a direct consequence of his baptismal experience. Somehow he had heard God's endorsement of himself as a "beloved Son." And this endorsement in the mind of Jesus, and among his followers later on, became the historical seed from which the Christian religion sprouted and grew.

The existential question that drove Jesus into solitude thus was a logical result of divine revelation: What does it really mean to be God's Son? The resolution at which Jesus arrived in the course of his wilderness solitude, by prayer and fasting, answers precisely this question. Thus, it is implied that Jesus rejected and condemned all "satanic" schemes of overlordship, such as military might, slavery, and all the vestments of grand domestication together with their concomitant institutionalized cultic legitimizations. Elsewhere Jesus

Copyrighted Material

identified his principal opponent as the "ruler of this world" (*John* 12:31; 14:30; 16:11).

For three thousand years, in the Near East, large civilizations had been emerging, blossoming here and there into mighty empires. Invariably they were organized by ambitious grand domesticators and were maintained, generally, with support from some kind of priestly hype. All these civilizations and grand domestication systems were supervised by leaders who played ambitious roles of god representation or god impersonation. Hereditary rulers insisted on being the legitimate sons of God, or gods.

During periods when separate religious organizations were strong enough to define *divinity* and *divine sonship*, the overdomesticator ambitions of "secular" military kings sometimes could be contained. Such kings were legitimized in a limited sense as human executive arms in the service of God, on earth. High priests in such grand domestication schemes claimed the status of "representatives" of God, and they insisted on being the mediators between God and humankind. In the best-balanced grand domestication systems such priestly representatives of God would keep the ruling impersonators of God, divine kings or "sons of God," somewhat in check.

Startled by his baptismal experience and revealed audition, and sensitized even more during his long fast in the desert, the man Jesus of Nazareth achieved clarity about his indeed being God's son. In addition, he resolved that his filial relationship with God did not call for grand domestication behavior, neither did it require aristocratic pretense or priestly hype. Unpretentiously he therefore got into the habit of addressing his divine Father in Heaven with the Hebrew-Aramaic "Abba!" This appellation was an expression of familiarity and endearment. In English it compares with "Daddy!"

No prudent grand domesticator would refer in public to his own divinized and mortal sire as if he were only a soft and gentle daddy. Grand domesticators always have ruled by sacerdotal hype, all the while fully conscious of their assumed honor and distinction. They have played their roles as heroes and gods and have so generated fear in the souls of their subjects.

Of course, when measured by the standards of average civilized and overdomesticated citizens, the self-awareness and personal theology of Jesus seemed conceited, if not downright perverted. And in relation to Pharisaic theology it appeared blasphemous as well. No

Copyrighted Material

transient penniless rabbi was entitled to such transroyal status, much less to intimate filial proximity with the one and only God on High.

Empires generate their own definitions, and definitions accepted by herds of people make, unmake, or reshape empires. Jesus staunchly taught the immediate arrival of heaven's kingdom—he announced a real and a more genuine kingdom than the ones that hitherto scored in the annals of human history. The meek, who ordinarily in kingdoms of this world reap scorn, were assured by Jesus that they would inherit the earth; that is, inherit an earth that increasingly would come under the influence of God's heavenly rule. People who were poor in spirit, who were not shrewd analytic predators or exploiters, would belong in this heavenly and real kingdom. It was a peaceable kingdom, where leaders behaved like humble servants, and where servants and masters had equal status. In short, it was a kingdom where even the majestic heavenly Father of Christianity's founder did not mind being "daddy" to the offspring of ordinary humankind. And this kind of an antithetical kingdom, Jesus insisted, was now at hand.

The words of the apostle Paul quoted at the beginning of this section proceeded to extend the divine kingdom, or humanly speaking the divinized human family under "Daddy" Almighty, to a point where it included all those who love God.

Surely, according to Jesus' own words which he spoke during his trial, and according to sound reasoning, such a kingdom was "not of this world." In the full English metaphorical sense it was something very much "out of this world." But precisely with regard to this kind of a kingdom Jesus claimed, unabashedly, that he was its "king." He could as well have claimed to be a slave in that kingdom—as Paul explained in *Romans* 15:8, and as in turn he also claimed to be a slave of Jesus Christ (*Romans* 1:1). King or servant, or servant to the servant, meant one and the same thing in that kingdom of heaven. All these teachings together express the absence of status and power play in the kingdom of God.

If that is so, why then has Jesus insisted explicitly on the title of "king" in that otherworldly kingdom? The answer is far more straightforward and obvious than most Christians and their detractors hitherto have comprehended.

As long as there were some kind of kingdoms or grand domestication systems in this world, and as long as people were abused in these systems by "Son of God" pretenders and divine representatives, Jesus deemed it necessary—inasmuch as he knew himself to be a different

Copyrighted Material

kind of Son of God—to insist on a different definition of "kingship." He based that new definition on his new definition of *kingdom*, relative to God and heaven, which was equally radical.

Jesus knew perfectly well that he was misunderstood by his judges. Yet, instead of trying to clear himself of the charge of sedition, he intentionally provoked and amplified their misunderstanding. Defiantly he put high priest and Sanhedrin on trial, and he threw into his cauldron of judgment the divine Roman emperor's procurator to boot. On behalf of his overall contrary message, Jesus refused to avoid an avoidable death sentence. He gave what to his accusers were obviously ambiguous answers; and his accusers, obligingly, convicted him.

All the while, as a result of Jesus having announced a "kingdom of heaven," a new socio-political order emerged and became a real fact of history. That which initially was "not of this world" produced a movement that was very much "in this world."

For Jesus, personally, the kingdom of heaven remained the normative Kingdom, by which all kingdoms henceforth were to be measured and judged. From the perspective of his revised Son of God consciousness, he explained his Father's kingdom to people who were still caught up in corrupt kingdoms of this world. With his view of universalized divine-human dignity Jesus confronted, and he judged, what he regarded to be an inverted divinized status of worldly emperors. Implicitly he rejected and undercut their fake heavenly mandates and their cruel empires.

Jesus was crucified for stirring up the people and speaking blasphemy. And indeed, if such unsettling and balancing activities deserve the death sentence, as often in civilized grand domestication systems they do, then Jesus at any rate received due process under civil law. It was his stubborn insistence on his divinely inspired and revised standards for *kingdom*, for *Son of God*, for *king*, for *King of kings* and *divine emperor*, that provoked condemnation by the Jewish as well as Roman authorities. His obstinate endurance, his unswerving commitment to act out a divine call and parody, to be another type of Son of God, in the final analysis, brought him the penalty of death.

The life and message of Jesus was based on his vision of a fulfilled *pan*theistic ontology, of a realized kingdom of heaven. His heavenly Father's claim on him proceeded on the basis of this vision. For the duration of his life on earth Jesus was caught up in an ordinary double-layered grand domestication system. Within that

Copyrighted Material

system all kinds of human victims were being judged and damned, here below, by judges who reigned as if speaking from on high. All the while, Jesus simply refused to live in their grand domesticated world. He refused to recognize their world as something real. By not recognizing earthly kingdoms he denied their legitimacy.[4]

In the new universalistic awareness that Jesus had of the kingdom of heaven, all grand domestication systems in the longer run stood damned and doomed. The historical records testify that impoverished folk listened to Jesus gladly. All the while, the status of grand domesticators was being undercut and eroded by his radical insistence on heavenly over earthly standards. The masses of people who followed Jesus grew larger, and it was only a matter of time before his "kingdom of heaven" definition became unbearably popular. On account of this new glimmer of egalitarian and rational insight, cast in the form of a religio-political parody, mighty emperors abdicated and disclaimed their divine status, eventually.[5]

Amazingly, the man Jesus who over and beyond the horizons of grand domesticated society has lived his life as a divinely graced parody, in opposition to established royal Sons of God, has electrified and even transcended human mortality itself—while he was at it. Divine-royal status, and return to the All-Father after death, were interdependent notions in orthodox Egyptian religion. Thus, after the dead body of Jesus hung transfixed at a Roman cross, and after his corpse had been laid to rest in a Jewish tomb, fresh excitement erupted among his followers while they were still in mourning. A few among them testified to the fact that the tomb of Jesus had been seen empty; and in consequence many more people told of encounters with their resurrected Lord.

---

[4]The incident given in *Matthew* 22:15ff frequently is mustered to demonstrate Jesus' support of the empire. In reality, his answer there is evasive at best. He let Caesar have his money, because money was not essential for his kingdom of heaven gospel. His advice at Capernaum, according to *Matthew* 17:24ff, to pay the half-shekel tax, is given also so as not to be unnecessarily offensive.

[5]The initial wavering and final resolution of the Emperor Constantine may be mentioned here as the classic example. For details see Ioannes Karayannopulos, "Konstantin der Grosse und der Kaiserkult" in Antonie Wlosok, *Römischer Kaiserkult* (Darmstadt, 1978), pp. 485–527.

Copyrighted Material

When speculating about the source of the Pharisaic belief in resurrection, scholars usually point to Iranian Mazdaism. Indeed, Persian influence on the history of Judaism is a fact of history, so too is Persia's contact with Egypt. Mircea Eliade was correct when he renamed the Iranian belief in the "resurrection of the dead" as "recreation of bodies." Elsewhere he has summarized how, according to Mazdaism, after the final judgment a human soul "will recover a resuscitated and glorious body."[6]

While influences from Mazdaism on Pharisaic Judaism and on early Christian belief need not be ruled out completely, the specific resurrection gospel that got Christendom started was definitely something more. First, the apparitions of Christ's resurrection body were temporary; they represented not a re-created and permanent state, precipitated on him by divine Judgment. His apparitions ceased when he returned to his Father. Second, in the Christian context, the savior's resurrection and ascension were notions very much dependent on his earlier descent. The Father's begetting and the Son's returning constitute a single gospel event, a single round-trip journey. From ancient Egypt we can derive the model for this entire round trip, whereas from latter-day Iran we can derive only the return journey. The probability of an ideological link with Egyptian soteriology therefore is considerably stronger.

Translated into Egyptian concepts, the Christian story of resurrection means that after Christ's resurrection as a *ba* apparition, between the moment of his resurrection and his ascension as *ka* essence to the Father, his *ba* appearances lingered a while longer. The neo-Egyptian Plotinus still understands this process very well.[7]

Joy of victory over the world's evils and death, wrought by God the Father who had raised his only-begotten Son, became the propellant of the revived Kingdom of Heaven movement from that first exciting Easter Sunday onward. Far and wide in the overdomesticated world Christian apostles proclaimed their kerygma: "Christ is risen!" and "Christ is Lord!"

---

[6]Mircea Eliade, *A History of Religious Ideas*, Vol. 1 (Chicago, 1978), p. 332 and Vol. 2, (1982), p. 320. He relies on passages in *Denkart* and refers to commentary by Zaehner.

[7]Compare the discussion of Ennead VI,4, in Chapter 14.

Copyrighted Material

Jewish leaders, particularly the Hellenized party of Sadducees whom the (Egyptianized) resurrection tale spoofed most of all, were infuriated about this resumption of irrational populist commotion. The Roman authorities, who had accommodated the Jewish accusers of Jesus, and who along a path of least resistance had furnished a death sentence in hope of maintaining order in the province, were puzzled even more by this ever-so-strange Hebrew behavior. They knew well how to deal with straightforward insurrection. Outright refusal to concede divine rights to the Roman emperor they could have identified and judged with reasonable precision. If someone shouted "Down with Caesar!" they knew how to crucify or behead the usurper, depending on his citizenship status within the empire.

But in this new commotion hundreds of people, and soon thousands, professed the puzzling kerygma of "Christ is risen!" The Roman civil authorities had no effective rational method with which to respond to this apparent absurdity. Christians therefore were alternately tolerated and persecuted in the provinces, and finally under Decius (250 C.E.) hunted with the full weight of Roman authority. Many lost their lives and, at the same time, many found the real fulfillment of their lives in the glories of martyrdom and heaven.

To this very day non-Christian philosophers, nesting comfortably in the underbrush that remains of the old forest of Christendom, still are puzzled by the fact that the Christian resurrection faith has spread so far and wide among genuine *homines sapientes*. Try as they may, they cannot ignore the fact that at a certain moment in Western history many educated Greco-Roman citizens converted to this absurdity that, back then, somehow must have seemed reasonable. But how was it reasonable?

The essence of this apparent foolishness lies with latter-day political naivete and the increasing distance from bygone reality configurations. Indeed, if viewed in the context of the larger evolutionary and historical process, within the commonsense context of classic Egyptian ontology, the resurrection kerygma of Christendom makes excellent political sense.

Finally, or "in the fullness of time" as the gospel writers expressed that sentiment, after three millennia of grand domestication efforts on the part of mortal tyrants who paraded as sons of God, the Christian resurrection story provided an alternate way of judging imperialism, militarism, human sacrifice, slavery, and other modes of overdomestication. And appraising the gospel story's intent, in

Copyrighted Material

light of Christendom's own subsequent lapses into methods of over-domestication, this kerygma of resurrection certainly was not destined to be the last of its kind.

For the time being, those who felt like damning the divine emperor in Rome no longer needed to join the small and hopeless schemes of zealotry or consistently suffer the bad news concerning setbacks among revolutions. In the company of angry freedom fighters, they no longer needed to shout "Down with Caesar!"

From Jesus they learned the secret of how to look at the brighter side of God's creation and evolutionary process. By welcoming the Father's intruding heavenly kingdom, they knew themselves to be on the winning side, for a change. Thus they subscribed to the divine power of positive political thinking. They could just as well shout "Christ is risen!" It was much more effective. It was much less dangerous. And in the longer run it meant and accomplished the same thing, even better.

By way of adapting to its new function as a check and balance to traditional imperial administration, this kerygma—with its new songs and prayers, learned from reformed angel voices and new visions of the kingdom of heaven—gradually reformed the rhythms and rites of life in Near Eastern, Mediterranean, and Western civilizations.

In its secularized form the Christian ethos still has been unfolding, in recent centuries, in the form of modern democratic ideals, even in democratic revolutions that have pitted reformed grand domestication presidents and folk heroes over against older houses of royalty. Violent democracies and republics have revolted against older violent and imperial sacerdotal enterprises. More threats and more sounds of guns, more reverberations from the primal greater-than-human Big Bang attested to by modern scientific mythology; and less songs of angels are being heard by human ears these days. More spectacular fireworks, flares, and less divine glories are being seen reflected in frightened human eyes.

Copyrighted Material

Copyrighted Material

17

The Gnosis Competition

Defining *gnosticism* or *gnosis*, humanly speaking, is an impossibility. It may be said that the task of studying gnosticism is even more difficult than, for instance, trying to comprehend a religion like "Hinduism." The latter generally is defined by a method of subtraction. One subtracts from all the religious life of India, past and present, those religious movements that can be classified under Jainism, Buddhism, Islam, Sikhism, and Christianity. What remains, for lack of any quick alternative, may be lumped together under the label of *Hinduism* or *Induism*. By comparison, a definition of *gnosticism* or *gnosis* is more difficult to attain because, thus far, the place of origin for this particular "*ism*" has not been ascertained or linked geographically with a known culture area, as this has been possible in the case of Hinduism in relation to India.

The reader will have noticed, however, that this situation gradually may be changing. No longer is it necessary to define *gnosticism* vaguely as a general milieu of thought or "syncretism" that somehow, as if coming from nowhere, permeated the Greco-Roman mixture of Hellenistic culture. Moreover, gnosticism's root notions hereby reveal themselves not merely as having belonged to a larger family of Near Eastern religions. We now know that ancient Egyptian religion was the matriarch of that family.

Gnosticism versus Christianity

In published commentaries, thus far, gnosticism still is being presented as the same many-headed hydra recognized already by the earliest Christian heresiologists. Such vagueness on the subject matter prevails because there never has been an organized "gnostic" church

Copyrighted Material

identified with certainty and to everyone's satisfaction; nor has an authoritative "gnostic" canon of scripture ever been compiled.

Gnostic "others" were first identified and classified as heretical folk by Christian catalogers of heresies—Irenaeus of Lyons (ca. 130–200) being foremost among them. They were people who had not adequately subscribed and conformed to the precepts and mores of the Christian majority. This fact naturally begs the question as to who, on the other hand, were that majority and these Christian heresiologists.

I already have explained how, during the first century C.E., a "kingdom of heaven" movement emerged from within Judaism and spread quickly. It then became dialectically involved with the larger Greco-Roman world of religious and political aspirations. Followers of that religion gathered in churches that initially were modeled after Jewish synagogues. Outsiders, disparagingly, began to call these church-going people *Christians*, that is, Christ followers. The label stuck and became a badge of honor for those who followed and worshipped Christ Jesus. And, of course, these Christians were "gnostics" in the sense that they "knew" something about God's saving revelation through Christ Jesus.

The ambiguity concerning gnosticism shows up, nowadays, as soon as one attributes an ability to know—thus "gnosis"—to *homines sapientes* in general. Christians knew a few things about God and his plan of salvation for humankind, whereas other folk knew a few other things about how God saves people from different predicaments. Faced by this wider ambiguity and the fact that other people were known to subscribe to other and yet similar soteriologies, Paul warned in *1 Corinthians* 8:1ff against an overreliance on gnosis. The deutero-Pauline pastoral letters have offered a similar warning against "gnostics" who do not really know what they say they know:

> O Timothy, guard what has been entrusted to you. Avoid the godless chatter and contradictions of what is falsely called knowledge, for by professing it some have missed the mark as regards to faith. (*1 Timothy* 20–21)

What is meant here by knowledge (gnosis) in contrast to false knowledge? What is false knowledge in contrast to the Christian faith? And is not faith the Christian equivalent of what may be recognized as revealed knowledge elsewhere? And what gnosis could
Copyrighted Material

not be regarded as also having been revealed? Such questions all were destined to quickly glide off into the realm of religious ontology. They had to be resolved as questions that require the ontological content of a distinct religious faith—or the entire field of gnosis.

There is at least a nominal difference between those who aspired to Christian faith and those who stood apart as gnostics. Faithful "Christians" clung to their name as a badge of honor and thereby became a distinct and identifiable group, whereas the so-called gnostics remained less organized and unspecified knowers at large. Although this superficial classification served the old Christian catalogers of heresies reasonably well, it has become quite misleading to later historians. There may never have been a religious movement, anywhere in the world, that reasonably could be distinguished from other religions in terms of certainty of "knowledge." To substitute the label of *gnosis* for *gnosticism* does not seem to resolve that basic difficulty.

Kurt Rudolph alerted us to the fact that already in 1699, with Gottfried Arnold's *Unparteiische Ketzer und Kirchen-historie*, "the ground was prepared for an independent consideration of the gnostics."[1] And indeed Rudolph himself still has treated gnosticism essentially as the same unique other-than-Christian phenomenon—as multiple syncretisms with many tributaries. It seems remarkable that the primary stream, ancient Egyptian orthodoxy, has not yet been recognized among these tributaries.[2] Indeed, that stream is so wide that it easily can be mistaken for the ocean itself.

---

[1] Kurt Rudolph, *Gnosis: The Nature and History of Gnosis* (San Francisco, 1987 [1977]), p. 30.

[2] Ibid., pp. 277–294. Among Gnosticism's primary historical sources and tributaries Rudolph has identified the fringes of Judaism; traits of Jewish monotheism; Jewish apocalyptic; Qumran; Jewish wisdom teaching; Jewish skepticism; Iranian Zoroastrian ideas; Greek philosophic enlightenment, especially Platonism and Middle Platonism; the Hermetica; Hellenistic mysteries; Orphism; Greco-Oriental syncretism, including "Syria or Egypt"; individualism and esoterism; spiritualization; economic conditions; the spread of oriental cults—Cybele, Isis, the unvanquished sun god, and Mithras; urban living; social protest; and religious intellectualism.

Copyrighted Material

Egyptian Christianity

The most problematic area for the study of early Christian history is Egypt—and that fact should alert students of that history to possible surprises. Of all the Christian mission fields, boundary lines between Christianity and "gnosticism" are most difficult to draw in the ancient land of Egypt.

In his *History and Literature of Early Christianity*, Helmut Koester commented on the apparent absence of Christianity in Egypt during the first decades of missionary expansion: "It is indeed unthinkable that the Christian mission should have bypassed Alexandria for decades." But then, as Walter Bauer already had suggested in 1934, our historical lacuna may have been determined by the different perspectives current within the early catholic church. Well defined perspectives on what had become orthodox Christendom, generally, have been used to sort out the source materials for church historians. "The beginnings of Christianity in Egypt"—so Koester summarizes Bauer—"were 'heretical,' and therefore Christian writings composed in Egypt in this early period were not preserved."[3] Fortunately for historians, copies of some of these early "heretical" Egyptian documents have since come to light. The Nag Hammadi library contains a number of them.

* * *

In a broad overview, such as is attempted by this book, it is not possible to revisit the entire field of gnosis studies. Let it suffice to say, however, that many apparently related data hitherto have been gathered, harvested like sheaves, and brought home under the rubric of "gnosticism." Academicians built a stately "gnosticism" barn to contain all these data. But then, the act of gathering a large mixed group of non-Christian "knowers," from the first century C.E. onward, into a single hypothetical barn, or sheave, may be an excellent task for barn builders and harvesters. But for most serious

---

[3]Helmut Koester, *History and Literature of Early Christianity*, (Berlin and New York, 1982), pp. 219-232. Copyrighted Material

historians the outcome of these labors has remained an indigestible and ambiguous plethora of "alldata."

Hans Jonas and more recently Kurt Rudolph brought a measure of order into the hypothetical "gnosis barn"—the construct into which a wealth of data from the early Christian era have been gathered. This book attempts no rebuttal of their accomplishments. The immense task of rebundling the total hypothetical sheaf of gnosticism, in light of distinct strains of ingredients, has been accomplished effectively by these two scholars. But, obviously, their work remains incomplete and must be carried forward and revised wherever fresh historical connections come into view.

Several fallout effects from Egyptian religion, for Israelite religion and Judaism, have been sketched already in Part Two. Part Three provided a similar revised sketch for Greek philosophy and Neoplatonism. As a result of new oblique "Egyptian light" streaming from those directions, much of traditional Christian theology now stands better illuminated as well. The distances between ancient Egypt, Christendom, and gnostic doctrines have been lessened in the process.

Also, with the discovery of the Nag Hammadi library, in Upper Egypt, the general profile of "gnosticism" has come into better view. All these texts eventually must be reexamined in light of possible ancient Egyptian antecedents. In addition to some specific Nag Hammadi texts that allude directly to Egypt—for example, "On the Origin of the World," "The Exegesis on the Soul," "The Gospel of the Egyptians," "The Thunder, Perfect Mind," "Asclepius," "Discourse on the Eighth and Ninth"—at least another dozen or so treatises contained in this "gnostic" library clearly are indebted to ancient Egyptian theology. Even a superficial discussion of all of these would call for writing another hefty volume.

Thus, instead of becoming sidetracked to yet another major enterprise, we shall rather turn to Simon Magus as an exemplary figure singled out by early Christian heresiologists as the foremost among these "gnostics." But before that can be undertaken it will be helpful to review how gnosticism has been summarized persistently by two prominent scholars, as containing a little of everything, dualism as well as monism. Before we can hope to understand the spiritual inheritances that have become the chosen content and subject matter for our academic disciplines, we must pay attention to the history of our presuppositions.

Copyrighted Material

Hans Jonas

Statements by this scholar have been quoted repeatedly in the Gnostic Studies field, especially his characterization of gnosticism as dualistic. This unfortunate misconception has to be put aside before anything more can be done.

In support of his "dualistic" definition, the gnosticism sheave of Hans Jonas contains strains of data garnered from as far away as Zoroastrianism. Iranian dualism has been counted, with Manichaeism serving as proxy, as having been an important dimension in the larger Hellenistic syncretism:

> The cardinal feature of gnostic thought is the radical dualism that governs the relation of God and world, and correspondingly that of man and world. The deity is absolutely transmundane, its nature alien to that of the universe, which it neither created nor governs and to which it is the complete antithesis: to the divine realm of light, self-contained and remote, the cosmos is opposed as the realm of darkness. The world is the work of lowly powers which though they may mediately be descended from Him do not know the true God and obstruct the knowledge of Him in the cosmos over which they rule. The genesis of these lower powers, the Archons (rulers), and in general that of all the orders of being outside God, including the world itself, is a main theme of gnostic speculation. . . . The transcendent God Himself is hidden from all creatures and is unknowable by natural concepts. Knowledge of Him requires supranatural revelation and illumination and even then can hardly be expressed otherwise than in negative terms.[4]

This much Hans Jonas has summarized concerning gnostic "theology" as such. He then proceeded to delineate gnostic cosmology, anthropology, eschatology, and morality. How much damage his fivefold imposition of categories has inflicted on the larger historical picture is still difficult to assess. Although we are concerned

---

[4]Hans Jonas, *The Gnostic Religion* (Boston, 1963 [1958]), pp. 42f.
Copyrighted Material

here with ancient Egyptian central notions, in theology and soteriology, we nevertheless have come to suspect, as a result of Jonas' approach, some unnecessary fragmentation of the larger phenomenon. Dualism has been projected into soteriology; that is, into its ontological dimension, where it least likely belongs:

> The radical nature of the dualism determines that of the doctrine of salvation. As alien as the transcendent God is to "this world" is the pneumatic self in the midst of it. The goal of gnostic striving is the release of the "inner man" from the bonds of the world and his return to his native realm of light.[5]

It is to his eternal credit that Hans Jonas has seen an obvious need to supplement his earlier abstraction, of cosmic dualism, with this postscript on soteriology. Now, after both cards have been placed on the table by him—dualism as well as soteriology—his authoritative pronouncement about gnostic dualism well may be in need of some backward adjustment. The entire problem reduces to the question of whether one is to think about this "dualistic gnostic" theology from the perspective of an estranged individual soul or rather listen to a reconciled soul who is returning home. In the former case the epithet *dualism* is appropriate, whereas in the latter instance the dualism of estrangement is in process of being overcome.

In any case, Hans Jonas has summarized some more his own summary of gnostic eschatology with a famous Valentinian formula. But incidently, this bit of gnostic advice reveals to us no "dualistic" worries on the part of its author. That person was concerned merely with getting from here to there within a rationally coherent dimension of reality:

> What liberates is the knowledge of who we were, what we became; where we were, wereinto we have been thrown; whereto we speed, wherefrom we are redeemed; what birth is, and what rebirth. (*Exc. Theod.* 78,2)[6]

---

[5]Ibid., pp. 44f.

[6]Ibid., p. 45.

Copyrighted Material

Kurt Rudolph

Responding obviously to Hans Jonas, and in some ways also echoing his words, this scholar has disassembled and rebundled the sheave of gnosticism by way of acknowledging a larger number of basic strains. To that effect he introduced his "basic framework" of gnosticism with an excellent trim quote from the 1966 Messina conference, On the Origins of Gnosticism. He points to the central idea, or the central myth, of gnosticism:

> the idea of the presence in man of a divine "spark" ... which has proceeded from the divine world and has fallen into this world of destiny, birth and death, and which must be reawakened through its own divine counterpart in order to be finally restored. This idea...is ontologically based on the conception of a downward development of the divine whose periphery (often called Sophia or Ennoia) has fatally fallen victim to a crisis and must—even if only indirectly—produce this world, in which it then cannot be disinterested, in that once again it must recover the divine "spark" (often designated as *pneuma*, "spirit").[7]

Amazingly, after this beautiful summary of what to us appears to be genuine monistic ancient Egyptian soteriology, Rudolph continues with repeating the old Jonas cliche to the effect that gnosticism is dualistic. Rudolph, for a moment, even pretends to derive dualism from the passage just quoted:

> From this quotation it is already clear that at the basis of Gnosis there is a dualistic view of the world which determines all its statements on a cosmological and anthropological level.... This dualism is carried along or, to put it more accurately, interwoven with a monistic idea which is expressed in the already mentioned upward and downward development of the divine spark and which is the basis for the identification of man and deity.... Imbedded in this "dualism on a monistic background" is the doctrine of God

---

[7]Quoted in Rudolph, *Gnosis*, p. 57.
Copyrighted Material

in Gnosis, which is determined above all by the idea of the "un-known God" beyond all that is visible or sensible, and incorporates a "fullness" (*pleroma*) of angels and other heavenly beings, be they personified ideas (abstractions) or hypostases.[8]

But wait a minute! That is not so! The scholar merely began with his conclusion of gnostic dualism to position it "on a monistic background." A puzzled reader might wish to ask why anyone could not begin, as well, with introducing gnosticism first as monism, and then worry about the secondary ambiguity of its "dualism" later. Whence, all of a sudden, came Rudolph's "monistic background"? Why could that background not be understood as the essence of gnosticism? If a universal monad is being contemplated, starting at one of its ends in terms of far and near, up and down, high and low, does that necessarily make it a dualism?

Nevertheless, one can only be impressed by the wonderful authoritative support Kurt Rudolph has provided for our thesis in spite of himself. He has, in fact, summarized the basic emanational unity of ancient Heliopolitan religion in gnostic teachings.

Simon Magus

Posterity probably will judge that too much attention is being given in this book to Simon Magus. Nevertheless, the necessary task of reexamining the "gnosis" phenomenon in light of fresh "Egyptian light" may begin just as easily with him as with any other. After all, Simon Magus scored in the history of Christendom as its one-time arch opponent. As the "father of all heresy," he must now be restudied not merely as an opponent, but also as a conspicuous competitor of Christ in the early Christian church—possibly even as a potential ally. Christian theology and christology together have driven their roots deep into ancient Egyptian religion, as had the theology of Simon Magus. From the fact of their common Egyptian heritage may be derived the very strength of Simon Magus's threat. The danger amounted to the possibility that he could be confused with

---

[8]Ibid., p. 57f.

Copyrighted Material

the Christ figure itself. The teachings of Simon therefore had to be differentiated unequivocally from the Christian gospel.[9]

Simon Magus, the person, is not a very sure historical datum. Nevertheless, his personal presence in history has been defined by Christian heresiologists as "father of all heresy." Thus, he definitely scores in our context as a historical datum in heresiology. Whether this arch foe of Christianity was identical with the personage in *Acts* 8 is difficult to discern for sure. On the other hand, the mere question of whether one is dealing here with a literary construct, a foil to Christian orthodox doctrine, or with a singular historical figure for the moment may be suspended. Both possibilities eventually will have to be reexamined in light of a common Egyptian religious heritage.

The Simon Magus cult mentioned in Christian heresiology, having emerged from the works of recent gnosticism scholars more clearly, has had—as it now turns out—its ideological roots deep in the theology of ancient Egypt. For the sake of beginning the Simon Magus discourse afresh we shall assume, for the moment, the historical identity of the personage mentioned in *Acts* 8 with the one described by later heresiologists. We engage in this hypothetical exercise because it is conceivable that "Egyptian light" may further illuminate the historicity of this personage. Definitive conclusions obviously will have to be left to future scholarship.

According to the Church Fathers Irenaeus and Hippolytus, the man Simon Magus was founder of a first century cult in Samaria.[10] As of late, this cult has been classified among the so-called gnostic religions. Actually, he was much more than only its founder. He was the movement's central divine figure, its messiah, and its God. The divine status of Simon was deduced directly from a variant of Egyptian ontology. For introducing Simon's basic teachings, and for

---

[9]It is customary, in Christian circles, to read the title *magus* literally, as denoting magician, sorcerer, or witch. However, such value judgments must be suspended during the opening stages of history of religions research. Similar denigrations have been used by outsiders against functionaries in many religions.

[10]Irenaeus, *Adv. haer.* I 23,1–4, and Hippolytus, *Refutatio* VI, 9–18. See Rudolph, *Gnosis,* pp. 294ff.

Copyrighted Material

the sake of brevity, we shall avail ourselves here of the masterful assortment Hans Jonas has compiled.[11]

"There is one Power, divided into upper and lower, begetting itself, increasing itself, seeking itself, finding itself, being its own mother, its own father... its own daughter, its own son... One, root of the All." This One, unfolded, "is he who stands, stood and shall stand: he stands above in the unbegotten Power; he stood below in the stream of waters, begotten in the image; he shall stand above with the blessed infinite power when his image shall be perfected."[12]

The ancient Egyptian root of this credal statement is difficult to miss. Even Hans Jonas, who divided Gnosticism into Syrian-Egyptian and Iranian branches, has exegeted here from all the Simon Magus documents something that very closely resembles ancient Egyptian process theology, without explicit "Syrian" or "Iranian" traces.

The most peculiar element in this Samaritan cult theology, of course, was the offspring that the ancient Egyptian "Tefnut-Mahet" hypostasis has engendered—the *Ennoia*.[13] It is necessary to review for a moment the Egyptian prehistory of this feminine dimension in the godhead.

The association of Tefnut with Mahet is as ancient as are the Coffin Texts.[14] In later Egyptian times the goddess Mahet, as a

---

[11]Jonas, *The Gnostic Religion,* pp. 103–111.

[12]Ibid., p. 105 (Hippol. *Refut.* VI.17.1–3), suggests that the dichotomy of "upper and lower" was derived by Simon Magus from a process that occurs within the primal being or godhead itself. Moreover, he considered this "a distinctive feature of the Syrian and Alexandrian gnosis, which"—according to Jonas—"starts from a dualism of pre-existent principles."

[13]Parallels pertaining to the Ennoia and the Barbelo, in the Nag Hammadi texts, may be consulted to round out the larger picture. A more complete and self-contained overview on these can be found in "The Exegesis on the Soul" in that same collection.

[14]See for instance Spell 80, in Chapter 4, on "Heliopolitan Orthodoxy in the Coffin Texts."

Copyrighted Material

personal manifestation of justice, right, rightness, order, and truth has been brought into companionship with Thoth, the masculine patron of knowledge and scribalism. She has become the feminine associate of Thoth. Some kind of reconciled male-female relationship, such as was supposed to exist between Mahet and Thoth, appears also to have stood as model for the theology and soteriology of Simon Magus.

But there was another important dimension to divine woman-hood—already embryonically present in traditional Egyptian religion. It went beyond the intellectual virtues expressed by the personification of Mahet. Isis, as mother of Horus and member of the Heliopolitan Ennead, represented divine womanhood in Egypt like no other goddess. She did so generally under the guise of her anthropomorphic *ba*, wearing a horned headdress. As the Enneadean goddess nearest to humankind, Isis embodied the basic function of feminine creativity as well as confidence. In offbeat traditions she did so even to the point of self-sufficiency in procreation.

For example, a late text of a typical "lamentation of Isis" mentions this self-sufficiency in relation to her generation of Horus. Hers was an almost parthenogenetic act. Isis says, "I made myself into a man, even though I was a woman."[15] The basic myth tells that it was Isis who retrieved the corpse of her brother-husband Osiris, it was she who gathered up his scattered portions. It was she who revived his sexual potency. According to Plutarch's later version, the phallus of Osiris was not among the gathered and reassembled parts. Isis therefore substituted on him a phallus of her own making whereby subsequently she conceived Horus. This could mean that Horus essentially was generated by her alone.

An even more free-spirited Isis can be found mentioned in a spell used against scorpion and snake venom, on a number of papyri from the Nineteenth Dynasty (1320–1200 B.C.E.). We find the goddess plotting for her share of power; that is, for status and partnership with the godhead Amun-Ra himself. Before the clever Isis took matters into her own hands, the godhead had not yet divulged his powerful secret name to any of the gods.

---

[15]Kees, *Lesebuch*, p. 30, in Hans Bonnet, *Reallexikon der Ägyptischen Religions-geschichte* (Berlin, 1952), p. 327.

Copyrighted Material

Now Isis was a clever woman. Her heart was craftier than a million men; she was choicer than a million gods; she was more discerning than a million of the noble dead.[16]

Isis knew everything in heaven and earth, like Amun-Ra himself, except his own hidden name.[17] In arranging her plot, Isis gathered up some of the God's spittle and kneaded it together with earth into a venomous snake. This most dangerous creature she laid, immobile, on the path the high deity frequented. The snake stung. The God became ill. And in return for his health the godhead "Atum and Horus-of-Praise" divulged to Isis his secret name.[18] Isis is the only one besides Amun-Ra himself who now knows this name. Of course, the God's secret is safe. Isis who, seen from a human perspective also functions in the cosmic dimension as Tefnut or Mahet, is very wise. Motivated by her own enlightened self-interest, she keeps the divine name secret from all the other gods. This measure assures her second-rank status and power in the created universe next to the godhead himself.

Thus the theme of the self-willed feminine hypostasis of the godhead, which was exploited by Simon Magus, has been well-enough foreboded in Egyptian religion and mythology. The name that Simon Magus gave to his feminine hypostasis was *Ennoia*. It is somewhat tempting to interpret this name historically as a feminine derivative from the larger Egyptian Ennead, but for the time being we shall refrain from doing so. In any case, this particular estranged female personage was the First Thought on God's mind. From what else we know about the incarnated godhead Simon Magus, she also might have been the foremost thing on his mind.

We must summarize Simon's gospel more coherently, and in doing so we shall avail ourselves of the synthesis of texts that Hans

---

[16]See John A. Wilson, "Egyptian Myths, Tales, and Mortuary Texts," in *Ancient Near Eastern Texts Relating to the Old Testament*, ed. James B. Pritchard (Princeton, N.J., 1969), pp. 12–14.

[17]See the Theban theology in Chapter 5.

[18]*Atum and Horus-of-Praise* identifies the God Amun still squarely with the Heliopolitan Ennead. Atum and Horus may be understood as representing the alpha and the omega of the Ennead.

Copyrighted Material

Jonas put together. In accordance with the gospel of this Samaritan cult, its founding magus has been identical with God Manifest. This quaint proclamation by the man Simon instantly will be brought into clearer focus, simply by transcribing it into his First Person Singular. For that purpose the text will be freely abbreviated here and paraphrased.[19] Simon Magus reasoned thusly and spoke:

My mind (i.e., God's mind) is captivated by this feminine hypostasis of mine (i.e., the Ennoia). Initially I had in mind to create angels and archangels through her. But, anticipating my intentions, this female Ennoia descended to the lowest regions of my outreach; and there this unruly divine female hastened to beat me to the act of procreation, by herself. Relying on her own feminine potentials alone, she generated angels and powers by whom, in turn, this world was made. And these her offspring, having been generated by her in estrangement and freedom from me, were totally ignorant of my presence; that is, of me who is the All-Father. Therefore, in turn, my Thought became preoccupied with those angels and powers, with those who had come into being through her—through her who is my first Thought and preoccupation. And my Thought thereby was dragged from its highest heaven down toward those secondary creative principalities who scurry about to alter phenomena in the nether regions of the cosmos.

The Ennoia, on the other hand, has suffered at their hands all manner of abuse, so that she might be hindered from returning home to me, the Father. And their abuse of her went so far as to even wrap her in human flesh. For centuries she migrated on earth from one female body into a next one. Thus degraded, in one instance, she was Helen on account of whom the Trojan War was fought. But as of late this Ennoia had been a whore in Tyre. And I, God Father, having descended to earth in human form as Simon Magus to find her, have come to save and return her home unto myself.

* * *

---

[19]The summary of Jonas utilizes *Iren.* I.23.2 including *Homilies* II.25; Hippolytus VI.19; and Tertullian's *De animo* Ch. 34.

Copyrighted Material

Let us hypothesize, for the sake of this discussion, a scenario by which Simon Magus has begun his religious career with Hebrew theology and a general Hebrew mind set, and that subsequently along the way he heard rumors of Philo's angelology. And then let us also assume that he might have become better acquainted with an extant strain of orthodox Egyptian theology. The upshot could have been his very musings about what possibly could have gone wrong in the Heliopolitan theogony. It became Simon's mission to fix that which at first possibly, and then definitely, must have gone wrong; namely, the estrangement of the entire female Tefnut-Mahet-Nut-Isis dimension from the masculine godhead.

With the mother of the world's creator-angels having been saved through the religion of Simon Magus, surely, the consequent world and humankind—that is, the more distant offspring of bastard creators born from the estranged spouse of the godhead—thereby also were given an opportunity to become reconciled again with God.

Hans Jonas and many other scholars doubt whether the gnostic Simon Magus could have been the Samaritan magician mentioned in *Acts* 8:9–24. Be that as it may, in light of the Egyptian background of Simon's theology, we now may be a little less sure about rejecting this possibility. According to our Christian source, this magician Simon formerly had amazed the nation of Samaria. But he lost his followers to a Christian teacher, Philip, and either in the aftermath of his followers' desertion or by honest momentary excitement, the magus himself is said to have joined the Christian movement.[20]

Perhaps after realizing that his followers have deserted him and perhaps because a process of aging had diminished his infatuation for his incarnate Ennoia, this opportunistic cult leader might realistically have assessed his possibilities.[21] If he ever was to become a religious

---

[20]It may be significant that this same Apostle Philip is depicted, a little later in that same chapter (26–40), as having taught and converted an Egyptian eunuch. This may mean that Philip was especially atuned to the Egyptian mission field.

[21]I recognize that this hypothesis goes against the contemporary current of opinion. It is quite obvious, of course, that a shrewd magus of Simon's caliber never could become an ordinary childlike follower of Christ. We need not judge this possibility. But for the sake of historical fairness, we also must assume the possibility that Simon's initial Ennoia gospel could have begun as a message similar to that of Hosea. This eighth century prophet married a harlot, Gomer, to demonstrate God's love for Israel.

Copyrighted Material

celebrity again, it would have had to be by joining the Christian movement to which his former admirers had converted. Nevertheless, the episode of a later visit by Peter and John (*Acts* 14–24) further humiliated and checked the flamboyant Simon Magus.

Our well-nigh literal consideration of the aforementioned narrative in *Acts*, for the sake of discussion, does not rely, as most commentators do, on the probability of whether the character of Simon could be reformed. The theological differences between the Simon of heresiology and the Christian gospel were not insurmountable. In fact, a Simon Magus in the generous tailwind of Egyptian theology could have adjusted to the christology of his competitors with relative ease. Egyptian theology had for its core notion a process of divine begetting. And on that orthodox Egyptian dimension, it appears, Simon formerly asserted his own identity with the godhead.

Christians, too, have asserted such an identity with the godhead on behalf of their Lord. Jesus Christ as Son of the Father, in the Egyptian theological context, would have added up to being Shu or Life (cf. *John* 1:4). In addition, all the followers of Jesus were adopted as fellow siblings; that is, as brothers and sisters of Christ and as divinized children of God.

Because of his chauvinism, Simon Magus initially may have divided his ontology, to match, into a male upper and a female lower portion. But let us give Simon the benefit of doubt. Let us assume for the moment that on joining the Christians he actually dropped for a time his outrageous self-theological posture. In that case his outright claim for divinity could have been redefined easily enough as brotherhood with Christ. After all, the hypostases of Atum, Shu, Geb, Osiris, and Horus were all manifestations of the same divine Enneadean masculinity.[22]

Moreover, the concept of a world symbolized by a whore in need of her Father's rescue and salvation—and the Father's damnation of her upon her refusal—has persisted in Hebrew as well as Christian

---

[22] And indeed, Jonas, in *The Gnostic Religion*, p. 108, found some passages by which Simon identified himself with Jesus as well as with the Holy Spirit. Whether *Acts* 8:9–13 represented thus a realistic Christian victory celebration over the cult of Simon Magus or whether it was premature and wishful thinking is not sufficiently clear. But Simon's Egyptian theological habit, of embracing every competing theology, is obvious enough.

Copyrighted Material

thought. That idea echoes from the eighth century prophet Hosea; it can be found prominently in Nag Hammadi texts; and it has been adopted by Christians, openly, in *Revelation* 17:1.[23]

Thus, when and if Philip encountered Simon Magus in Samaria, both their gospels would have been based on the same internal logic, derived from the Egyptian theogony. They both would have been indebted to the mythological fact of a godhead's extended self-begetting. Both cults would have appeared logical and convincing over against this Egyptian background.

Moreover, because both Christ and Simon have identified their own persons with the godhead, more or less, both their cults implicitly also would have preempted the claims of grand domesticator kings and emperors, of being legitimate special sons of God. The gospels of both founders so would have managed to dance, nay gyrate, circles around established grand domesticators whom summarily they judged as serving some lower "principalities and powers." Their respective divine claims parodied the mandates of imperial Sons of God.

The greatest difference between the two cult founders lay in Simon's opportunistic effrontery, of course. His ontology and theology had been adapted all too flippantly to suit his infatuation with this uninhibited woman whom he had picked up in Tyre to keep him company.

In sharp contrast, the divine claim of Jesus had been established with deadly seriousness. It had been paid for with the founder's own life and blood. As a result, Christian salvation not only had been more dramatically established, it also was more unselfishly universalistic. Christian salvation could not be bought with silver—hence the balancing addendum of *Acts* 8:14–24. Christian soteriology went far beyond the privilege of founders and leaders to ensure everyone's rescue from sin and death. It embraced and exceeded everything that might have pertained to salvation within the scope of Simon's

---

[23]In contrast to the "God versus Whore" theme, it is necessary to also consider the counterpoint over against which that theme has been meaningful; namely, the proper marital union of God-Father with the Tefnut-Nut-Isis line. In Christendom Mary links up with Isis, and Holy Spirit and Church become manifestations of that same divine dimension. The divine wedding paradigm, which was basic for ancient Egyptian theogony and cosmology, figures conspicuously in the canonical parables of Jesus, as well as in the Nag Hammadi texts.

Copyrighted Material

gospel—the gospel of a playboy savior. Christian soteriology embraced the fact of death as well as resurrection.

The depth of Jesus's existential involvement over a larger range of possible human problems, including the agony of his real death—with the subsequent joy of resurrection added for contrast—is what gave Christendom its popular advantage. More lighthearted gnostic cults, such as Simon's, thereby were put morally on the defensive. They had no other choice but try, whenever they could, to undercut this greater relevance of the Christian gospel. They therefore, in principle, denied that Jesus Christ actually died his impressive sacrificial death.

It remains noteworthy that specifically Christ's death, not his resurrection, evoked the most severe objections to Christianity from the side of the gnostic competition. The resurrection of an incarnate God posed no problem to minds who already reasoned on the basis of orthodox Egyptian theology. Such resurrection was self-evident and a matter of common sense.

We must return to the Simon story in *Acts* to ask only one more question: Is it really improbable that the notorious Simon Magus would at some time have been welcomed by the Christians? The question may be asked and answered as well the other way around. Where else but in Christianity, at the time, would the founder of a defunct competitor cult have been welcome? Where else but under an extremely gracious and reconciling Father-god? The theological reaches and embracings of Simon Magus were surpassed by the even more magnanimous and practical embrace offered by the Christ story and the Christian community.

Does this sound unbelievable? Not at all. We know that another far more deadly enemy of Christendom, Saul of Tarsus, succumbed to that embrace and became a leading apostle, Paul. Thus, *Acts* 8:9–13, even if as a literary product it may express wishful thinking, signifies nevertheless the Christian welcome extended ideally to all of its former opponents. Such openness and love was a direct consequence of the new and expanded vision of God the Father Almighty and his kingdom. The gospel of Jesus presented the godhead as the loving Father of estranged humanity and the world.

Copyrighted Material

18

The Kingdom of Heaven Spreading

I came to cast fire upon the earth; and would that it were already kindled! (*Luke* 12:49)

And there appeared to them tongues as of fire, distributed and resting on each one of them. And they were all filled with the Holy Spirit and began to speak in other tongues, as the Spirit gave them utterance. (*Acts* 2:3–4)

The first of these introductory quotations renders words of Jesus that express his hope that Kingdom of Heaven enthusiasm might spread. He envisioned his good news to spread like fire—like an all-consuming Hebrew wildfire. The second quotation provides a glimpse of an early moment in Christian history when that Kingdom of Heaven wildfire had begun to spread beyond the confines of Judaism. Its flames in northern gentile lands were sustained by the presence of "spirit," a category of thought that had become especially significant in dualistic Indo-European contexts, including Hellenic philosophy.

Jewish Piety a Challenge to Hellas

How did the skirmish between philosophy and the remnant gods of Greek grand domestication finally end? This battle never came to a real conclusion. The gradual demise of philosophy in Greece was accompanied by a new round of grand domestication and conflict, beginning with Alexander the Great. Even this very book is being written and will be read and criticized still in the melee of ensuing hopes and conflicts. Cronos with his progeny of analytic imitators and

Copyrighted Material

critics, and the All-Father with a great variety of priestly imitators and reformers still are facing each other on the same battlefield.

It is a curious war in which most people change sides, eventually. The same combatants desire to be left in heavenly peace as, intermittently, they become accustomed to thinking of themselves as redeemed and harmless grazing animals, sheep or such like. But then again they rise up to celebrate victory as if, all along, they had been justified predator-heroes, crusaders, and holy warriors. Their uniforms and methods of aggression, their slogans and battle cries, often are altered. Now you find wolves in sheepskins, and then again you can find sheep clothed in wolfskins. But it is still a war similar to that which has erupted, some four to five millennia ago, between roaming cowboy-bandits on horseback and sedentary planter folk (see Chapter 11). The conflict is faith in weapons versus faith in a dignified and peaceful perpetuation of sedentary life, holistically understood.

Fortunes in this "battle of Hellas," won early on by Cronos and his grand domesticator progeny at the level of basic mythology, were reversed by a simple gospel rumor that began to spread from along the eastern shore of the Mediterranean Sea. This rumor sharply undercut the Hesiodic narrative that proclaimed the severance of Father Heaven from Mother Earth at the hand of Cronos—of Cronos the divinely begotten son of the old Greek religion.

Jewish and Christian folk knew differently. They knew that humankind, having eaten from the forbidden tree of life and the tree of analytic knowledge, by their own fault generated their estrangement from God. Jews and Christians knew that earth, not heaven, had been spoiled and mutilated by this process of human emancipation. They also knew, contrary to Hesiodic tradition, that God on High himself has actively pursued an independent plan to heal the human-made wounds of rebellion and separation.

Half a millennium after Socrates, the philosophical battlefield of Hellas was still strewn with the mutilated bodies of gods. Mythologists had castrated them. Sculptors had chiseled, melted, cast, and left them transfixed, immovable, and sometimes in rather compromising positions. Later poets have ridiculed these artistic caricatures as if they were the actual remains of gods and as if these artifacts were their immediate manifestations. Undoubtedly, to earlier faithfuls in Hellas their gods had been vibrantly alive. But in the end philosophers inflicted their analysis on the entire culture of artistic

Copyrighted Material

mockery; that is, on these concretizations and cadavers of divine mythological personages.

At the same time, philosophers generously undertook to "upgrade" ancient gods and rescue them from popular ridicule. They elevated them to an altitude of respectable philosophical "concepts" or "principles." To that end they transformed ancient personal gods into abstractions. Inevitably, by doing so, they reduced them as well to the size of thinkable entities, to principles or concepts small enough to be grasped by finite human minds. Everywhere in the world philosophical principles are but abstracted and recycled caricatures of ancient gods, who formerly were known to be alive. In Greece these abstractions were conceptualized by professed "lovers of wisdom"; they were worked over by the wily minds of Cronos' younger human progeny.

For a number of centuries Near Eastern peoples have come under the spell and mission of Alexander the Great and his cultural expansion. Alexander's military and cultural campaigns, presumably, were inspired by the self-confident display of Greek genius. Part of their Hellenic confidence was inspired by the impressive mental legacy of Greek philosophers, such as Socrates and Plato, or by Aristotle who was Alexander's one-time mentor.

By contrast, Jews by and large remained devoutly monotheistic. But even at that, as members of the *Homo sapiens* species, some among them have been wondering a thing or two about the personal life-style of their God who, singularly, was known to sit enthroned in heaven. They wondered about him in conjunction with what they had learned from other Mediterranean and Near Eastern mythologies. According to prevailing Hellenistic traditions, including those of Egypt, certain ancient father-gods were reputed to have begotten human sons.

Although down-to-earth Jewish prudence suggested that one could expect only a human messiah, one who was an offspring of good old king David, the actual political liberation of a god-fearing minority within the larger Greco-Roman environs demanded something more. In the wider Mediterranean world divine kings flaunted several millennia old traditions and claimed to have been born of human as well as divine parentage. Many of these kings sat on imperial thrones as sons of God. Therefore, a stronger antithetical role than "Son of Man" eventually was required of the founder of Christian universalism. Only a corporeal and an equally divine Son of God, a more

Copyrighted Material

decent one, could hope to eventually usurp the divine mandate of seated imperial grand domesticators—of Son of God pretenders.

Suddenly during the first century C.E., across the Hellenistic battlefield littered with impotent divine bodies and corpses from an earlier grand domestication era, a fresh religious breeze, a whiff of new life—or "Shu"—blew in from the east.

On the Hellenic battlefield, strewn with mutilated divinities, the new Christian rumor generated stirrings of fresh life. It spread as a theistic gospel foremostly along the Mediterranean coastlands, and it triumphed precisely in lands where the aggressive builders of Hellenistic culture, philosophers and scientists, in the wake of their rationalism had left a severe religious void—the rationalized castration legacy of Cronos. Notwithstanding the chisels of skilled artists, the analytic habits of philosophers, and the sharp scalpels of butchers, barbers, and scientists alike, the earth on which common people lived continued to produce myriads of living and growing creatures. The colorful spectacle of clouds, of azure heaven, of life-giving breath and heavenly sunlight continued unperturbed.

Together, all these wonderful phenomena demonstrated to sensitive Hebrews how their God, who created heaven and earth, has been coaxing earth into "bringing forth" continuously. The question arose, necessarily: Should among all of God's creatures the human species alone remain forever estranged, analytically and rebelliously, from the total glory of this creative heavenly splendor? The answer of faith was: Of course not!

The new Christian rumor spread with commonsense ease. It spread as "good news" concerning the recent stirrings of the only God and creator of the world. It spread on the basis of ancient Egyptian theological presuppositions.

God, the Father in Heaven, and the Creator of our world is alive and well! He has in reality never been transfixed into a craven or artificial image. He has never been defined or reduced by human wit to the manageable dimensions of philosophical abstractions or principles. He has never been castrated by tellers of ever so wondersome Greek tales.

The heavenly Father of Jesus Christ, who by extension of his divine grace is recognized as the Father of all humankind, has shown himself to be more than just a contemplative Aristotelian first mover. God the heavenly Father has demonstrated anew how his life and his virility endure, that he is alive and well, forever. As proof to that

Copyrighted Material

effect he has begotten, and has presented for the whole world to see, his son Jesus Christ!

Many hitherto insignificant people—most of them sons, under-standably—since that time have risen to testify to this fact. And it was this simple and concrete theophany, the birth of a different and kinder Son of God, that breathed new life and hope into the religiously depleted and overanalyzed world of Hellenism.

Some among the followers of Jesus recognized his divine status—"his glory, the glory as of the only begotten of the Father" (*John* 1:14). And thanks to Egyptian theology, by means of which the analytic temper of Greek philosophy was discretely pushed into the background, all of this made good sense.

All the while, the essentially holistic Christian gospel, the story of the heavenly Father who sent his Son, had to be communicated to a predominantly dualistic Indo-European audience. This audience consisted of people who were in a habit of radically distinguishing between "soul" and "body," and between "spirit" and "matter." The basic Hesiodic severance—that is, the castration, abstraction, or "spiritualization" of Father Heaven and his severance from an increasingly "materialized" Mother Earth—could not be avoided when Christian apostles began to communicate and to explain their gospel to people who reasoned abstractly and philosophically.

Greco-Roman philosophers naturally criticized the Christian story from their own dualistic perspective. Thus, for purposes of communi-cating and defending the Christian gospel in Hellas, the spirit-matter dichotomy had to be acknowledged first, as Paul had done in *1 Corinthians* 15:44, and had to be skirted subsequently at the abstract philosophical level. The Christian apostles had no choice but to define deity as being somehow "spiritual." To communicate a Father-Son theophany, in Indo-European lands, was an impossible task without first acknowledging spirituality as an essential divine attribute. Paul's treatise in *1 Corinthians* 15 on the resurrection of "spiritual bodies"—of all things!—is an early instance of this very necessary communicational adjustment. A holistic Father-and-Son story, which concluded with the resurrection of Christ Jesus as a whole person, had to be explained in Hellas nevertheless half dualistically, as if body and spirit were at once separate and unified.

The doctrines concerning the Holy Spirit and the Holy Trinity represent the larger theological umbrella of this missionary accomo-dation. With these doctrines it has become possible to discuss deity
Copyrighted Material

as being "spiritual." Theologically, the Christian doctrine of the Holy Spirit therefore may be explained as a necessary emergency revelation sent by God Almighty, specifically to impress Indo-European dualists and accommodate them in the Christian fold.

Beyond trinitarian theology it remains historically also significant that much of Mediterranean Christendom has continued to revere, alongside the predominantly masculine trinity of Father and Son, and the feminine-neuter Spirit, also a "Mother of God." Her full name has been kept conveniently ambiguous. Her official title is *Mother of God*—an appellation that, over against the backdrop of Egyptian-Hellenistic process theology, specifies precisely neither human nor divine attributes. For many among simple and faithful folk the descriptive title *Virgin* has become her first name. The name *Mary*, which according to tradition has been her given name, consequently was shifted to the position of a middle name. She has become *Virgin Mary Mother of God*.

Meanwhile some stalwart catholic Christians have become convinced that she has now caught up with her divine Son and ascended into heaven as well. Indeed, this dogma may be evaluated as a significant achievement for Christians who belong to the feminine gender or to an egalitarian persuasion!

Universal Salvation Religion

Reactionary universalistic tendencies toward reform have been evoked in all oppressive grand domestication systems from the start. Human self-respect and dignity were not simply surrendered to the first grand domesticator who happened to come along.

Nevertheless, most "civilized" peoples have fallen under the sway of grand domestication enterprises voluntarily and often with great enthusiasm—in moments before grand domesticators became selfish overdomesticators. Then in the course of time some reactionary murmurs and protests, some liberating notions of universalistic salvation, surfaced in Egyptian as well as Hebrew grand domestication religion. They were present even in Greek philosophy.

Grand domestication, as it has been defined earlier in this book, means that domestication efforts have been overdone. Domestication tricks have been turned against groups of humankind and inflicted on even the guardian gods of such groups. Wherever in this world the

Copyrighted Material

injustices of this sort are on the increase, there the human spirit in some way or other will resist. Alterations in people's religions, that is, changes in their general retreat behavior and retreat thinking, therefore provide the first signals of dissatisfaction and hope for a better lot. Oppressed people will lament to their God long before they will endanger themselves by complaining directly to their over-domesticators.

Thus, the readiness for universal salvation religiosity begins invariably in response to oppressive overdomestication. It begins with only weak stirrings at first. But universalism may eventually consummate its destiny with a more complete reformation of a people's hopes, mores, and rites of living.

Seen within a narrower historical perspective, the universalism of Christianity has had its initial beginnings in the religiosity of ancient Israelite rebel prophets—also in tendencies within postexilic Judaism. It was the eventual outcome of the collective aspirations of prehistoric patriarchs, of Moses, priests, warrior kings, scribes, prophets, and a founder who dared to be a different kind of Son of God.

In Greater Asia

In a wider historical perspective, it is important to note that domestication cultures have matured into grand domestication civilizations at several places on the globe. At one time or other all these civilizations degenerated into oppressive overdomestication schemes. In the Near East, South Asia, and China, protest movements of the universal salvation type sprang up almost contemporaneously during the first millennium B.C.E. Thus, some of the murmurs and protests that have predisposed the Mediterranean world in the direction of Christendom can be detected in other grand domesticated areas of the world as well; for example, in fifth century India and China.

Five centuries before the Christian era, South Asia became the cradle for a number of universalistic religious movements. Hippie-monks there dropped out from civilized society in droves. They followed universalistic paths of escape, of asceticism and yoga for spiritual liberation. The religiously bankrupt theology of the Vedic grand domestication cult, managed by groups of Brahmana priests, had degenerated to the point of near homonymy between the name of their caste and the name of their godhead, Brahmana and Brahman.

Copyrighted Material

Implicitly, regarding their personal religiosity, these priests thereby reduced the godhead to their own kind of "brahmana power," and as a matter of course, they thereby inflated their priestly authority. Exploitative theology of this sort was rejected emphatically by the new generation of sensitized religious dropouts.

The universalistic salvationism of reform-minded reactionaries in India, of the fifth century B.C.E., therefore frequently was tinged with atheism. Gotama, the Buddha, denied the reality of Brahman. He even denied the reality of the human "soul." Apparently the Buddha felt a need to block the path on which a grand domesticator's deity, once denied, might somehow return under the guise of "soul."[1] Such a remote possibility was left open in Jainism and in some other Hindu universalistic teachings.

Impulses from Indian ways on Mediterranean thought and culture were not unknown during the centuries preceding Alexander's military campaign eastward. Pythagorean philosophy and some of Plato's dialogues attest to this fact. Nevertheless, as a backlash effect against Alexander's "missionary" campaign, South Asian ideas began to trickle more freely into the Near East. Indirectly they might even have affected religious ferment in Judaism.

In Palestine

But, in contrast to Indo-European theologies, Jewish theology evolved and was institutionalized as a reaction specifically against Near Eastern overdomestication schemes, especially against Egypt. As such, especially among Pharisees and Essenes, it had not yet become as bankrupt as Brahmanic theology had become by way of justifying the extravagances of the Vedic sacrificial cult. Nevertheless, John the Baptizer and Jesus of Nazareth came as close to being an Indian dropout as such a thing was possible in Palestine at the time among sons of pious Jewish parents. One must remember that John and Jesus still had inherited a viable Jewish theology for their ideological

---

[1]Of course, the Buddha's no-soul doctrine also was necessitated by his nirvanic experience. Viewed from the perspective of nirvanic bliss, the human soul or ego appears nonexistent—or belongs beyond the range of analytic perception. Religious proportionality was maintained negatively, by subordinating a no-soul under a greater-than-human no-Brahman. *Copyrighted Material*

umbrella.[2] Their universalistic reactions, as far as theology was concerned, therefore easily could remain on the theistic side.

All the same, Jesus ventured as far from Jewish orthodoxy as a wandering hippie-rabbi could, modifying high Jewish theology along the way by insisting on lowly and selfless intimacy, for himself, with the traditional God on High. Jesus approached the supreme deity as his "Daddy." In addition, the kingdom of heaven ideal that inspired his life-style contradicted and challenged every kingdom on earth. It challenged every grand domestication scheme and civilizational organization. The harbinger of such a radical heavenly kingdom, of course, was promptly put to death.

Measured by the standards of cultural progress Jesus was an apparent failure. But at the moment when he died his real contribution to human history had only begun to take form. His dying was part of his life, as much as were his teachings. Followers of Jesus suddenly proclaimed that, though he was crucified and had died, their Lord remained alive by the eternal power of his Father God. This meant that some of Jesus' followers finally had gotten the point their rabbi was trying to make all along—that the kingdom of heaven was a contrary kingdom and, therefore, not subject to the rules by which ordinary grand domestication kingdoms were run.

The utter selflessness of Jesus, his poverty and vulnerability, made him an ideal, different, and most desirable king of the down-trodden. He was well suited to be king of this new anti-imperial kingdom that he himself had proclaimed. Moreover, the only good king (of the overdomesticator type) being a dead king, one who somehow has died, Jesus competed with them on that negative score as well.

In any case, with having an earthly loser now enthroned as eternal king, the Christian kingdom movement indeed was, demonstrably, not of this world. But it nevertheless was in the world to stay. During the centuries that followed, other God-kings were dethroned right and left, on account of people who preferred this loser king.

---

[2]Such thorough theological bankruptcy within the Judeo-Christian tradition and large-scale atheistic alternatives may have begun taking shape among ruling circles of Sadducees. But, on the whole, for Jewish tradition such stark theological decay and atheism had to wait for the nineteenth and twentieth century scientisms, in the Western world.

Copyrighted Material

Copyrighted Material

19

Bequest of
the Mother Religion

"Out of Egypt have I called my son," a sentence from *Hosea* 11:1, was quoted in *Matthew* 2:13-15 to support the story about the flight of the holy family into Egypt. Has this brief addendum to the nativity tradition of Christ Jesus been intended to hint at the broader nativity of Christian theology in Egypt? Did some of the first Christians actually sense the Egyptian direction into which their theologizing tended to move? A turning point in sacred Jewish history, an Exodus in reverse from Palestine to Egypt, is implied even in the surface meaning of this story.

Subsequently, there in Egypt—if we permit ourselves an additional historical allegory—Isis as the Egyptian divine madonna with her Horus child (see Figure 11), as a representative of the feminine Enneadean "Tefnut-Nut-Isis" lineage, passed on her mantle to the unsuspecting mother of Jesus. Let us leave these obvious hints aside, for a while, and turn to less tangible and nevertheless historical glimpses.

Undeniably, Christianity was first inspired by Hebrew "kingdom of heaven" radicalism. But the first apostles of Christ drew their enthusiasm not so much from their Lord's teachings about the kingdom of heaven as from his personal participation in death and resurrection. With a few exceptions, the apostle Paul discontinued mentioning the "kingdom of God." He preferred the less political and more personal "body of Christ" mysticism instead. This provided Christians an opportunity to participate more intimately in the death and resurrection of Christ—and in Christianized Egyptian soteriology. The kerygma—of God having begotten a Son, of that Son having been born, having died, risen, and ascended to the Father—is what has

Figure 11. Isis with the Horus child. Together these two Egyptian divinities were prototypes for the Christian madonna with child. Drawn after Ions and Bonnet.

an encouraging resonance from the broad background spectrum of ancient Egyptian ontology.

It long has been suspected by historians of religions that a general knowledge about death and resurrection, associated specifically with Osiris mythology in Egyptian religion, may have aided the success of the Christian story in the wider Hellenistic world.[1]

The well-established structure of ancient Egyptian ontology, eschatology, and soteriology, which was widely regarded as common sense, made it possible to believe that the Son of God rose from death (as his essential *ka*) and thus returned to the Father. It explained also why for a while, before he completely ascended into heaven, some of the Christ apparitions have been seen as a visible *ba*. Also in tune with Egyptian logic was the notion that, even though Christ Jesus had

---

[1]See Ninian Smart, *The World's Religions* (Englewood Cliffs, N.J., 1989), p. 199.

Copyrighted Material

now returned to the Father, he nevertheless eternally remains present among his followers. Deceased Egyptian pharaohs continued to dispense divine Mahet (Maat) in a similar manner. Christ had been present, emanationally speaking, as Father essence or *ka* in the Son, and he continued to radiate this same essence as divine love and holy spirit. The radiation of this divine light is celebrated, visibly, with many symbolic candles and Easter sunrises.

When Greek philosopher minds listened to the apostle Paul in Athens (*Acts* 17:32), they mocked him as soon as he began to talk about Christ's resurrection from death. For Hellenic dualists, and rationalists, the human soul was being separated at death from its material body. In contrast, Paul, who reasoned after the mode of Egyptian *ka* essences and *ba* apparitions, saw the visible world still contained in the larger emanation of divinely given life, redemption, and resurrection. In his Christian "Egyptianness" the apostle Paul was essentially free from the Greek Hesiodic habit of radically distinguishing Father Heaven or spirit from a material realm beneath.

On the one hand, Indo-European dualism has forced the category of "spirit" into prominence within Christendom. On the other hand, Egyptian ontology and logic have made it possible to believe in one God as Father, Son, and Holy Spirit. The presence of the Holy Spirit in the Holy Trinity was not only a missionary adaptation of the concept of deity to Indo-European dualism, as has been suggested earlier; in addition, the third person in the Christian trinity could be recognized as well in the institution of the Christian church, the new visible "city of God" on earth. As such the three divine hypostases together resemble closely the Egyptian trinity of Atum the Father, Shu the Son, and Tefnut-Mahet the divine wisdom and the congregational order. Thus, the Holy Spirit within the Christian Holy Trinity gradually absorbed into itself all of the following: the kingdom of heaven as it was represented in the communion of saints and the church, the Indo-European domain of spirit, as well as the entire Hand-Tefnut-Nut-Isis dimension of the Enneadean godhead.

We now are ready to contemplate Paul's own amplification of his doctrine of resurrection, according to the aforementioned episode in *Acts* 17. And we are given no uncertain hints that Paul's reasoning about these matters was a spinoff from Egyptian theology, by way of Epimenides and Aratus. Their words communicated to Paul what appeared to be true theology:

Copyrighted Material

In him we live and move and have our being . . . [and that] . . . we are indeed his offspring. For being indeed God's offspring. . . . (*Acts* 17:28)

Egyptian theology, based on a theogony of emanation and begetting, made it possible for educated Hellenistic Christians to believe in an only-begotten Son who came into the world as the *logos*, as the divine creative command, or the Word made visible. It seems safe to say that in all the religious literature from the so-called Hellenistic Period, there is no better summary of ancient orthodox Egyptian theology than the prologue to the Gospel of *John*:

In the beginning was the Word, and the Word was with God, and the Word was God. He was in the beginning with God; all things were made through him, and without him was not anything made that was made. In him was life, and the life was the light of men. The light shines in darkness, and the darkness has not overcome it. (*John* 1:1–5)

Another favorite creed from this same, and most Egyptianized among the Christian gospels, resonates still in perfect harmony with ancient Egyptian soteriology. And what harm is there in knowing, now, that this love which the Father has shown toward his world has been anticipated, millennia earlier, by the creative fatherly activity and the self-love of Atum? That divine sentiment was described clumsily, and inconsistently enough, by the ancient Heliopolitan theologians to have remained a mystery. The incarnation of Christ still is explained in terms of a quasi-sexual metaphor as well, that is, as a process of divine begetting—as a fact to be believed if not understood. Nevertheless, the total pattern of divine activity—of God's creation by *logos*, of God begetting his Son, and his presentation of eternal life to wayward humankind—are Egyptian soteriology throughout. Here is an orthodox Christian summary statement:

For God so loved the world that he gave his only Son, that whoever believes in him should not perish but have everlasting life. For God sent not the Son into the world to condemn the world, but that the world might be saved through him. (*John* 3:16f)

Copyrighted Material

Although on the one hand, the Christian "kingdom of heaven" enthusiasm was internalized by Egyptian-style soteriology, its political dimension eventually was compromised in exchange for a new kind, a more livable, Holy Roman Empire. This Christianized empire, at the same time, was checked and balanced and stabilized by whatever retreat-oriented counterweights the Christian religion could provide. As the Holy Roman Empire evolved, amidst philosophized remnants of Indo-European dichotomies, Christendom's reliance on proven ancient Egyptian theological structures became even more obvious. The Egyptian theological heritage, as it has been philosophized by Neoplatonism, provided the emerging Christian church organization and the Holy Roman Empire with much-needed doctrinal structure and ontological substance.

Following the lead of earlier Alexandrian theologians, Augustine of Hippo infused Egyptian ontology into Christian soteriology to a point where its presence no longer can be overlooked. He personalized Egyptian soteriology and thereby clarified how all estranged human hearts, while they live here on earth, are doomed to be restless until they will have found their rest in God.

Thus, at the hands of Christian apologists and church fathers, Neoplatonism was destined to become the serum with which the Christian doctrine immunized itself against Hellenic philosophy's own god-killing venom. The scarcely disguised brand of Egyptian mystic philosophy, in Neoplatonism, shielded Christian theology against philosophy's own digestive acids of more arrogant analysis. Because the designation *Neoplatonism* appeals to Plato as the school's god-father, the same secular cover that at one time protected Ammonius and Plotinus at Alexandria against the bonafide Greek intelligentsia continued to protect Christian apologists against the same.

A full history of Christian beginnings, in Egypt, would have to pay special attention to pioneer theologians in Alexandria, such as Clement, Origen, Dionysius the Great, and others—and to their influence upon the belief systems of later North Africans such as Tertullian of Carthage and Augustine of Hippo. Any attempt to do justice to all of these, in this book, obviously would lead beyond its present scope. In light of what already has been suggested concerning Egyptian antecedents, other scholars sooner or later will want to reconsider all of these church fathers, one by one.

This book is intended merely as a rough sketch of four large Near Eastern religious and philosophical traditions, viewed together over

Copyrighted Material

long periods of time. Therefore, Part Four of this book hopes to provide no more than bare hints of Egyptian influence on early Christian theology. The remaining tasks must be left in the hands of specialized historians of these traditions.

From here on the general Egyptian influence can be sketched more boldly if one skips the first few centuries of Christian history and points directly to what the Christian orthodox creed actually has become. The formative struggles for Christian theology, christology, mariology, and numenology all demonstrate the intrusion of ancient Egyptian emanationalism among Mediterranean peoples, who at the time also had been challenged by Indo-European dualism. These struggles and controversies demonstrate the gradual triumph of basic notions that once belonged to the theological legacy of Egypt. The strong theological bequest of Christendom's mother religion has evoked, quite expectedly, a series of very interesting birthright controversies. You may think of them as ideological birth pangs, if you like.

The Arian Controversy

In Christian history texts the "Arian Controversy" (318–381 C.E.) sometimes is explained as a crisis during which two extreme Christian factions rode roughshod over a silent majority of Near Eastern bishops—especially during the second phase of the conflict (325–361), which ensued between Arius and Athanasius. Presumably the majority, either for pragmatic reasons or lack of perception, remained satisfied with Origen's christological ambiguities.[2]

After the manner of ancient Egyptian process theology, Origen at Alexandria taught "the eternal generation of the Son," a christology that dualistic northerners could not quite fathom. And then, still in harmony with his larger Egyptian theological inheritance, Origen also referred to the nature of Christ, in snapshot fashion along the larger Egyptian expanse of eternal emanation, as a "second God and

---

[2]For example, Williston Walker, *A History of the Christian Church* (New York, 1959), pp. 106ff; and Karl Heussi, *Kompendium der Kirchengeschichte*, 12th ed., (Tübingen, 1960), p. 97. Copyrighted Material

creature."[3] Although this formulation was innocent enough in the context of the Egyptian theological heritage, it raised havoc with the northern-educated mind of Arius.

The Arian controversy was unavoidable, considering the massive differences between the two world-views to which Christianity, largely unawares, had fallen heir. All still could have gone well, had the new gospel spawned a religion that spread either only among people of the Egyptian persuasion or only among dualistic Indo-European folk. Instead Christianity spread into the geography of the larger Roman Empire. In the north the minds of fledgling Christian theologians were being troubled by Hellenic dualism, inflamed by Hebrew fire and accentuated by Iranian and Mithraic apocalyptic dualisms. The alternative to northern dualism was the ancient monistic world-view that continued to radiate from the ancient Egyptian homeland, in the south.

It should surprise no one to find that in the Hellenistic-Egyptian meltingpot, in the city of Alexandria, the dualistic and monistic ideological extremes engaged in more severe wrangling than elsewhere. Egyptian process theologians, and Hellenizers who reasoned disjunctively and for whom separate names and separate acts of creation signified separate realities, found only a haphazard medium for communication in the international Greek language. Reconsidering the controversy from the Egyptian perspective, one might note that the Greek language was a little too well suited for doing unnecessary analysis and making unnecessary distinctions.

Both sides, of course, also had recourse to Platonic philosophical categories, to eternal norms and "ideas," which had ambiguous communicational value between the two sides as well. Underneath their lingual symbols of communication, the world-views of the two sides continued to draw from radically different mythological presuppositions. Both sides drew their axioms from ancient world perspectives, from which their rational structures had been drifting away for several millennia.

It is not an accident that Arius, whose christology became the northern focal point of this controversy, was educated in Antioch

---

[3]Walker, *A History of the Christian Church*, p. 106.

under Lucianus—and became aggravated in Alexandria. And it is even less of an accident to observe how solidly, on the other hand, Athanasius identified himself and his cause with monasteries in the Egyptian hinterland; namely, with those very contemplative brotherhoods of mystics who were spawned, so to speak, among the diminishing remains of traditional Egyptian piety. Christian brotherhoods and a variety of Gnostic associations, at the time, began to fill the void that the decline of the royal, subsequently democratized, ancient Egyptian soteriology left in its wake.

Christian orthodoxy was engendered by the gospel of Christ's resurrection, a logical derivative of Egyptian holistic emanationalism. In Indo-European lands that basic orientation was pressured into discomfort by extreme disjunctive and dualistic philosophizing. In its struggle to maintain its resurrection kerygma, Christian orthodox theology was predestined to settle, eventually, far within the former camp of ancient Egyptian grand domestication theology. Christ as *homoousion*—who was begotten, not made, and who was of one essence with the Father—was a reasonable Egyptian mode of including Christ within the greater godhead. Theology in ancient Egypt always has been reasoned in this manner.

By contrast the strictly "created" Christ figure of Arius was conceptualized more as a human person than as God. Such a christology seemed rather irrelevant to traditional Egyptian mystics. By the time Arius came along, Egyptians had been switching from an already democratized Osiris-Horus soteriology to the still more democratized version of the Christ-Jesus gospel. The Christ hypostasis, characterized as *homoousion to patri*, could be accommodated within the eternal and unnameable Egyptian godhead as easily as, during earlier millennia of Egyptian religion, the Osiris hypostasis could be accommodated.

In this same context, it seems significant that Athanasius' objection to the christology of Arius was not so much concerned with christology for christology sake, as it was troubled by the unsatisfactory doctrine of salvation implied by Arius' christology. According to Athanasius, "He (Christ) was made man that we might be made divine."[4] By contrast, the christology of Arius threatened to interrupt

---

[4]*Incarnation*, 54:3. Quoted in Walker, *A History of the Christian Church*, p. 110.

the Father's saving outreach in the direction of humankind; thus it threatened to interrupt the full Egyptian U-turn that leads from cosmogony to soteriology.

The democratic tendencies already present in the Egyptian funerary cult, whereby during the New Kingdom lesser folk insisted on being saved by the old Osirian royal incantations, were democratized further and radically overhauled or "fulfilled" by the Christian gospel. For Egypt, Christ had come to be the savior, the new Horus-Osiris, expressly for all the people and not especially for royalty, aristocracy, or wealthy patricians. True to its Hebrew prophetic inheritance, the early Christian gospel was anti-overdomestication and offered salvation to the weak, the meek, and the poor.

And yes, the essential and structural continuity between the old Egyptian religion and its Christian replacement remained intact. The Christ event happened under the same, one and only, generative, and ineffable godhead. It happened within the same integrated theological, ontological, and soteriological structure.

All the while, the emperor Constantine has tried hard to use Christianity as clue with which to cement together his fragmented empire. Understandably, he was perturbed by the seeming lack of rationale on either side of the Arian controversy. His bewilderment was expressed by his actions when, alternately, he banned proponents from either side of these puzzling arguments. Without really knowing what they were up against, Roman emperors in fact moderated between opposing world orientations that had evolved differently over many millennia. They varied over a much greater territory than either Constantine, Arius, or Athanasius at the time could have surveyed.

The Arian controversy concerned not only the nature of Christ. Its outcome decided what Christians were to believe concerning the nature of the triune God and their salvation. Was God engaged in battle within a dualistic universe, was he faced with a world dominated by its own principalities and powers, forever? Or, was he an All-god of the unitary and universal Egyptian sort who could influence his creation within and throughout? In spite of having located its major institutional power centers in dualistic Indo-European lands, orthodox Christendom gradually chose and moved in the direction of what used to be persuasive Egyptian theology.

Copyrighted Material

The Nestorian Controversy

The metaphysical rift, which during the Arian controversy gaped, in Hesiodic fashion, between God and his acclaimed only-begotten Son, in Constantinople (428–433) erupted anew during the Nestorian controversy. It happened in dialogue with Alexandria. The focus of this new conflict transferred the christological problem superficially to another personage.

Was Mary the mother of Jesus a "Mother of God" (*theotokos*) or was she only a "Mother of Christ" (*christotokos*)? A closer scrutiny of this issue reveals the same implication that already had haunted combatants during the Arian controversy. The difference between "Mother of God" and "Mother of Christ" pertained directly to the difference between God and Christ and thus, again, to their interrelatedness. The appellation *Mother of Christ* could have admitted the possibility that her Son inherited a severed Hellenic "dual nature," even one with the human aspect being the dominant one. The "Egyptian" theologians could have said *Mother of God* or *Mother of Christ*, but they would have had to insist on both. The latter was contained in the former, but did not necessarily imply the former.

Stated in terms of our present historical reconstruction, the real question was whether Mary, the mother of Jesus, has been a representative of the entire Tefnut-Nut-Isis continuum, reconciled with the All-God; whether she could give birth to a son with similar divine nexus; or, whether perchance she could have been a self-willed Isis type, or even an estranged Ennoia of the Gnostic variety (cf. Chapter 17). This mariological question was crucial, because the latter options would have endangered not only orthodox christology but the entire All-God theology along with it.

The Monophysite Struggle

The same problem surfaced again, and it pitted ancient Egyptian sentiments over against the dualism of the Indo-European west. As the name of the most conspicuous party in these struggles suggests, the "monophysites" insisted on the "one" as over against the "two" natures, or essences, that supposedly composed the person of Christ. One divine emanation, a *mono-physis*, was called for by traditional Egyptian theological reasoning.

Copyrighted Material

All the while by northern standards, by which the monophysite case had to be argued, this ancient Egyptian theology no longer was understood. It therefore no longer could be acknowledged in the surface-consciousness of Christian minds. What nevertheless remained of the Egyptian heritage in Christian theology was an orientation toward a cosmic emanational process; albeit, philosophically cleansed of all the old Egyptian personal divine names and labels. Eastern Christendom continued to insist on seeing Christ as the only-begotten Son who has remained in traditional Egyptian unity with the godhead. Thus, as in earlier controversies, so too in the monophysite struggle, the entire All-God theology was at stake.

The policy of the emperor Constantine, of using the Christian religion to cement together his empire, basically had been sound strategy. However, during the turbulent debates between the inheritors of ancient Egyptian monism and of Indo-European dualism, agitated initially by the spreading wildfire of a Hebrew "kingdom of heaven" gospel, the basic theological tenets of Christendom as frequently were obscured as they were elucidated. It is a pity to see how all these good people were fated to resolve their differences, unknowingly, in the context of someone else's world-view: Egyptian, Greek, and Hebrew-Aramaic.

The Filioque Clause

The same East-West (originally south-north) differences, which had erupted during the famous christological and mariological controversies, surfaced as well in relation to the third person of the Holy Trinity. In the west the credal addition of the "filioque" clause, to the effect that the Holy Spirit proceeds from the Father *and the Son*, was adopted first by the church of Spain (589) and the Frankish church (809) and finally by Rome (1014).

Understandably the Eastern Orthodox Church, still living more directly in the afterglow of ancient Egyptian theology and logic, rejected the "filioque" clause outright. The reason for their stern response is obvious in light of their Egyptian heritage. Just as Shu and Tefnut (Mahet) were known to have proceeded from the godhead Atum, so in the Christian replication the Son (as Shu) and the Holy Spirit (as Tefnut-Mahet) would both proceed from the Father.

Copyrighted Material

Had the Egyptian theology been exceedingly fine-tuned, easterners conceivably could have agreed to the Son proceeding from the Father and the Spirit, inasmuch as Tefnut was Hand and Order and occasionally also thought to have come forth "behind" Shu. But they could never have consented to the other way around. It nevertheless is doubtful whether even Christian theologians, in the east, at that time still had the finer details of ancient Egyptian theology in focus. In any case, Spanish theologians and Frankish monks who disputed with eastern monks in Jerusalem obviously knew still less than their Greek and Roman predecessors about the theological roots of Christendom in ancient Egypt.

The Egyptian Theology of Augustine

Meanwhile, in the west, the church father Augustine (354–430) completed his life's work of returning the Western portion of Christendom, theologically, homeward in the direction of Egyptian monotheism and grand domestication religion—unknowingly, it seems. Augustine's first conversion, from dualistic Manichaeism to Neoplatonism, was soon followed by his next conversion from Neoplatonism to Christianity.

The broader indebtedness of Neoplatonism to ancient orthodox Egyptian theology has been sufficiently shown in Part Three of this book. Augustine's acceptance of Neoplatonic emanationalism, his conversion to Christianity, and his prompt reintegration of the Neoplatonic *nous* hypostasis into the Mind of God composed the rationales for his devotion to Christianity. This theology rehabilitated for Augustine the Christian godhead's incarnational link with humankind along the downward path of procreative emanation. This measure also opened to Christian thinkers, with the same stroke of the pen, the upward and homeward Egyptian path of salvation—for restless yearning hearts, on earth, to find rest in the eternal heart of God.

As a Latin theologian, Saint Augustine of course was obligated to take some courteous bows toward northern dualism. Brilliantly he took hold of the two Indo-European metaphysical realms of "spirit" and "matter" and, together, replicated them as concrete precipitates in the realm of practical politics. He acknowledged the fact of dualism by institutionalizing it in a "church-state" dichotomy. He

Copyrighted Material

established this political duality concretely, in check and balance fashion, as the "City of God" over against the "City of Man."

Having executed this balancing act, Augustine, behind this solid dualistic curtain, could accept Egyptian monotheism under the guise of monism. Egyptian mysticism and soteriology, abstracted by Neoplatonism, thereby came to serve as framework for his Christian theology. Under the guise of neutral Neoplatonic philosophy, which the selfsame Augustine had already harmonized allegorically with his personal Christian faith, Western civilization was given theological checks and balances that, during a long three millennia earlier, already provided structure and stability to Egyptian civilization.

Roman leaders had an empire to tend and to balance, and the reactionary Hebrew "kingdom of heaven" wildfire, by itself, was clearly unsuited for the larger imperial organizational task. Fortunately, for another millennium and beyond, Augustinian-Egyptian theology was able to contribute ontology and stability toward the balance of Western civilization.

An Epilogue of Hope

With historical hindsight the christological, mariological, and numenological controversies may be understood as birth pangs for the Christian religion. These ancient birth pangs, although they now are almost forgotten by the offspring, nevertheless were real labor pains on the part of Christendom's mother. They were suffered as a matter of course by the expiring matriarch of Near Eastern religions. Our old Egyptian mother died in the centuries during which her vigorous offspring emerged and began prospering in the Mediterranean world. Her labor pains were her death pangs.

Strands of ancient Egyptian-Augustinian theology still are very much alive and with us today. Saint Thomas Aquinas with his dual theories of knowledge, natural and revealed, probably was still more Augustinian than his own students made him appear. Then, the Protestant Reformation under Luther began essentially with a holistic Augustinian-Egyptian theological orientation. And finally, certain modern atheistic refractions and reactions may have been indebted to Augustinian-Egyptian theology more than we think. Form and mold, figure and reflected image, thesis and antithesis, together always testify to a common reality or event.

Copyrighted Material

For example, the existential philosophy of Jean-Paul Sartre reads in places as though it had been written to display a negative mold from which the theology of Saint Augustine has just been removed. By the same token, the atheistic ideologies of Ludwig Feuerbach, Sigmund Freud, Karl Marx, and Friedrich Engels—especially of the latter two—were agitated and motivated by the broader Egyptian-Hebrew-Christian ethos, minus its theological checks and balances. The presence of old theistic checks and balances are taken for granted nevertheless, unthinkingly, in most modern systems of ethics and laws and in political ideologies.

As the manuscript for this book is being readied for publication, people are dancing on the Berlin wall and celebrating the demise of a Communist bureaucracy. But before they could cast off the empty mold of atheistic party ideology, the people in East Germany had been returning to their churches in troves to find there, again, God as the personal source and content of their existence. To God they appealed for more reliable checks and balances in the human order. From their churches the masses emerged then, carrying candles. And so the story of emanational theology continues and survives. Cautious historians will require another few centuries before they can discern what religion or ideology is presently being born, or reborn, what divinity is dying or is rising, or is in labor to give birth.

Copyrighted Material

Bibliography

Aldred, Cyril. *Akhenaten, King of Egypt.* London: Thames and Hudson, 1988.

Alford, Garth. "The Origin and Development of a Foreign Eschatological Concept in Archaic Greek Literature." Dissertation, University of Washington, 1987. Ann Arbor: University of Michigan Microfilms.

——. "Elysion—A Foreign Eschatological Concept in Homer's Odyssey." Unpublished manuscript, 1989.

Allen, Thomas George, trans. *The Book of the Dead or Going Forth by Day.* Studies in Ancient Oriental Civilization 37. Chicago: University of Chicago Press, 1974.

Anderson, Bernhard W. *Understanding the Old Testament,* 3d ed. Englewood Cliffs, N.J.: Prentice-Hall, 1971.

Andrae, Thor. *Mohammed, the Man and His Faith.* New York: Harper Torchbooks, 1960.

Anthes, Rudolf. "Mythology in Ancient Egypt." In *Mythologies of the Ancient World*, ed. S. M. Kramer. Garden City, N.Y.: Doubleday and Co., 1961.

Armstrong, A. H., trans. *Plotinus,* in 7 volumes. Cambridge, Mass.: Harvard University Press, 1966–88.

Benjamin, Don C. "Israel's God: Mother and Midwife." *Biblical Theology Bulletin* 19 (1989).

Copyrighted Material

——. "The Adam and Eve Story." Unpublished manuscript copyrighted 1990.

Berchman, Robert M. *From Philo to Origen: Middle Platonism in Transition.* Chico, Calif.: Scholars Press, 1984.

Bernal, Martin. *Black Athena: The Afroasiatic Roots of Classical Civilization,* Vol. 1. The Fabrication of Ancient Greece 1785–1985. New Brunswick, N.J.: Rutgers University Press, 1987.

Bonnet, Hans. *Reallexikon der Ägyptischen Religionsgeschichte.* Berlin: Walter de Gruyter, 1952.

Bowman, Alan K. *Egypt after the Pharaohs.* Berkely: University of California Press, 1986.

Brehier, Emile. *The Philosophy of Plotinus,* trans. Joseph Thomas. Chicago: University of Chicago Press, 1958.

Breasted, J.H. *Development of Religion and Thought in Ancient Egypt.* New York: Charles Scribner's Sons, 1912.

Bretall, Robert. ed. *A Kierkegaard Anthology.* Princeton, N.J.: Princeton University Press, 1946.

Burkert, Walter. *Greek Religion.* Cambridge: Harvard University Press, 1985 (German ed. 1977).

——. *Ancient Mystery Cults.* Cambridge, Mass: Harvard University Press, 1987.

Burleigh, John H. S., trans. *Augustine: Earlier Writings.* Philadelphia: Westminster Press, 1953.

Burnaby, John, trans. *Augustine: Later Works.* Philadelphia: Westminster Press, 1955.

Casson, Lionel. *Ancient Egypt.* New York: Time Inc., 1965.

Copyrighted Material

Charlesworth, James H., ed. *The Apogrypha and Pseudepigrapha of the Old Testament*, Volume 2. Oxford: Clarendon Press, 1913.

——, ed. *The Old Testament Pseudoepigrapha, Apocalyptic Literature and Testaments*, Volume 1. Garden City, N.Y.: Doubleday and Co., 1983.

Clark, R. T. Rundle. *Myth and Symbol in Ancient Egypt*. London: Thames and Hudson, 1959.

De Buck, Adriaan. *The Egyptian Coffin Texts*, Volume 2. Chicago: University of Chicago Press, 1935-61.

Dodds, E. R., et al. *Entretiens Sur L'Antiquite Classique*, Volume 5, Les Sources de Plotin. Geneva: Foundation Hardt, 1960.

Doerrie, Heinrich. "Ammonios, der Lehrer Plotins." *Hermes* 83 (1955): 439-477.

——. "Was ist 'spätantiker Platonismus'? Überlegungen zur Grenzziehung zwischen Platonismus und Christentum." *Theologische Rundschau* 36, no.4 (1971): 285-302.

Eliade, Mircea. *A History of Religious Ideas*, 3 volumes. Chicago: University of Chicago Press, 1985.

Erman, Adolf. "Der Leidener Amonshymnus." *Sitzungsberichte der Preussischen Akademie der Wissenschaften* 11 (1923).

——. *Die Religion der Ägypter: ihr Werden und Vergehen in Vier Jahrtausenden*. Berlin and Leipzig: Walter de Gruyter, 1934.

——. *The Ancient Egyptians, a Sourcebook of Their Writings*, trans. Aylward M. Blackman. Gloucester, England: Peter Smith, 1978 [1966].

Faulkner, R. O. *The Ancient Egyptian Pyramid Texts*. New York: Oxford University Press, 1969.

Copyrighted Material

——. *The Ancient Egyptian Coffin Texts.* Warminster, England: Aris and Phillips, 1973.

Frankfort, Henri. *Ancient Egyptian Religion: An Interpretation.* New York: Harper and Row, 1961 [1948].

——. *Kingship and the Gods: A Study of Ancient Near Eastern Religion as the Integration of Society and Nature.* Chicago: University of Chicago Press, 1978 [1948].

Geldner, Karl F. *Der Rigveda.* Harvard Oriental Series, Volumes 33–36. Cambridge, Mass.: Harvard University Press, 1951.

Ginzberg, Louis. *The Legends of the Jews.* New York: Simon and Schuster, 1961 [1909].

Goetze, Albrecht. "Hittite Myths, Epics, and Legends." In *Ancient Near Eastern Texts*, ed. James B. Pritchard. Princeton, N.J.: Princeton University Press, 1955.

Gottwald, Norman K. *The Tribes of Yahweh: A Sociology of the Religion of Liberated Israel, 1250–1050 B.C.E.*, Maryknoll, N.Y.: Orbis Books, 1979.

Guthrie, W. K. C. *The Greeks and Their Gods.* Boston: Beacon Press, 1955 [1950].

——. *A History of Greek Philosophy,* 6 volumes. Cambridge: Cambridge University Press, 1962.

Guttmann, Julius. *Philosophies of Judaism,* trans. David W. Silverman. Garden City, N.Y.: Anchor Books, Doubleday, 1966 [1964].

Hamilton, E. and H. Cairns. *Collected Dialogues of Plato.* Princeton, N.J.: Princeton University Press, 1963.

Harris, R. Baine, ed. *Neoplatonism and Indian Thought.* Norfolk, Va.: International Society for Neoplatonic Studies, 1982.

Copyrighted Material

Henry, Paul, "The Place of Plotinus in the History of Thought." In *Plotinus: The Enneads*, trans. Stephen MacKenna. New York: Pantheon Books, 1962.

Hesiod. "Theogony." In *Hesiod, the Homeric Hymns and Homerica*, trans. H. G. Evelyn-White. Cambridge, Mass.: Harvard University Press, 1977.

Heussi, Karl. *Kompendium der Kirchengeschichte*, 12th ed. Tübingen: J. C. B. Mohr Verlag, 1960.

Holte, Ragnar. "Logos Spermatikos. Christianity and Ancient Philosophy according to St. Justin's Apologies." *Studia Theologica* 12 (1958): 109–168.

Hornung, Erik. *Geist der Pharaonenzeit*. Zürich: Artemis Verlag, 1989.

Ions, Veronica. *Egyptian Mythology*. Middlesex, England: Hamlyn Publishing Group, 1968.

Jonas, Hans. *The Gnostic Religion: The Message of the Alien God and the Beginnings of Christianity*. Boston: Beacon Press, 1963 [1958].

——. *Die mythologische Gnosis—Mit einer Einleitung zur Geschichte und Methodologie der Forschung*. Göttingen: Vandenhoeck and Ruprecht, 1964.

——. *Gnosis und spätantiker Geist—von der Mythologie zur mystischen Philosophie*. Göttingen: Vandenhoeck and Ruprecht, 1966.

Koester, Helmut. *History, Culture and Religion of the Hellenistic Age*. New York: Walter de Gruyter, 1982.

——. *History and Literature of Early Christianity*. New York: Walter de Gruyter, 1982.

Kramer, Samuel Noah, ed. *Mythologies of the Ancient World*. Garden City, N.Y.: Anchor Books, Doubleday, 1961.

——. *Cradle of Civilization.* New York: Time Inc., 1967.

——, trans. "Enki and Ninhursag: A Paradise Myth." In *Ancient Near Eastern Texts,* ed. James P. Pritchard. Princeton, N.J.: Princeton University Press, 1969.

Lichtheim, Miriam. *Ancient Egyptian Literature,* 3 volumes. Berkeley: University of California Press, 1980.

Lowrie, Walter. "Fear and Trembling: A Dialectical Lyric by Johannes de Silentio" [1843]. In Robert Bretall, ed., *A Kierkegaard Anthology.* Princeton, N.J.: Princeton University Press, 1946.

Luckert, Karl W. *The Navajo Hunter Tradition.* Tucson: University of Arizona Press, 1975.

MacKenna, Stephen, trans. *The Enneads,* by Plotinus. 3d ed. by B. S. Page. New York: Pantheon Books, 1962. Copyright by Faber and Faber Ltd., London.

Mallory, J. P. *In Search of the Indo-Europeans: Language, Archaeology and Myth.* London: Thames and Hudson, 1989.

Matthews, Victor H. *Manners and Customs of the Bible.* Peabody, Mass.: Hendrickson Publ., 1988.

Miller, J. Maxwell and John H. Hayes. *A History of Ancient Israel and Judah.* Philadelphia: Westminster Press, 1986.

Morenz, Siegfried. *Ägyptische Religion.* Stuttgart: Kohlhammer Verlag, 1960.

Nahm, Milton C., ed. *Selections from Early Greek Philosophy.* New York: Appleton-Century-Crofts, Inc., 1962.

O'Meara, Dominic J. *Neoplatonism and Christian Thought.* Norfolk, Va.: International Society for Neoplatonic Studies, 1982

Oppenheim, A. Leo, et al., eds. "Akitu" in *Assyrian Dictionary,* Volume 1, pp. 267–272. Chicago: The Oriental Institute, 1964.

Outler, Albert C., trans. *Augustine: Confessions and Enchiridion.* Philadelphia: Westminster Press, 1955.

Pagels, Elaine H. *The Gnostic Gospels.* New York: Random House, 1979.

Pearson, Birger A., and James E. Goehring, eds. *The Roots of Egyptian Christianity.* Philadelphia: Fortress Press, 1986.

Pritchard, James B. ed. *Ancient Near Eastern Texts Relating to the Old Testament,* 3d ed. Princeton, N.J.: Princeton University Press, 1969.

Redford, Donald B. *Akhenaten, the Heretic King.* Princeton, N.J.: Princeton University Press, 1984.

Renfrew, Colin. *Archaeology and Language: The Puzzle of Indo-European Origins.* New York: Cambridge University Press, 1987.

Ringgren, Helmer. *Israelitische Religion.* Stuttgart: Kohlhammer Verlag, 1963.

Robinson, James M., ed. *The Nag Hammadi Library.* San Francisco: Harper and Row, 1981 [1977].

Ross, W. D. *Aristotle, a Complete Exposition of His Works.* Cleveland: Meridian Books, 1962 [1959].

Rudolph, Kurt. *Gnosis: the Nature and History of Gnosticism.* San Francisco: Harper and Row, 1987.

Ryne, Linn. "The Faistos Disc—Norwegian Researcher Unravels Ancient Mystery." *Norway Now,* no. 6 (1990).

Sabloff, Jeremy A., and C. C. Lamberg-Karlovsky. *The Rise and Fall of Civilizations: Modern Archaeological Approaches to Ancient Cultures.* Menlo Park, Calif.: Cummings Publishing Co., 1974.

Copyrighted Material

Sakellarakis, Yannis and Efi Sapouna-Sakellarakis. "Drama of Death in a Minoan Temple." *National Geographic* (February 1981), pp. 204–222.

Sethe, Kurt. *Übersetzung und Kommentar zu den Ägyptischen Pyramidentexten,* 6 volumes. Hamburg: J. J. Augustin, 1, 1962.

——. "Amun und die acht Urgötter von Hermopolis." *Abhandlungen der Preussischen Akademie der Wissenschaften* (1929):4.

Skinner, John. *A Critical and Exegetical Commentary on Genesis.* Edinburgh: T. & T. Clark, 1969 [1910].

Smart, Ninian. *The World's Religions.* Englewood Cliffs, N.J.: Prentice-Hall, 1989.

Smith, Jonathan Z. "A Pearl of Great Price and a Cargo of Yams: A Study in Situational Incongruity." *History of Religions* 16, no. 1 (1976): 1–11.

Theiler, Willy. *Forschungen zum Neuplatonismus.* Berlin: Walter de Gruyter & Co., 1966.

Thomas, D. Winton, ed. *Documents from Old Testament Times.* New York: Harper and Row, 1958.

Trigg, Joseph Wilson. *Origen: The Bible and Philosophy in the Third-Century Church.* Atlanta: John Knox Press, 1983.

Turnbull, Grace H. *The Essence of Plotinus: Extracts from the Six Enneads and Porphyry's Life of Plotinus.* Westport, Conn.: Greenwood Press, 1934.

Van den Broek, R. and M. J. Vermaseren, eds. *Studies in Gnosticism and Hellenistic Religions: Presented to Gilles Quispel on the Occasion of his 65th Birthday.* Leiden: E. J. Brill, 1981.

Van Seters, John. *The Hyksos, a New Investigation.* New Haven, Conn.: Yale University Press, 1966.

Copyrighted Material

Waddell, W. G., trans. *Manetho*. Cambridge, Mass.: Harvard University Press, 1971.

Walker, Williston. *A History of the Christian Church*. New York: Charles Scribners' Sons, 1959.

Wilson, John A. *The Burden of Egypt*. Chicago: University of Chicago Press, 1951.

———, trans. "The Theology of Memphis" and "Egyptian Myths, Tales, and Mortuary Texts." In *Ancient Near Eastern Texts*, ed. James B. Pritchard. Princeton, N.J.: Princeton University Press, 1969.

Wolfson, Harry Austryn. *Philo: Foundations of Religious Philosophy in Judaism, Christianity, and Islam*. Cambridge, Mass.: Harvard University Press, 1962 [1947].

Wolters, Albert M. "Survey of Modern Scholarly Opinion." In *Neo-Platonism and Indian Thought*, ed. R. Blaine Harris. Norfolk, Va.: International Society for Neoplatonic Studies, 1982.

Wlosok, Antonie. *Römischer Kaiserkult*. Darmstadt: Wissenschaftliche Buchgesellschaft, 1978.

Copyrighted Material

Copyrighted Material

Index

Copyrighted Material

Copyrighted Material

Copyrighted Material

Copyrighted Material

Copyrighted Material

Copyrighted Material

Copyrighted Material

Copyrighted Material

Copyrighted Material

Copyrighted Material

Copyrighted Material

Copyrighted Material

Copyrighted Material

Copyrighted Material

Copyrighted Material

Printed in Germany
by Amazon Distribution
GmbH, Leipzig